Target-Centric
Network Modeling

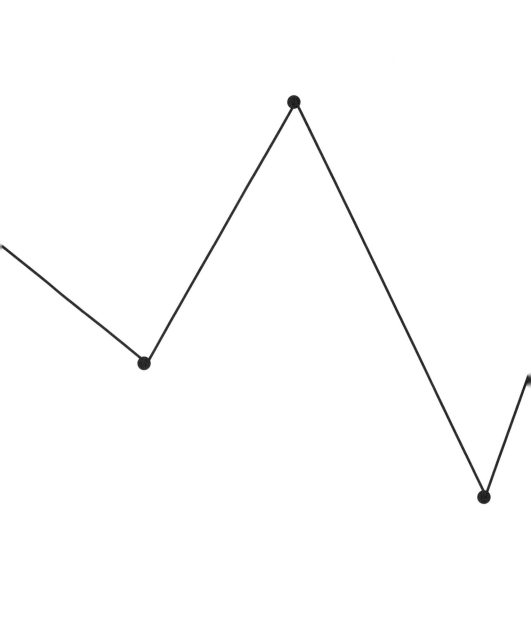

Target-Centric Network Modeling

Case Studies in Analyzing Complex Intelligence Issues

Robert M. Clark

William L. Mitchell

Los Angeles | London | New Delhi
Singapore | Washington DC | Boston

Los Angeles | London | New Delhi
Singapore | Washington DC | Boston

FOR INFORMATION:

CQ Press

An Imprint of SAGE Publications, Inc.

2455 Teller Road

Thousand Oaks, California 91320

E-mail: order@sagepub.com

SAGE Publications Ltd.

1 Oliver's Yard

55 City Road

London EC1Y 1SP

United Kingdom

SAGE Publications India Pvt. Ltd.

B 1/I 1 Mohan Cooperative Industrial Area

Mathura Road, New Delhi 110 044

India

SAGE Publications Asia-Pacific Pte. Ltd.

3 Church Street

#10–04 Samsung Hub

Singapore 049483

Printed in the United States of America

A catalog record of this book is available from the Library of Congress.

ISBN 978-1-4833-1698-7

This book is printed on acid-free paper.

Acquisitions Editor: Suzanne Flinchbaugh

Editorial Assistant: Davia Grant

Production Editor: David C. Felts

Typesetter: C&M Digitals (P) Ltd.

Copy Editor: Megan Markanich

Proofreader: Pam Suwinsky

Indexer: Molly Hall

Cover Designer: Michael Dubowe

Marketing Manager: Amy Whitaker

15 16 17 18 19 10 9 8 7 6 5 4 3 2 1

Contents

Tables and Figures

About the Authors

Robert M. Clark currently is an independent consultant performing threat analyses for the U.S. Intelligence Community. He is also a faculty member of the Intelligence and Security Academy and a professor of intelligence studies at the University of Maryland University College. He previously was a faculty member of the Director of National Intelligence (DNI) Intelligence Community Officers' course and course director of the DNI Introduction to the Intelligence Community course. Dr. Clark served as a U.S. Air Force electronics warfare officer and intelligence officer, reaching the rank of lieutenant colonel. At the Central Intelligence Agency (CIA), he was a senior analyst and group chief responsible for managing analytic methodologies. Clark holds an SB from MIT, a PhD in electrical engineering from the University of Illinois, and a JD from George Washington University. He has previously authored three books: *Intelligence Analysis: A Target-Centric Approach* (4th edition, 2013), *The Technical Collection of Intelligence* (2010), and *Intelligence Collection* (2014).

William L. Mitchell's military and intelligence career spans three decades including operations in Afghanistan, the Balkans, Iraq, Africa, and French Guyana. Dr. Mitchell is currently an active member of Danish Defence and an all-source specialist, researcher, instructor, and lecturer. At the Royal Danish Defence College (RDDC) he is responsible for the synchronization of theory, practice, and education regarding intelligence and joint operations. He is a member of the RDDC Research Board and supports NATO and US Department of Defense research, education, and doctrine development programs. He has several publications on intelligence and battlespace agility, and was part of the NATO Science & Technology Organization group awarded the 2014 NATO Scientific Achievement Award. Dr. Mitchell has a BA, an MA with Distinction from Kent University, and a PhD from Aarhus University in Political Science. He is a decorated war veteran of two countries, with one citation and several medals, including the French Croix de Combatant and the Danish Defence medal.

Preface

This workbook is designed to complement the textbook *Intelligence Analysis: A Target-Centric Approach,* as well as other existing course texts on intelligence analysis. It is about creating and sharing models of intelligence problems and intelligence targets. Creating target models is something that intelligence analysts do routinely in the course of their work. The workbook further focuses on a specific class of target—networks—because most intelligence problems today in any field (such as national, military, law enforcement, and even commercial) concern networks.

The workbook is focused on the practical training and development of intelligence students and analysts. Its mission is to teach them to put the principles of target network modeling and analysis into practice. Through case studies and scenarios, readers will learn tools to succeed at defining the problem, decomposing it into constituent parts, and creating and using a target network model to produce finished intelligence. They will realize the value of collaboratively sharing the model. In short, they will learn how to create high-quality, defensible answers to a customer's question. The workbook also includes an optional step of developing a collection strategy.

Part I of the workbook includes a brief review of intelligence analysis methodology, stressing the general basics of intelligence problem definition, model building, and the creation of network models. Chapter 1 briefly introduces two analytic concepts—the problem definition model (PDM) and the target network model (TNM)—and explains their importance. It concludes with a discussion of model sharing and how to do it effectively. Chapter 2 is an overview of how the cases in Part II can be used to create and use these models.

Part II comprises case studies based on detailed scenarios that allow students to develop competence in critical elements of intelligence analysis. Different exercises emphasize different parts of the intelligence analysis process. Some focus on problem definition and dealing with a customer's poorly defined problem; others on getting the problem breakdown right; and others on the modeling or collaborative problem-solving stages, for example.

Target audiences for the book include the following:

- intelligence analysis students and instructors
- active intelligence analysts from all organizational environments
- collectors who must develop targeting strategies and productively work with analysts

The workbook differs from others in three ways:

It Is Internationally Relevant

The customer set and cases include international, national, military, and law enforcement customers of intelligence. Many texts on intelligence assume a U.S. audience and are targeted specifically at national policy or military intelligence analysis. The case studies presented here allow users to select from a wider cross section of intelligence customers.

It Employs Realistic Intelligence Reporting

Each case study contains raw intelligence that is designed to give students a feel for the type of reporting they can expect in the real world. Students must deal with ambiguity, uncertainty, conflicting and contradictory reporting, and denial and deception.

It Allows Instructors Extensive Flexibility

The workbook is tailored to provide ease of use for teaching the following:

- The material adapts to a standard semester or a short course: the text as a whole includes ample material to encompass a full semester, but each case study easily stands on its own for shorter courses.
- The design allows curriculum flexibility: instructors can choose analytic problems best suited to their classes by stressing or skipping steps in the analysis process.
- The format encourages assignment flexibility: cases can be assigned as whole-class, individual, or team projects.
- Multiple valid solutions exist: most exercise problems have more than one possible answer, as usually is the case in real-world intelligence issues.
- Many of the cases are easily adaptable to military doctrine: they can be used to generate standard documents such as an intelligence preparation of the battlespace (IPB), Intelligence Collection Plan (ICP), high-value target lists (HVTLs), and target sets.

The cases in this workbook are based on fictitious scenarios. Many place names, equipment names, and organization names exist in the real world, but the events described in the cases generally are apocryphal.

All statements of fact, opinion, or analysis expressed are those of the authors and do not reflect the official positions or view of the Central Intelligence Agency (CIA) or any other U.S. government agency, the Royal Danish Defence College (RDDC), or any other Danish government agency. Nothing in the contents should be construed as asserting or implying U.S. government authentication of information or agency endorsement of the author's views. This material has been reviewed by the CIA to prevent the disclosure of classified information.

This book would not have existed without the initiative and extensive inputs from Dr. Clark's wife, Abigail, and we both appreciate her unstinting efforts. Dr. Clark also thanks his former colleagues in the DNI's Intelligence Community Officers' Course—Dr. Donald Cummings, John Allison, Peter Oleson, Marcia Barkell, and Dr. Gary Goodrich—whose efforts inspired the Democratic Republic of the Congo case studies. Dr. Mitchell would like to acknowledge the Danish Defence forces and the many there who have, over the years, facilitated a renaissance in military intelligence learning and practice, both in the classrooms of the Royal Danish Defence College, and on operations overseas. In this regard, his special thanks go to Brigadier General Lennie Fredskov Hansen, Lieutenant Colonel Thomas Funch, Lieutenant Colonel Hans Henrik Møller, Major Niels Petersen, Commander Søren Spodsberg, and Chief Advisor Søren Kirkbak. We also wish to thank Suzanne Flinchbaugh, acquisitions editor; Davia Grant, editorial assistant; David C. Felts, production editor; and Megan Markanich, copy editor at CQ Press, for shaping the finished product.

PART I

Process and Methodology

1

Introduction

There are no single node targets in intelligence. Even when we are concerned just with a person, organization, object, or location, our target is associated with some network—usually with many networks—that are essential to understanding the target. These networks have become more complex over the years, largely because of advances in communications technologies. The ones of intelligence interest now are transorganizational and transnational.

The toughest job for intelligence analysts in any field—national policy, military operations, or law enforcement—is to deal with networks. Most of the major challenges facing governments today come from organized networks with established and identifiable infrastructures. These networks are well adapted to their operational environment and capable of surviving and accommodating substantial military, economic, and political changes. Countering them is a difficult task and requires an intense intelligence effort.[1] For this reason, the cases in this workbook are devoted to analyzing target networks.

A formal methodology for dealing with complex networks is outlined in this chapter and the next: target network modeling is an answer to one of intelligence's most pernicious problems today: how to make sense of and quickly communicate to other members of the intelligence team (and to customers) the morass of disparate pieces of intelligence that comprise any complex problem. The term *customer* is used in this workbook to refer to the intelligence customer in general (who may be a military commander, government leader, or law enforcement executive). In some cases, one type of customer, such as the military commander, will be specified.

Target network modeling provides a blueprint for understanding and operating against a well-defined activity—such as conventional or unconventional warfare, militant extremism, counterinsurgency, terrorism, and organized criminal activity. Reduced to its basics, the methodology relies on decomposition and visualization

---

[1] U.S. Joint Forces Command "Commander's Handbook for Attack the Network," Joint Warfighting Center, Suffolk, VA, May 20, 2011, http://www.dtic.mil/doctrine/doctrine/jwfc/atn_hbk.pdf.

techniques to facilitate the development and communication of a shared situational awareness (SA) and understanding:

> Situational awareness ensures the customer (particularly in the military theater) has the right level of knowledge to put new data and information into context to make rational decisions and take appropriate actions.

> Situational understanding goes beyond that: it concerns the perception and interpretation of the particular situation which provides the context, insight, and foresight required for effective decision-making.[2]

The two concepts sound similar, and in fact, they draw from the same target network model (TNM). The difference is that SA is more descriptive, while situational understanding (SU) is more analytical, leading to the foresight needed for accurate prediction. Consider an insurgent group that the intelligence customer might wish to negotiate with. SA is achieved by a network diagram identifying the group's decision makers and their objectives (descriptive). SU comes from a deeper analysis of the model such as recognizing that all of the decision makers in the group are men past middle age, indicating that the target organization is patriarchal in nature or their social relationships are driven by men (explanation). Therefore, the customer knows to choose an elderly male to negotiate with the group. As another example, SA can be achieved by a list of high-value targets for attack to decimate a terrorist group (descriptive). SU is derived by having the contextual insight or foresight that attacking some of the targets on the list would have severe political or social repercussions, perhaps offsetting the military gains achieved.

The decisive advantage of target network modeling for intelligence teams is timeliness. In rapidly evolving situations, a TNM can be amended and disseminated within seconds. Long written narratives are cumbersome and tend not to get read after the first iteration.

In tackling an intelligence issue, TNMs are used first as a means to assimilate data into an organized format by the analyst who creates them to promote his own understanding. Second, TNMs facilitate the communication of that understanding to others who can help improve the model—fellow analysts, intelligence collectors, decision makers, operational planners, law enforcement professionals, and military commanders—across organizational boundaries. And, perhaps most critically, TNMs are a vehicle for conveying the complexity of a situation to customers in a fashion that they can understand.

Target network modeling is also groundbreaking because it inherently provides a mechanism for tracking the historic development of targets, operational environments, or narratives over time. Why is this important? It is because the crux of intelligence is *not* about looking at a snapshot. It is about analyzing patterns over time

---

[2]NATO Allied Joint Publication 2.0 Version 2, 2012.

(several years, a couple of weeks, or even a day when tracking terrorists) in order to engage in informed estimative analysis.

Target network modeling makes use of the target-centric approach to intelligence analysis that is detailed in the companion textbook by Robert M. Clark, *Intelligence Analysis: A Target-Centric Approach.* It employs three overarching concepts: problem modeling, target network modeling, and collaboratively sharing the models, which are briefly outlined next.

THE PROBLEM MODEL

An intelligence analyst cannot develop a TNM properly without first thinking critically about the intelligence problem or issue. If this step is skipped, the analyst may later exclude things that should be part of the TNM or include things that should not be part of it. In the first case, the analyst answers the wrong question. In the second case, she produces answers that don't help her customer.

The exercises in this workbook provide statements of the intelligence problem or issue upfront in each case study. These statements are typical of what customers provide to analysts. They are very general and usually reflect the customer's view of the problem. For example, the military scenarios present the problem statement in the form of a "commander's intent," which simply states the commander's objective. The job of the intelligence analyst is to flesh out this general guidance by creating a problem model. The customer's question or guidance is just a starting point. Sometimes the customer asks the wrong question. Even when the initial question is well posed, intelligence customers seldom are able to think about all of the factors that bear on the problem. That becomes the analyst's job.

Intelligence problems always have several factors that have to be considered at the beginning. That happens because we must deal not only with networks but also with systems—which have a definite meaning and a special significance in intelligence analysis. So let's spend some time upfront explaining just what we mean by a "system."

Major weapons systems employed by a military force are comprised of many interacting subsystems, often causing them to be referred to as a "system of systems." A main battle tank, for example, requires ammunition and fuel. It must be operated by a crew. The crew requires training. The tank needs frequent maintenance and repair of battle damage. It has to have sensors to detect, identify, and attack targets and also communications to permit it to function effectively in the battlespace. Without all of these things—and more—that comprise the weapons system, the tank is just an ineffective hunk of metal.

Many systems of intelligence interest have little or nothing to do with the military, though. There are health care systems, law enforcement systems, and financial and banking systems; the list is very long. The case studies in this workbook all deal with networks, but they also deal with systems. Criminal cartels and gangs—the subjects of Chapters 3, 4, 7, and 11—are both networks and systems of systems.

Some case studies deal with military systems, or a mix of military and nonmilitary systems—Chapters 10, 13, and 14, for example. The case study in Chapter 12 focuses on a single military system, but even there civilian matters intrude.

The development of systems theory and systems thinking goes back many decades. In the 1960s, the U.S. military defined four top-level systems through which a state exercises its power, which the military called "Instruments of National Power": political, military, economic, and psychosocial. Over the years, there have been several iterations of this breakdown. The current one, used frequently in this workbook, is political, military, economic, society, infrastructure, and information, or PMESII.

Rarely, if ever, will an intelligence problem only include one of these factors or systems. Complex international issues typically involve them all. The events of the Arab Spring in 2011, the Syrian uprising that began that year, and the Ukrainian crisis of 2014 involved all of the PMESII factors. But PMESII is also relevant in issues that are not necessarily international. Several of these factors are in play in local law enforcement events such as the Mara Salvatrucha (MS-13) gang case in this workbook.

Once the issue has been thought through, the next step is to formulate a problem breakdown, which will create a problem model, almost always in the form of a hierarchy. How that breakdown might be done is discussed, with examples, in Chapter 2.

THE TARGET NETWORK MODEL

Beginning from the problem model, the next step is to create a TNM. Target network modeling has two distinct advantages over other paradigms in terms of flexibility.

First, it is not bound by one structure—there are any number of different types of target models from which to choose to represent any given problem. In fact, for most situations, the analyst will begin by building interacting models of the target. A relationship model, such as the one that helped in going after Osama bin Laden, is common in intelligence. A relationship model will generally lead to a model on patterns of living—where do the people in those relationships live, conduct their business, practice their religion, or send their children to school? This intelligence will lead to geospatial models and so on. It is the intersection of these target models that will bear fruit along the way and in the end. *Intelligence Analysis: A Target-Centric Approach* devotes considerable time to detailing various model categories and the use of alternative models. Chapter 2 of this workbook presents a few of these.

The second advantage of building target models, already noted, is that they are easily and quickly modified—something that is not true of finished intelligence reports (INTREPs), for example. All intelligence situations are fluid; new information arrives and pieces of existing intelligence, having been proven invalid or irrelevant, must be discarded. The TNM provides a rapid means for the analyst to update the picture and disseminate it to working partners and/or customers. This capability is essential in the military theater or in a fast-developing situation such as the Boston Marathon bombing of 2013.

The target network is broadly defined here. It includes the opposing forces, persons, organizations, and their allies, of course. But you may, in some instances, need to include a model of your allied networks and neutral networks too. In fact, intelligence often has the job of assessing neutral and friendly networks, considering all of the PMESII dimensions.

Intelligence organizations, in fact, have a long history of assessing friendly and neutral as well as hostile networks. Over two millennia ago, Chinese military strategist Sun Tzu observed the following: "We cannot enter into alliances until we are acquainted with the designs of our neighbors." During and immediately after World War I, British intelligence relied on the human terrain knowledge and diplomatic skills of T. E. Lawrence (known as Lawrence of Arabia) and Gertrude Bell in assessing the tribal networks of Arabia and Iraq. Without the intelligence that they furnished about friendly networks, the British probably would have had considerably less success militarily and diplomatically during and after the war. And, of course, without a good upfront understanding of the intelligence problems that the British had, Lawrence and Bell probably would not have obtained the needed intelligence.[3]

The need for understanding neutral and friendly networks is especially important for military analysts and law enforcement officials in multinational operations. There, the intelligence customer often lacks critical information about his own allies or potential allies, and intelligence has to supply it. A few examples of how to create the opponent's network model appear in Chapter 2. The case studies that follow Chapter 2 will also provide some opportunities to create target models that include friendly or neutral networks.

SHARING TARGET NETWORK MODELS

Intelligence sharing among analysts has become commonplace in intelligence organizations. So, many of the exercises in this workbook require collaborative sharing of TNMs among fellow analysts. Perhaps less commonplace, but more important, is the sharing of these models with customers, collectors, and increasingly, with allies including nongovernmental organizations (NGOs).

The requirement for modern intelligence to provide and share accurate and timely SA and understanding with the customers as well as their respective operational planning departments has not changed since the time of T. E. Lawrence and Gertrude Bell. What has changed is the challenge that Lawrence and Bell faced in getting their military and civilian customers to accept and use their intelligence. The ability to share with customers both the target model of a situation and the supporting evidence for that model has improved substantially since WWI. That

---

[3]Janet Wallach, *Desert Queen* (New York: Anchor Books, 2005).

advancement has facilitated the effectiveness of our customers in what has become the dominant conflict of our time: *netwar.*

INTELLIGENCE SHARING IN NETWAR

During the 1990s, RAND researchers John Arquilla and David Ronfeldt articulated the concept of netwar. Today, it has become a universal concept. As they originally described it, the term referred to societal conflict and crime, short of war, in which the antagonists are organized more as sprawling networks than as tight-knit hierarchies. Netwar, they observed, was a preferred mode of operation for terrorists, criminals, extremist fundamentalists, and ethno-nationalists, all of whom were developing netwar capabilities.[4] The information revolution led to the rise of network forms of organization, with implications for how societies are organized and conflicts are conducted. Netwar was the consequence. Arquilla and Ronfeldt subsequently expanded the definition. Netwar, they observed, includes conflicts waged both by highly structured organizations and by groups that are actually leaderless—civil-society activists (such as cyber activists or Occupy Wall Street protestors), for example. What distinguishes netwar is the networked organizational structure of its practitioners and their quickness in coming together in swarming attacks. To confront this new type of conflict, the authors argued, it is crucial for governments, military, and law enforcement to begin networking themselves.[5]

Retired U.S. Army general Stanley McChrystal, former commander of the U.S. Joint Special Operations Command, has endorsed the netwar concept, observing that "it takes a network to defeat a network."[6] He also made a cogent observation about sharing while he commanded the U.S. Joint Special Operations Command: "The more people you shared your problem with, the better you'd do in solving it."

Clark's target-centric approach is designed to deal with sharing in netwar. Specifically, it requires that intelligence analysts provide SA and understanding that focuses on the target and its environment. Target network modeling, as described in this workbook, is the "engine" for doing that. Figure 1.1 illustrates how the process works in netwar. The participants in your network—customers, collectors, processors, and fellow analysts—are in a sense standing around a (electronic) table examining a model of the target network and exchanging their knowledge about it.

The group titled "Your network" in Figure 1.1 has become more inclusive and therefore more complex over the years. Gone are the times when countries operated independently and police agencies operated individually. Customers, in

---

[4]John Arquilla and David Ronfeldt, *The Advent of Netwar* (Washington, DC: RAND Corporation, 1996).

[5]John Arquilla and David Ronfeldt, *Networks and Netwars* (Washington, DC: RAND Corporation, 2001).

[6]General (Retired) Stanley McChrystal, *Foreign Policy,* March/April 2011, http://www.foreign policy.com/articles/2011/02/22/it_takes_a_network.

FIGURE 1.1   Intelligence Sharing in Network Versus Network

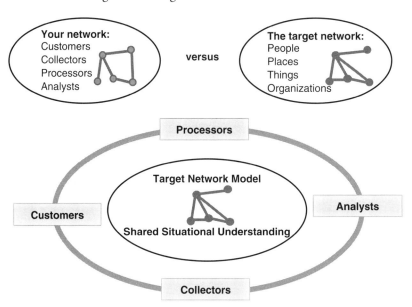

today's context, may include allies or other partners as well. They include coalition partners in military operations; other law enforcement groups in dealing with transnational criminal organizations; and political allies in defusing international crises, for example. All of these customers typically need to reach a common level of SU if they are to arrive at an effective solution to modern intelligence issues.

Intelligence sharing of TNMs also is an essential part of operations in what is called the *observe-orient-decide-act (OODA) loop,* discussed next.

Intelligence Sharing in the Observe-Orient-Decide-Act Loop

Target network modeling has an increasingly explicit role in warfighting and is of paramount importance to the organizations designing and executing military actions and operations. Obviously, it is detrimental to operations for two or more *different* organizations, looking at the same situation or target, not to define the problem at hand in the same way nor be in agreement as to the major issues involved. However, it also is detrimental to mounting effective operations if a unitary organization's command, intelligence unit, and planning unit do not share a common understanding about the situation or target. Target network modeling as a formal approach for communicating shared SU between the commander, his intelligence support, and his operational planners, increases the warfighting efficacy of the organization. For example, if we place target network modeling for easy reference within the context of the popular OODA loop, all three functions, the commander, the intelligence analysts, and the planners, should have a shared SU for the organization to be effective in the battlespace. Figure 1.2 illustrates the intelligence process in the

FIGURE 1.2   Intelligence in the Observe-Orient-Decide-Act Loop

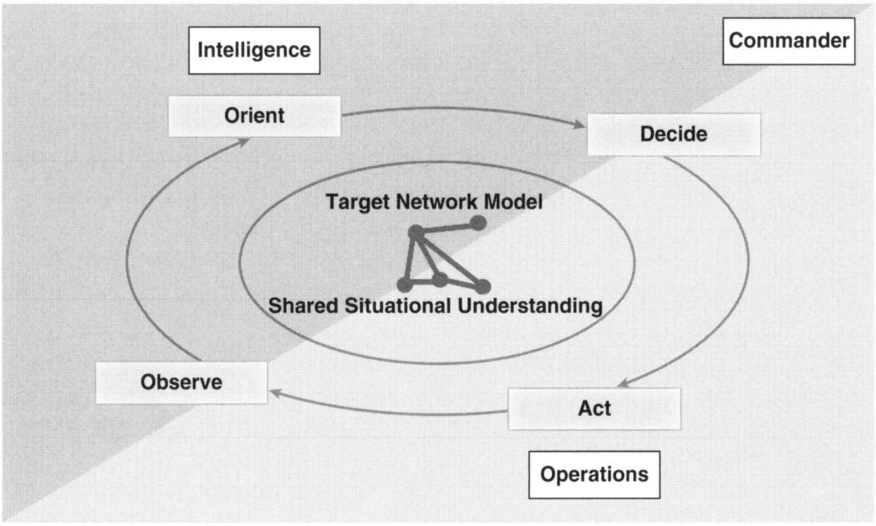

OODA loop.[7] The role of intelligence here is in observing (gathering information) and orienting (developing and assessing hypotheses about an opponent's activities and intent).

Configuration Management in Sharing

The broad sharing of models among stakeholders, described previously, was less practical in earlier years. But communications networks now allow the creation and sharing of a rich set of target models without the historical constraints of physical boundaries.

There can be a challenge in such a sharing process: thorough analysis of a complex problem may mean creating a sizable set of alternative models and sub-models. This presents the same issue that software developers are intimately famil-iar with: configuration management. The lead intelligence analyst has to keep track of the models and know which one is most accurate—usually the most current version. The solution is much like that used in the software industry—to make use of an annotation that indicates uniquely the nature of the model and the specific version.

The approach used by intelligence teams in combat zones and law enforcement is to use a configuration indicator for the shared models. A generic model (explained in the next chapter) carries a designation. For example, a generic target model of narcotics trafficking cartels might be labeled "narcotraffickers."

---

[7]John R. Boyd, *Destruction and Creation* (Fort Leavenworth, KS: U.S. Army Command and General Staff College, 1976).

For most intelligence problems, though, a single generic model is insufficient. There are likely to be several alternative generic models. The easy answer is to number the alternatives. "Narcotraffickers 3," for example, would indicate the third alternative model that has been shared. Other designation techniques include the following:

- Variant models—that is, generic models that have been customized to deal with (for instance) a regional variation—would carry additional designators. For example, assuming that southwest Asian narcotraffickers generally have a different network than Latin American narcotraffickers, these two network models might be distinguished as "Narcotraffickers SW Asia" and "Narcotraffickers Latin America."
- Submodels will also need a designation. For example, narcotraffickers typically have a money laundering system in place. Such a submodel might carry the designation "Narcotraffickers Money Laundering" or "Narcotraffickers SW Asia Money Laundering."

The result of sharing annotated generic target models, over time, is something that every intelligence analysis organization should have: a library of generic models to draw from. This is vastly different from past decades where the memories of a singular veteran analyst might be the best or only source of previous models. As part of the mentoring process, they shared their conceptual models with novice analysts. The difference is that with TNM methodology, these models will be routinely made available to any cadre of new analysts.

From generic models, we advance to specific TNMs. Continuing the example of narcotraffickers, a target model of the Zetas drug cartel might carry the designation "Zetas 4," indicating that it is the fourth model that has been customized to represent the structure of the Zetas cartel. The model can then be identified in a message. For instance, Texas law enforcement communicating with the U.S. Drug Enforcement Administration (DEA) could text the following: "I can see that you are working on Zetas 4. There is some new reporting on it at . . ."

When working through these exercises in a group setting, you will experience how model creation and sharing works in practice. Several of the exercises are arranged to facilitate that.

2

Working with the Case Studies

Many different types of case studies are presented in this workbook. They cover a wide spectrum of issues and differ in regard to their focus, length, detail, style, and organizational environment. Some are more attuned to civilian and law enforcement intelligence agencies while others are more familiar to military intelligence organizations. This is intentional for two reasons: (1) to stress the universality of target network modeling and its inherent advocacy of critical and adaptive thinking that should be part of every analyst's basic skill set and (2) to reflect the real-world dictate and growing popularity of inter-agency intelligence environments.

Because the primary purpose of this workbook is to develop competence with target network models (TNMs), all of the exercises entail, at a minimum, using the scenario and intelligence reporting to define the given problem and create appropriate TNMs. Steps 5 and 6 in the process are open to a good deal of innovation according to whatever your instructor would like to accomplish in terms of analytical training and delivery of various intelligence products.

The focus of this chapter is to guide you on the most lucrative approach to working through each case study. Figure 2.1 indicates a rather linear six-step process, and to some extent, that's the way it works, but note that as in any problem-solving process, the work is also iterative. For the exercises here, as in the real world, you will frequently go back and revisit steps—jumping from a TNM or an intelligence assessment back to redefining the problem, for example.

Following is a discussion of each step in the process with some examples.

STEP 1: READ THE SCENARIO

Reading the scenario is the first step to understanding the setting or environment. The scenario (which usually includes some background readings at the end of the case) has the necessary background material to help you work through all of the exercise phases. It also forms the context for the intelligence that is included with each case. It contains explanatory material to help in defining the problem and guidance in the form of an organizational mission or customer's guidance (such as a commander's intent) that will help you create relevant TNMs. In many of the cases,

FIGURE 2.1   Working with the Case Studies

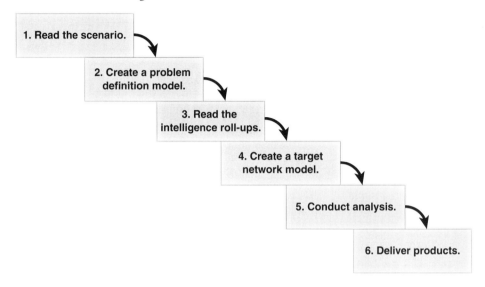

some additional explanatory material is included that will be of use such as a money laundering generic model; weapons performance assessment guidance; how terrorist networks organize, get funding, plan, and conduct attacks; or, how gray arms traffickers conduct business. Some scenarios may reflect real-world characteristics in terms of who, what when, where, and how; others are completely fictional but reflect real-world issues.

While these are not current intelligence cases, many of them encompass accurate historical details and include published names of public officials and criminals. Much effort has been expended to make the exercises as authentic as possible. But they all include a mix of fact and fiction (with the exception of those cases that are completely fictional). Resist the temptation to perform any Internet-enhancing research. The intelligence needed for developing all of the activities in this workbook is developed from the scenario. Do not fight the setting particulars.

Knowing as much as possible about the scenario in which target networks operate is key when working real-world intelligence problems. Most operational environments are shaped by varying degrees of interaction among political, military, economic, society, infrastructure, and information factors. As noted in Chapter 1, military organizations summarize these factors using the acronym PMESII. The construct can be applied to describe the environment in which most networks of intelligence interest operate, and that is how we will use it in this text. As indicated in Figure 2.2, it is not only the different dimensions themselves that provide the situational understanding (SU) for target network modeling but the nature of relationships between them. PMESII is not the only analytic framework—far from it—but it is a starting point for those analysts who do not have one, with something that has been tried and tested in theory and practice since 2008. There are many frameworks to assist you, but the point is that you have to adapt some sort of system of systems approach to ensure a holistic understanding and to create sufficient mental room for your critical thinking. We will revisit the particular benefit of PMESII in a brief section on structured analytic techniques (in step 5).

FIGURE 2.2   PMESII System of Systems Framework

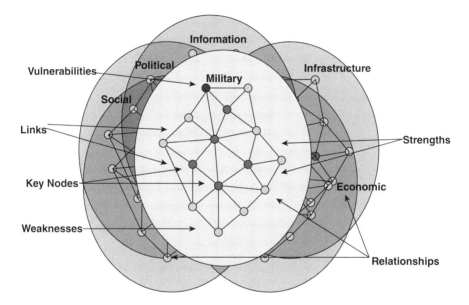

STEP 2: CREATE A PROBLEM DEFINITION MODEL

The purpose of the problem definition model (PDM) is to decompose and visualize the information in the scenario in order to create a common understanding of an operational environment. The shared model is the basis for further direction and guidance to intelligence managers, collectors, analysts, and any partnering intelligence organizations.

For almost any intelligence problem, there exists one or more *generic* PDMs that apply. This is true because the problem has been solved several times over the years in different settings. Starting from a generic model, an analyst can create a specific problem definition that applies to the scenario being considered. So that you have a basic foundation before being asked to use this technique, let's go through an example that describes how one might do a problem definition at both the generic and the specific levels.

Problem Definition Model Example 1: Cyber Attack

Suppose that your assignment is to assess cyber threats to a country's infrastructure. The first step would be to identify potential sources of an attack: those countries or nonstate actors that have the motivation, means, and intent to make such an attack. Next, you would probably contemplate the most likely targets of an attack (which might include these sectors: military, energy, financial, government, media, or transportation infrastructures). Finally, it would make sense to try to ascertain possible means of attack (such as denial of service [DoS] or computer sabotage) and assess the likelihood of each. So at the top level, the problem definition could look like Figure 2.3.

FIGURE 2.3   Cyber Threat Assessment Generic Problem Definition Model

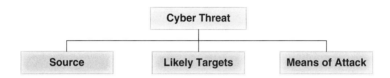

This figure is an example of a generic problem definition; it would be much the same for any cyber threat assessment. To prepare a problem definition for a *specific* country, the next step would be to proceed to lower levels and make those levels relevant to your target. Following is an illustration of such a definition.

In 2007, the country of Estonia was the victim of a series of cyber attacks. The Estonian parliament, banks, newspapers, and news portals all were hit with attacks that included DoS, flooding of websites, and sabotage to individual computers. The attacks were believed to originate from inside Russia and Transnistria (a breakaway part of the country of Moldova). An assessment of potential future sources, based on past experience, would include those in Russia and Transnistria, as well as Belarus (a prime source of cyber crime). The resulting cyber threat problem definition for Estonia could look something like Figure 2.4. The next level definition after this

FIGURE 2.4   Cyber Threat to Estonia Problem Definition Model 1.1

might identify, for example, specific Belarusian cyber criminal groups known to be targeting Estonia; specific financial centers believed to be most vulnerable to attack; and some preferred means of attack by the criminal groups. It is important to get into the habit of annotating your PDM for two reasons: (1) it is very useful when referencing communication between different organizations, authorities, and colleagues about your understanding of the situation, and (2) it creates an archive for the future. Following the model annotation concept described in Chapter 1, this iteration would be designated "Cyber Threat to Estonia Problem Definition Model 1.1." In reality, an organizational identifier would also be included to eliminate any confusion about the model's origination.

Note that most, if not all, of the PMESII factors are present here. The sources include both political and economic opponents. The targets are political, economic, informational, and infrastructure. The means of attack fall into the military category.[1]

Problem Definition Model Example 2: International Trade

Let's take an example from the field of economic intelligence as a starting point for dealing with a different type of threat. The primary intelligence concerns about international trade involve supporting trade negotiations and identifying trade activities that affect a country's economic and political interests. A generic PDM would include identifying other governments' strategies in either bilateral or multilateral trade negotiations, warning of attempts to circumvent trade sanctions, indicating unfair trade practices, and examining potential industrial espionage practices. The resulting generic PDM could look like Figure 2.5.

A lower-level problem definition might focus on a specific country (as in the previous example of the cyber threat to Estonia) or on only one part of the definition shown in Figure 2.5. Let's choose an example of such a sub-element definition, and carry the example through the remaining case study steps (3, 4, 5, and 6) shown earlier in Figure 2.1.

Consider the example of Sierra Leone in the late 1990s. The country had been torn by conflict between the government and the Revolutionary United Front (RUF) since 1991. In 1992, the United Nations (UN) imposed sanctions on the transfer of

FIGURE 2.5   International Trade Issues Generic Problem Definition Model 1

---

[1]"Military" in the PMESII context often refers to actions that are not traditionally thought of as military; it includes cyber attacks, as here, or uses of force in law enforcement, for example.

arms to Sierra Leone. In this case, the problem definition narrows to a single issue: *efforts to circumvent sanctions.* Trade negotiation strategy, unfair trade practices, and industrial espionage are not issues of intelligence interest here.

One method for a country to undermine sanctions is to use the services of international criminal networks. Regional and international networks of front companies, unethical businessmen, and crime groups specialize in evading trade, military, and financial sanctions by facilitating shipments of embargoed products (usually weapons) and executing financial transfers. The usual method of defeating arms sanctions is to acquire arms through either the gray arms market or the black arms market.

Most illegal arms transfers worldwide are completed through the gray arms market. This market is controlled by individual brokers and their arms brokering firms. Gray market arms transfers make use of legitimate export licensing processes. The broker typically uses falsified documentation to obtain an export license. The documentation usually will conceal the identity of the end user or the military nature of the goods involved. The fraudulent license allows the broker to make a transfer appear legitimate so that the broker can arrange payment and international transportation for transactions.[2] (This is in contrast to black market arms transfers, which do not go through an export licensing process. Instead, smugglers rely exclusively on hiding contraband arms from government officials. The chief difference is that a falsified end user certificate must exist for gray arms transfers.)

The generic PDM of Figure 2.6 indicates a problem definition (of the topics on which the customer wants intelligence) for gray arms transfers.

FIGURE 2.6   Circumventing Sanctions PDM 1.1

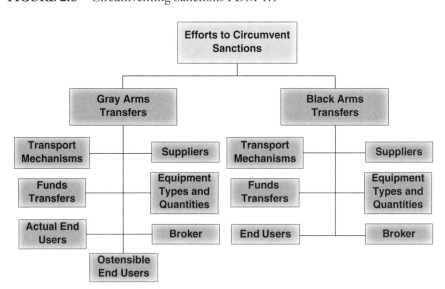

[2]Federation of American Scientists, "International Crime Threat Assessment," www.fas.org/irp/threat/pub45270chap2.html.

Problem Definition Model Example 3: Military Operation

To illustrate that PDMs can take many forms, let's look at a different approach to problem definition.

Establishing a shared situational awareness (SA) and understanding in the battlespace is critical to the planning and conduct of all military operations. Today's adversary is a dynamic, adaptive foe that operates within a complex, interconnected operational environment. Conflicts are constantly evolving and mutating, stretching from conventional warfare to peacekeeping, and increasingly posing new challenges for the military.

In this example, suppose that you are an intelligence analyst under the commander of Joint Task Force (JTF) 76, assigned to a battlespace in the fictitious West Hiber Region. Using Figure 2.7 as a starting point, you are tasked with identifying the conditions, circumstances, and influences that affect the employment of JTF 76's capabilities, relative to the commander's intent, or tasking. Specifically, in this particular situation, JTF 76 has been given the mission to establish a safe and secure environment in its area of responsibility (AoR). You have already determined that the political situation in the country of Tyronia is playing a key role in the destabilization of the region.

JTF 76 Operational Environment PDM 1 (Figure 2.7) is the beginning phase for creating a knowledge base of what JTF 76 knows about the operational environment

FIGURE 2.7 Joint Task Force 76 Operational Environment PDM 1

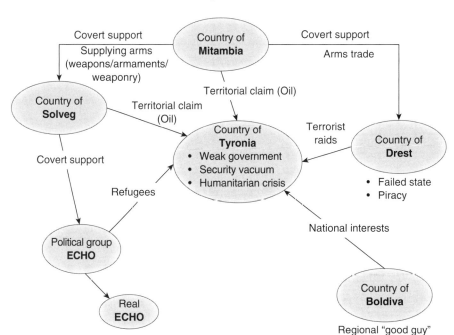

based on the system of systems PMESII framework. For example, the model presented in Figure 2.7 is derived from the following information:

- **Political:** Tyronia has a weak government; Mitambia has territorial claims to areas of Tyronia; and Solveg has territorial claims to oil reserves that also are claimed by Tyronia.
- **Military:** Solveg is believed to provide covert military support to Real ECHO, the militarized wing of the political group ECHO. Drest is conducting terrorist raids on Tyronia. Heavily armed Drest pirates limit freedom of the seas.
- **Economic:** Mitambia is believed to be sending arms covertly to Solveg and Drest. Drest piracy is also negatively affecting trade and driving shipping prices up in the region.
- **Social:** Tyronia faces a humanitarian crisis, in part due to a refugee influx caused by Real ECHO insurgency and terrorist raids sponsored by Drest. In some coastal Drest villages, pirate and terrorist organizations recruit and indoctrinate young men actively and in some cases are the main social service providers for the village.

Note that certain topics link several PMESII dimensions together, such as piracy that has a clear impact on the military, economic, and social dimensions of the battlespace. The PDM has visualized this very complex situation in a way that would require very little explanation if given in a short briefing of the situation JTF 76 is facing.

Also note that the friendly, adversarial, and neutral PMESII systems and their subsystems have been identified for a sufficient SU so that the commander can determine and state further objectives. More importantly, that will allow a holistic understanding as to the effects of any actions or nonactions on the operational environment.

Figure 2.7 shows the operational environment that JTF 76 must engage. But not all of the issues shown are ones that JTF can do anything about—territorial claims or refugees, for example. So the next step is to narrow the focus to those issues that will require TNMs. Figure 2.8 represents a subset of JTF 76 Operational Environment PDM 1, categorizing the issues that JTF 76 can act upon because of its capabilities (i.e., force of arms). For simplicity, we're now back to a hierarchy of issues that can be broken down in detail. However, Figure 2.7 is a more valuable starting point because it gives a picture of how the issues are interrelated.

Different PDMs created for the same scenario can look very different because individuals interpret and weight information differently. However, there should be an expectation that a specific scenario, no matter how broad the visual depiction may appear, will have certain commonalities.

FIGURE 2.8   Joint Task Force 76 Operational Environment PDM 1.1

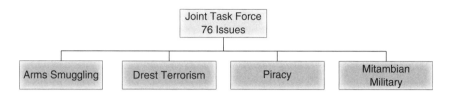

Problem Definition Models: Rationale

These three examples illustrate the importance of beginning any analytic effort by thinking through the problem rigorously. With a well-stated problem definition, it is much easier to create TNMs because the problem definition ensures that critical elements of the target network have not been missed. After the production of a PDM or two, the target model is a straightforward step, as we'll see in step 4. But to get to step 4, you have to make use of intelligence reporting, discussed next.

STEP 3: READ THE INTELLIGENCE REPORTING

A package of intelligence reporting from relevant collection disciplines about the target is presented after the scenario. This raw intelligence (and some finished analysis) takes the form of brief summaries of Human Intelligence (HUMINT), Communications Intelligence (COMINT), cyber collection, Open Source (OSINT), and technical collection reporting (primarily Imagery Intelligence, or IMINT). Added to the scenario, this intelligence reporting is used to develop the TNM or TNMs.

To illustrate how the raw intelligence is used in the exercises, let's continue the example, introduced earlier and loosely modeled on a real-life event: the illicit transfer of gray arms from eastern European sources to a Sierra Leone rebel group, the RUF, in 1998 and 1999. Following is the raw intelligence (all of which is notional, though many names and organizations are drawn from the actual scenario). This same set of reports will be used in the target network modeling example in step 4 that follows.

Rep #	Date-Time Group	Text
R1	HUMINT October 6, 1998	The Revolutionary United Front (RUF) currently controls a large swath of territory in eastern and southern Sierra Leone, an area rich in alluvial diamonds, and is using forced labor to mine the diamonds. (Source: History of reliable reporting)
R2	COMINT November 3, 1998	Former Soviet air force airplanes, registered as Air Cess, Centrafican Airlines, and San Air General Trading, are being used to deliver attack helicopters (AHs), armored vehicles, and anti-tank mines to Liberia from an airport in Bulgaria. The end use of the weaponry is unknown.

(Continued)

(Continued)

Rep #	Date-Time Group	Text
R3	OSINT December 2, 1998	Air Cess first appeared in Belgium in 1996, although it was registered in Monrovia, Liberia, with Viktor Bout as its head. Bout also is believed to own Centrafrican Airlines and San Air General Trading. (Source: Paris AFP [World Service] in English—world news service of the independent French news agency Agence France-Presse)
R4	HUMINT January 4, 1999	Charles Taylor's regime in Liberia is supplying weaponry that includes AK-47 automatic weapons, AHs, and armored vehicles to a Sierra Leone rebel group, the RUF. (Source: Liaison service, believed reliable)
R5	COMINT April 2, 1999	International arms dealer Viktor Bout received a funds transfer from Liberia's international ship registry of $12 million on March 23, 1999.
R6	HUMINT May 20, 1999	During late 1998, Bulgarian arms dealer Peter Mirchev was providing arms broker Viktor Bout with military weaponry for an unspecified African country. Mirchev's company, KAS Engineering, was handling the transfers. The weapons, which included assault rifles and anti-tank mines, were airlifted from Burgas Airport in Bulgaria. (Source: Believed reliable, but has no prior reporting history)
R7	HUMINT June 13, 1999	In July 1998, KAS Engineering, a Bulgarian company, had end user certificates, ostensibly issued by Togo, for the shipment of heavy military equipment to that country from Bulgaria. A check with Togo government officials revealed no record of the issuance of such certificates. (Source: Reporting derived from multiple sources)

Note: HUMINT = Human Intelligence; COMINT = communications intelligence; OSINT = Open Source Intelligence.

Intelligence Reports (INTREPs) can come in many different formats. The format varies from one intelligence service to another, and even within intelligence services, typically depending on the type of source. The reporting example here resembles what might be encountered by an analyst at the national level or at the military operational theater level. Such analysts typically have high-level security clearances, so the reporting includes substantial detail. Another type of format is encountered in combat theaters at the tactical level. Those reports, usually called "tear line" reports, have been sanitized for release at a lower security classification level. As a result, they are very brief, perhaps one or two sentences. Many of the case studies in this workbook use intelligence reporting in tear line format.

Drawing analytic conclusions directly from a set of raw intelligence is not an easy task, even with this limited set. It is far more difficult when the relevant raw material runs into the hundreds of reports, as sometimes is the case. Some form of TNM is needed as a framework for organizing and collating the raw material, as discussed next.

STEP 4: CREATE A TARGET NETWORK MODEL

The scenario and background reading, your problem model(s) and the raw intelligence, are the necessary elements that allow for the development of a preliminary TNM. (Some exercises also will encourage the creation of several collateral models, such as process models or geospatial models as well.)

Most issues of intelligence interest can be modeled in the abstract. That is, a generic model of the issue can be selected, populated, refined, and transitioned into a specific TNM. Continuing the Sierra Leone Gray Arms example will illustrate the way it works.

Target Network Model Example 1: Gray Arms Shipments to Sierra Leone

Figure 2.9 is an example of a generic network model template that could be used for any gray (or black) market commodities case. It reflects the problem definition shown in the PDM titled "Circumventing Sanctions PDM 1.1" (Figure 2.6). In this example, the template is closely related to that PDM. It exhibits the gray arms broker's network as a social network consisting of the actors in the trade: suppliers, brokers, end users, financiers, and transport agents.

To make the model specific, we populate it using the raw intelligence from step 3.

FIGURE 2.9 Generic Arms Transfer Network Model

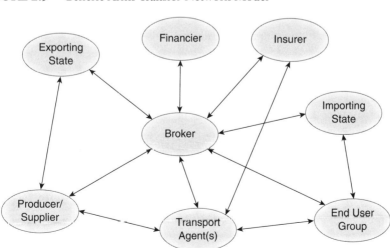

Figure 2.10 is the populated version of Figure 2.9. Note that the identity of the insurer is not given in the raw intelligence (it may be that Bout was self-insured). This would be an intelligence gap, to be addressed in any future collection plan.

Again, remember that it's important to annotate and track your modeling work to facilitate communication of the models themselves; this gray arms example uses the simplest notation, but increasing levels of granularity are most useful: origin, title, date, and time, for example. The TNM is a means to an end. Its purpose is to create a quickly shared awareness among all stakeholders.

FIGURE 2.10   Viktor Bout Arms Transfer Target Network Model 1.1

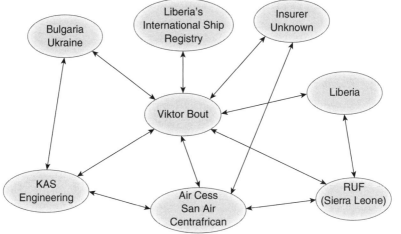

Note: RUF = Revolutionary United Front.

Target Network Model Example 2: Joint Task Force Operational Environment

In this TNM example, we consider the JTF 76 Operational Environment PDM 1 created earlier in step 2 (in Figure 2.7) within the context of the INTREPs. The goal is to identify the critical vulnerabilities of the target network that the intelligence customer can possibly affect or influence. These could include structures, communications, popular support, motivation, members, leaders, and infrastructure amongst others. Your job is to develop only the TNMs that are relevant to what your organization can do with its capabilities; JTF 76 as a military organization clearly has the means of coercion to tackle adversaries that are essentially armed and dangerous (also understood as threat networks).

In the problem model (Figure 2.8), four TNM topics were identified: arms smuggling, terrorism, piracy, and the Mitambian military. However, it makes sense to populate just three models since INTREPs indicate that there is a very close connection between the terrorist groups and arms smuggling. TNM 1 could establish the tracking and guidance collection on those together as illustrated in Figure 2.11. TNM 2 could focus on the piracy network as represented in Figure 2.12. And,

FIGURE 2.11   Joint Task Force Arms Smuggling Target Network Model 1

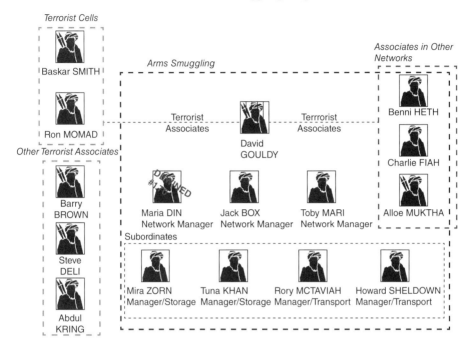

FIGURE 2.12   Joint Task Force Pirating Target Network Model 2

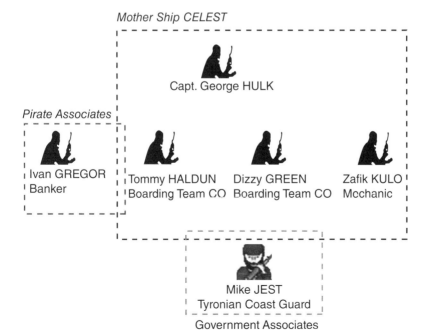

TNM 3 could address the Mitambian military conventional forces as is the case in Figure 2.13.

TNM 3 (Figure 2.13) shows how conventional forces can be modeled with TNMs. This step really is not much different from traditional Order Of Battle (OOB) work, with maybe a little more attention given to social networks within the military organization. These TNMs can also be broken into sub-TNMs as needed and

FIGURE 2.13   Joint Task Force Mitambian Military Target Network Model 3

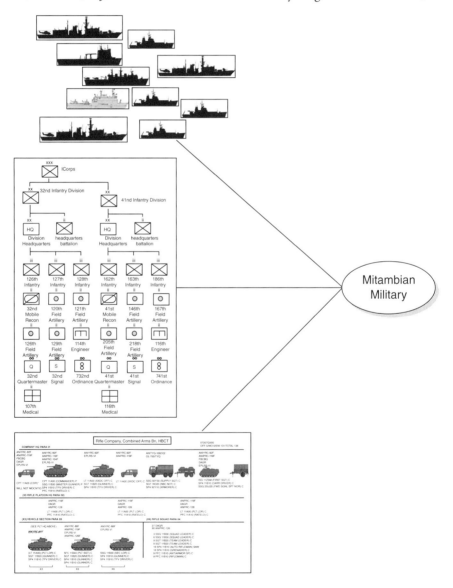

distributed to forces to quickly illustrate what is known and where knowledge gaps exist, in order to build shared SU.

As you can see, there is no set design for TNMs. However, they should be sufficiently stand-alone to indicate relationships between entities; groups of entities; and, of course, structures, functions, and organizations.

As intelligence comes in, you will populate and update your TNMs as required, in terms of functions, structure, and organization. For those who are accustomed to working with products such as target lists or intelligence collection plans (ICPs), it does not take a great deal of imagination to see how TNMs can be used to help deliver these and other products for the scenarios in this workbook. However, before generating these, some sort of intelligence assessment or analysis usually must be done—which shortly will be discussed in the step 5 section on analysis.

Caveats to Keep in Mind When Populating Target Network Models

Answering Who-What-When-Where-How-Why Questions   TNMs are particularly valuable for answering questions that begin with *who*. One common way to create a network model is to first create an association matrix. It portrays the existence of an association, known or suspected, between individuals, organizations, places, and things. Analysts use association matrices to identify those personalities and select the associations needing a more in-depth analysis to determine the degree of relationships between nodes.[3]

Answering questions that begin with *how* and *why* usually requires digging a bit deeper into the model. Typically, you have to look in detail at individual nodes as well as the relationships among them, a process referred to as nodal analysis or individual component analysis. It focuses on activity taking place within a specific node in a specific geographic area. Often the purpose is to determine how nodes in a system function in relation to one another and which nodes are critical—that is, where your intelligence customer can act to influence the situation favorably.[4] These nodes, in a generalized or functional network, can be places or objects. Sometimes, nodal analysis involves assessing performance of an object—aircraft, missile, etc. The node can be an organization, and your job might be to assess the role of the organization within the larger network.

Because there are no single-node intelligence problems, a seasoned analyst always will include one or more network models. But the analyst often will be called upon to answer all of the classic intelligence questions identified previously. Some of those require additional types of generic model templates. In general, pattern analysis

---

[3]U.S. Joint Forces Command, "Commander's Handbook for Attack the Network," Joint Warfighting Center, Suffolk, VA, May 20, 2011, chap. IV, http://www.dtic.mil/doctrine/doctrine/jwfc/atn_hbk.pdf.

[4]Ibid.

models such as process models, timelines, and geospatial models answer what-when-where questions:

- Process models show the sequence of activities in graphical form—the "what" question.
- Timelines, or time event charts, are chronological records of individual or group activities. Analysts use these charts to help analyze larger scale patterns of such things as activities and relationships, establishing the "what" and "when."
- Geospatial models, such as incident maps, focus on the "what" and "where" of an event.[5]

Looking again at the Sierra Leone Gray Arms example, the target network Viktor Bout Arms Transfer (TNM 1.1) model in Figure 2.10 is necessary for the proper overview. But additional models would represent an even more complete picture by showing what is happening from a process, spatial or time point of view, for example:

1. a process model that goes from the source of the arms to the end user

2. a geospatial model, showing the routes of movement of the arms on a map

3. a timeline model showing the transit times of weaponry from the exporting state to the RUF

No one type of model template fits all, and some fact situations naturally lend themselves to certain types of templates. Think about money laundering, for example. Like gray arms traffic, it involves a network of companies, financial institutions, criminal organizations, and individuals. Obviously, network models are appropriate. But money laundering is a process that typically involves three phases: placement, layering, and integration, so it makes sense to also create a process flow model.

Source Evaluation   In the real world, populating the models often requires that analysts evaluate the intelligence reporting. Fitting information into the existing model template can mean a three-step process: evaluating the source; evaluating the communications channel through which the information arrived; and evaluating the quality of the information itself. Here are some questions that analysts keep in mind: What are the source's credentials? Did the source have proper access to get the information? Does the source have any bias or vested interest? How did the information arrive? How many times did the information change hands before you received it? Do you trust the organizations or people the information flowed through? And finally, how would you weigh the information? Is it rumor, hearsay, or an eyewitness account? Can it be corroborated by other accounts?

---

[5]Ibid.

For the purposes of this workbook, the majority of cases do not require evaluation. The cases where that element is highlighted will be noted in the assignment section.

The intelligence reporting in tear line form (Chapters 3, 4, 13, and 14) makes use of the standard HUMINT evaluation schema shown in Table 2.1. This standard annotation for HUMINT sources frequently will include a reference to the source by number. For example, a report might be labeled "HUMINT 020–B2" indicating that it is from source 20; that the source is judged as usually reliable (B); and that the report is judged as probably true (2).

Table 2.1 6 × 6 Source Evaluation and Rating Schema

Reliability of the Source	Credibility of the Information
A. Completely reliable	1. Confirmed by other sources
B. Usually reliable	2. Probably true
C. Fairly reliable	3. Possibly true
D. Not usually reliable	4. Doubtful
E. Unreliable	5. Improbable
F. Reliability cannot be judged	6. Truth cannot be judged

Network Modeling Tools   Network modeling tools such as IBM Analyst Notebook or Palantir Gotham allow analysts to populate a network template electronically. There are also many Geographic Information Systems (GIS) tools that allow geospatial modeling and software packages for creating timelines. If more sophisticated tools are not available, all of these models can be created using PowerPoint and electronically shared among students. In working intelligence units, it could be said that the single greatest benefit of target network modeling is the facility to share electronically. However, if all else fails, the model templates in this workbook can easily be created the way that they have been for decades: with pencil and paper (and the frequent use of an eraser). In the classroom, sharing the model in hard copy can work fine.

STEP 5: CONDUCT ANALYSIS

The analysis of the scenario, development of the problem definition, assimilation of the INTREPs, and the development of your TNM all require the application of critical thinking. Those activities, along with the generation of other intelligence products (to be discussed in step 6), also entail the use of structured analytic techniques. A brief note about each is included here as a reminder that all beginning analysts need to have some basic knowledge of the concepts.

Critical Thinking

Much has been written on critical thinking—going back to 400 BC and Socrates. Critical thinking, under different names, was dealt with repeatedly during the

Middle Ages and the Renaissance in Europe, and again extensively in the eighteenth, nineteenth, and twentieth centuries. Most educated populaces understand that without training in the discipline, societies are doomed to fail. Many academics and professionals alike have devoted careers to and written books about the subject and the behaviors needed to apply critical reasoning methods. Most often, authors distill their recommendations into ten steps or actions (much like books on effective management or leadership) toward the practice of critical thought.

For the intelligence analyst, critical thinking requires at least two core character traits or inherent inclinations that encourage the practice. First, it requires a predisposition toward inquisitiveness, an almost limitless curiosity about any and all subjects or processes. Curious minds tend to stay open to possibilities. And second, it requires an ability to rigorously pay attention to details and to stay focused. With those two attributes in the foreground, the following are some time-tested standard critical reasoning competencies (many more than ten items), framed around the process of creating an intelligence product and expressed in terms that are appropriate for intelligence analysts.

Defining the Problem   Never accept the problem definition stated by the customer as is. Ask clarifying questions. Restate the problem in your own words to the customer to see if you really understand what they are asking for. This will often result in additional information that may narrow or widen the scope of their original request. Pay close attention for any statements that indicate a customer is hoping for a particular outcome. Systematically break down the problem into sub-elements and model those. Ask yourself if the model is applicable, and if not, begin again with an alternative model.

Having a Perspective on the Problem   Approach the problem objectively, and employ a systematic method for maintaining that approach. Begin by immediately considering your belief systems and potential biases (especially political and cultural views) surrounding the issue and detach from them. Do a periodic check to ensure that life experiences are not coloring your perspective. Guard against inevitable stereotypes. One strategy for maintaining an open mind is to think like a scientist. The scientific standard is to observe and report without judgment.

Approaching the Evidence or Intelligence Reporting   You will rarely have proof of anything and most certainly have to work with limited data. Decide on a systematic construct to evaluate, weigh, and integrate evidence. Intelligence analysis is about looking for patterns. Look for convergent evidence. Are there reports that seem to be in alignment? Conversely, be aware of divergent reporting. Examine the sourcing, logic, timing, and any other parameters that indicate a potential presence or absence of credibility. Consider the context surrounding the reporting. Distinguish between fact and opinion (or rumor), but do not automatically disregard the latter. Do discard evidence that upon reflection or testing you find to be irrelevant.

Generating Hypotheses   Most important is to understand that the first hypothesis is a *beginning* point. All hypotheses are based on incomplete information, which is why testing is required. A hypothesis has to be formulated logically, through finding relationships and connections between the limited and variable evidence provided to you. Have you made assumptions, and are they defensible? Use clear, simple, precise language, absent of any generalizations. Fewer words are more effective than more.

Testing Hypotheses   In the intelligence business, ego is the foremost enemy of critical thinking. Mentally or emotionally anchoring to the initial hypothesis and coming to premature closure will create bad outcomes. Think creatively to prove an alternative, opposite, or even slightly different position. Work to find any flaw or inconsistency in your chain of reasoning. Can the conclusions that you have drawn be traced to supporting intelligence? If the conclusions cannot be articulated succinctly and the line of reasoning is not immediately apparent, then your support for them should be reassessed.

Structured Analytic Techniques

There are many established structured or descriptive analytical methods discussed in numerous published sources, including entire textbooks. A researcher investigating analytic methodologies in use in the U.S. Intelligence Community identified at least 160 separate techniques.[6] Numerous commonly understood methods are easily employed in this workbook, such as Key Assumptions Check or Analysis of Competing Hypotheses, or Timeline Analysis. Force Field Analysis and decomposition and visualization are staples in target network modeling. But, as discussed in Chapter 1, referred to in this chapter, and cited in many of the case studies, one of the most straightforward yet powerful structured analytic techniques for intelligence applications is the PMESII paradigm. Because it is especially important in target network modeling, let's examine it in some detail.

Structured Analytic Techniques: PMESII

PMESII is used to describe the foundation, features, and activities of adversaries and the relationships between them and, as discussed in Chapter 1, of friendly or neutral groups. It can help determine strengths and weaknesses of all these groups; therefore, it is an invaluable tool to support decision making, operational planning, and targeting to deal with all networks of intelligence concern. While it has become one of the most popular systems of systems analysis tools in modern military doctrine, it has proven equally as applicable in intelligence that supports national policy or deals with criminal groups. Though the *M* in the acronym stands for "military," in nonmilitary contexts it generally refers to the threat or use of force.

[6]Rob Johnson, *Analytic Culture in the U.S. Intelligence Community* (Washington, DC: Center for the Study of Intelligence, CIA, 2005), xviii.

Both PDMs and TNMs inherently will reflect one or more of the PMESII dimensions. The methodology's application was highlighted earlier in PDM Example 3. To illustrate its efficacy in a different context, we return once again to the Sierra Leone Gray Arms example. Let's use the PMESII breakout to approach analyzing the Viktor Bout Arms Transfer Target Network Model 1.1 in Figure 2.10.

The Sierra Leone Gray Arms Target Network Model 1.1 (Figure 2.10)
Political: The embargo on arms shipments to Sierra Leone is a political action. The intelligence customer might wish to know how the embargo could be modified to reduce gray arms traffic after learning how the embargo is being defeated. The relationships among the countries involved (Bulgaria, Liberia, and Sierra Leone) are political also, and those relationships could be altered by political actions to reduce the arms traffic.

Military: The capabilities, performance, and quality of the weapons being transferred are important in assessing the outcome of the Sierra Leone conflict. The likely end use of the weaponry is also of intelligence interest.

Economic: Issues here include the funds transfers connected to the arms sales and funding sources that the Sierra Leone rebels (the RUF) are using to pay for the arms (reportedly diamond traffic—a separate TNM could be developed to map the RUF illicit diamond trade).

Social: The nature of the relationship between Liberia's leader, Charles Taylor, and the RUF rebels is significant in determining the future of the arms shipments. The strength of the relationship between Viktor Bout and arms dealer Peter Mirchev is also important.

Infrastructure: Transportation routes for arms and the means of transport fall into this category. Also of intelligence interest are the support capabilities for weaponry in the field.

Informational: Issues of intelligence significance include the use of falsified end user certificates and international perceptions created by mainstream and social media reports that contribute to an overall negative narrative for Liberia. An example of the latter would be a narrative built on the story of how rebels receive arms through Liberia and how the arms facilitate the RUF use of forced labor to mine diamonds.

PMESII Templates   An additional level of analytic structure can be added by creating a matrix of PMESII versus other factors. For example, activity-based analysis focuses on geospatial and temporal activities. An analysis template like Table 2.2 might be useful, for example, in analysis of the upcoming Chapter 3 case (Narcotics and the Afghan Insurgency).

One more detailed such matrix, often used by intelligence officers supporting coalition operations, is called PMESII/ASCOPE (area, structure, capabilities, organizations, people, and events). Table 2.3 is an example template again illustrating the issues to be examined in dealing with the Narcotics and the Afghan Insurgency case study.

Table 2.2   PMESII for Activity-Based Analysis

	Political	Military	Economic	Social	Infrastructure	Information
Geospatial	Regional and district boundaries; party areas	Military controlled areas; incident locations	Markets; industrial sites; banking centers	Housing sites; schools; recreational areas	Water supply; transport routes	Radio and TV media coverage
Temporal	Elections; political meetings	Deployments; force movements	Harvests; business hours	Prayer meetings; holidays	Construction programs	Information campaigns

STEP 6: DELIVER PRODUCTS

Developing and populating target models is both challenging and rewarding. An analyst is no longer working in a vacuum. Target network modeling is a giant leap forward in the ability to share an easily understandable picture of an intelligence issue and either give or get help from all stakeholders. The target-centric approach to analysis demands skill in developing TNMs. But the real challenge and reward comes in creating the intelligence products that your TNM facilitates.

In practice, many types of intelligence products are derived from completed TNMs. Your customer depends on you for some form of what we in the profession call "actionable intelligence." Your law enforcement or military customer needs to discriminate among too many potential targets. While the explicit training focus is to develop facility in creating, populating, and sharing TNMs, the assignments in this workbook also require generating a product. The product assignments are deliberately kept simple; following is some background on three that are common to the cases.

Intelligence Assessments

Obviously, one objective of target network modeling is to produce an intelligence assessment or finished INTREP that answers the questions posed by your customer or military commander. If your intelligence assessment is unclear or misunderstood, the consequences could be dire. Good writing is hard work. But hard work on your part is essential to make your customer's decision-making process easier.

Following are some general guidelines for a proper intelligence assessment.

1. Systematically organize your thoughts.

2. Use declarative sentences. Avoid the passive voice. There are two extremes to avoid: stilted writing and the opposite extreme—informality that detracts from the message or affects its credibility.

3. Begin with your statement of major findings and conclusions. Immediately get to the point; do not build up to it. And never wait until the end. Put another way—give your answers *before* explanations and conclusions *before* details.

Table 2.3 Example PMESII/ASCOPE Template

	Political	Military	Economic	Social	Infrastructure	Information
Area	Regional and district boundaries; party areas	Military controlled areas; incident locations	Markets; industrial sites; banking centers	Housing sites; schools; recreational areas	Water supply; transport routes	Radio and TV media coverage
Structure	District centers; shuras	Government buildings; military and police barracks	Food storage sites; access routes	Hospitals; recreational and religious centers	Roads; bridges; airports; electrical lines	Television; telephone; print shops
Capabilities	Dispute resolution; leadership	Military and police leadership; integrity; reliability	Electrical capacity and reliability	Strength of tribal, religious, and political groups	Ability to build and maintain roads and utilities	Literacy and access to media
Organizations	Government political parties, organizations, and NGOs	Structure and governance of military and police forces	Industrial and service industries; unions	Tribes; families; clubs; sports organizations	Government ministries; construction industries; NGOs	Media, government, and religious centers
People	Governors; mullahs; elders	Military and police leadership, integrity, and reliability	Banking and industrial leaders; corruption; opposition	Leaders in family; religion, political, union, and social activities	Builders and construction firms; skill base; division of labor	Controllers of media in government, opposition, and religious groups
Events	Elections; political meetings	Deployments	Harvests; business hours	Prayer meetings; holidays	Construction programs	Information campaigns

Note: NGOs = nongovernmental organizations.

4. Support every analytic conclusion. Provide, explain, and emphasize key insights. The customer should be able to follow your reasoning at every turn.

5. Your customer expects logical and objective arguments. Make it abundantly clear when you move from fact to analysis. Your customer should never be in doubt whether he is reading facts or analysis.

6. Don't use acronyms without defining them. Even standard acronyms in common use throughout an organization may cause problems for readers outside the organization.

7. If you feel that it's appropriate, you can include a graphic or table, but then be sure that you explain or refer to it in your text.

8. Make sure that your grammar and spelling are spot on. The most powerfully constructed bit of analysis can be totally destroyed by errors in either.

9. Recognize that the finishing-up process—polishing—takes longer than any other part. Good writing most often means rewriting. You are close to the subject, so your results are clear to you; be sure that they will be clear to someone who does not have your familiarity with the data. Written assessments do not give you the opportunity to clarify that you have in a verbal presentation.

Intelligence assessments can be very short—one or two paragraphs—or can extend to several pages by providing both the conclusions and the supporting evidence. Continuing the Sierra Leone Gray Arms example, let's make use of TNM 1.1 shown in Figure 2.10. A short assessment drawn from this TNM might read as follows:

Sierra Leone arms sanctions are being circumvented by a network managed by arms dealer Viktor Bout. Funding to pay for the arms appears to be derived from illicit diamond traffic and flows through the Liberian International Ship and Corporate Registry. The arms, coming primarily from sources in Bulgaria and the Ukraine, are being supplied by a Bulgarian company, KAS Engineering. The arms are transported via Bout-controlled airlines to Liberia under forged end user certificates and from there find their way to the RUF in Sierra Leone.

Intelligence Collection Planning

Another common product, aside from assessments, involves intelligence collection planning. Such planning can take a number of forms, from the very general to the detailed and highly specific.

To help achieve SU, the intelligence process has to be a learning process—that is, it must develop knowledge iteratively. This requires that analysts be prudent in identifying what they do not know and in identifying ways to use collection to fill the gaps. Once a TNM is established, it can be used also to help manage this process, simply by visually illustrating what is known and not known. Following is a discussion of collection planning products that are assigned in some of the case studies.

Intelligence Gaps and Requirements   All collection planning starts from intelligence requirements—usually based on gaps in knowledge that are derived from examining the TNM. The requirements typically must be prioritized, because available collection means seldom if ever are adequate to satisfy all requirements.

For example, many intelligence assessments conclude with a section identifying gaps in knowledge—the first step in collection planning. In the Sierra Leone Gray Arms example, gaps might include the following:

- quantities of arms supplied
- supply routes between Liberia and Sierra Leone
- funds transferred to pay for arms
- identity of insurer, if any

Intelligence Collection Plan   The ICP is a detailed breakdown of how each intelligence requirement is to be satisfied in terms of direction and collection. It contributes greatly to ensuring shared SU among collection managers and analysts as to what is needed and why. TNMs facilitate this construction of ICPs by providing a framework for the visual identification of intelligence gaps. The TNM also can be used to develop hypotheses (based on relationships depicted) that should be tested through collection.

The ICP, then, is a formal way of matching intelligence requirements with collection capabilities. In its simplest form, it can be a list of gaps or requirements along with a tasking of specific collection means to fill the gap or requirement. It frequently takes the form of a matrix (requirements versus capabilities). Table 2.4 illustrates one format for an ICP, derived from the first two gaps (now priority intelligence requirements) listed previously for the Sierra Leone Arms issue.

Operations Targeting

Another common product of target network modeling is operations targeting. Operations targeting supports military, covert actions, and law enforcement operations.

For those experienced with national or military intelligence products, the concepts discussed previously—intelligence gaps and ICPs—may be familiar. Terms such as *target sets* and *HVTLs,* discussed next, may be less familiar and may also seem to be more tied to operational planning than to traditional intelligence roles. The advent of netwar, introduced in Chapter 1, has led to a blurring of these traditional roles, especially in fields such as counterterrorism, counternarcotics, and counterproliferation. Today, intelligence analysts frequently are called upon to develop products that formerly were not their responsibility. In particular, intelligence analysts in military and law enforcement units now do a great deal of operations targeting.

Table 2.4   Intelligence Collection Plan: Sierra Leone Gray Arms Traffic Matrix

Priority Intelligence Requirement	Information Requirement	Sources	Specific Information Requirement
Determine quantities of arms supplied to Sierra Leone rebels.	How many attack helicopters (AHs)? How many armored vehicles?	HUMINT, IMINT, COMINT, OSINT	What are the types? What is their operational status? Where are they located?
	How many anti-tank mines? How many assault rifles?	HUMINT, COMINT, OSINT	What types of mines are there? What are the types or models of assault rifles?
Identify supply routes for arms transfers between Liberia and Sierra Leone.	Where are the main border crossing points for smugglers?	IMINT, MASINT, HUMINT	Is Roberts International Airport a likely entry point for smuggled mines and rifles? Is the Port of Monrovia a likely entry for helicopters and armored vehicles?
	Determine transshipment points and transportation means between entry point and rebel forces.	IMINT, HUMINT, Liaison	Are the roads between Liberia and Sierra Leone used at night for smuggling? Are the bridges and fords across the Mano River used for smuggling? Does the Sierra Leone military have special knowledge of known smuggling routes?

Note: HUMINT = Human Intelligence; IMINT = Imagery Intelligence; COMINT = communications intelligence; OSINT = Open Source Intelligence; MASINT = Measurement and Signature Intelligence.

Following are some examples of products that are widely used in operations targeting and are assigned in selected case studies.

Target Sets   Making lists of target nominations—a target set—primarily serves two purposes. First, it ensures that all participating units have visibility into the targeting process. Second, it facilitates timeliness; with preapproved target sets, targets do not have to be approved individually. Target sets are most useful for larger military formations engaged in a battlespace to ensure unity of effort. Table 2.5 is a partial target set that could be created from the Sierra Leone Gray Arms TNM.

Table 2.5   Partial Target Set: Sierra Leone Arms Traffic

Target	Desired Effect	Justification
Charles Taylor	Influence	Taylor reportedly fears UN intervention in Sierra Leone. Publicizing reports of gray arms shipments would likely pressure him to back off permitting the shipments.
Air Cess Centrafrican Airlines San Air General Trading	Disrupt	These Viktor Bout-controlled airlines depend on airports in North Africa for refueling stops. The countries involved may be willing to deny transit.
Peter Mirchev	Influence/ Disrupt	The Bulgarian government may ignore Mirchev's arms dealing but appears vulnerable to adverse publicity and international pressure to deal with Mirchev.

High-Value Target Lists   High-value target lists (HVTLs) are a prioritized list of targets, derived from the target set, that have been scrutinized and the risks assessed against the overall objectives of the mission. An HVTL might look much like Table 2.5, with the addition of a priority justification. There should be some sort of standard evaluation framework for determining the priority of one target over another. The HVTL communicates shared objectives and helps to determine resource use and intelligence collection planning. Once TNMs are populated, identifying the HVTs should be relatively simple. Again, the list can be used for kinetic and nonkinetic targeting.

Additional examples of all three types of products (intelligence assessment, intelligence collection planning, and operations targeting) are introduced in the case studies. Some of the best learning experiences for students who have completed the case studies in this workbook have resulted from the comparison of TNM products produced by different individuals or groups for the same cases.

A BRIEF EXAMPLE CASE: RUNDOWN FLATS

Let's conclude by moving through the steps reviewed in this chapter, using a brief example from the field of law enforcement in a domestic crime case.

Educational Objectives

This exercise provides practical experience in the following:

- practicing developing target network modeling using social network analysis (SNA)

- practicing identifying and using PMESII elements for target network modeling
- creating a brief (one or two paragraphs) intelligence assessment using target network modeling as support

Assignment

In this example, you are an intelligence analyst with the white-collar crime unit of the Federal Bureau of Investigation (FBI). The U.S. Department of Housing and Urban Development (HUD) has requested that you investigate a series of property transfers that have resulted in the loss of several million dollars in HUD-guaranteed loans. HUD officials are concerned about the possibility of fraud in the transfers.

Scenario

The property in question is called Rundown Flats. It is located in Pine Ridge, Arkansas, a mid-sized city (population 57,000) in an agricultural region having a depressed economy. Most residents live below the poverty level; a small segment of landowners and merchants possess most of the wealth. The city has one of the highest crime rates in the United States.

Rundown Flats is a public housing complex in the poorest section of the city and is one of the three in the city that qualify for HUD financial backing.

The file you received from HUD contains the following series of transactions.

REP #	DTG	TEXT
R1	June 1988	Rundown Flats was purchased by James Brinson and Susan Smythe, DBA Caswell Properties, LLC, on June 3, 1988, for $1.23 million. Walridge Enterprises Financial provided a HUD-guaranteed mortgage on the property for $1.1 million.
R2	August 1988	Caswell Properties, LLC, paid $235,000 to Jackson County General Contractors for repairs to Rundown Flats.
R3	July 1989	Caswell Properties, LLC, declared bankruptcy. Walridge Enterprises Financial took possession of Rundown Flats, subsequently selling the property to Philip McCain and Sharon Sloan, DBA Milestone Corporation, for $243,000 and being reimbursed by HUD for the mortgage loan loss. Milestone Corporation obtained a $224,000 mortgage from Walridge Enterprises Financial to purchase the property.
R4	November 1989	Milestone Corporation paid $277,000 to Jackson County General Contractors for repairs to Rundown Flats, obtaining an HUD-backed mortgage from Walridge Enterprises to finance the repairs.

(Continued)

(Continued)

REP #	DTG	TEXT
R5	October 1990	Milestone Corporation declared bankruptcy. Walridge Enterprises Financial took possession of Rundown Flats and was reimbursed by HUD for the repairs and loan losses.
R6	November 1990	Walridge Enterprises sold Rundown Flats to John Briscoe and Samuel Fisk, DBA New Age Holding Company, for $1,323,000. Walridge Enterprises Financial provided an HUD-guaranteed mortgage on the property for $1.11 million.
R7	January 1991	New Age Holding Company paid $313,000 to Jackson County General Contractors for repairs to Rundown Flats.
R8	February 1992	New Age Holding Company declared bankruptcy. Walridge Enterprises Financial took possession of Rundown Flats and was reimbursed by HUD for the repairs and mortgage loan losses.
R9	March 1992	Walridge Enterprises sold Rundown Flats to Mike McCarthy and Ellen James, DBA Southport Properties, LLC, for $1,170,000.

Note: DTG = date-time group; DBA = doing business as; HUD = U.S. Department of Housing and Urban Development.

Problem Definition

The guidance you are given is to investigate the transfers for any evidence of criminal activity that caused the HUD losses. From this general guidance, a simple problem definition would include these elements:

- the nature of the property transfers
- the nature of relationships among the mortgage company and successive buyers
- the series of costly repairs to the property

The Target Network Model

In this case, as in a number of the workbook's case studies, you don't have a target network template to work with or may not know what template is the proper one to start with. There is no one "right" way to proceed—often it is a trial and error process—but the approach described next usually works.

Target networks generally are composed of nodes (people, places, things, organizations, and activities) and links (the relationships among the nodes). One way to begin creating the network model is to select one of these node categories and diagram (link) all of the relationships among those nodes. From that starting point, you would add in the other nodes and the links among them.

In the case of Rundown Flats, it seems logical to start with the organizations involved in the property transfers. There are five of them, including the mortgage company that funded each transfer. The five, with the linkages showing the transfers, are depicted in Figure 2.14, the beginning of a network model.

Next, you would add names of the owners of each company involved in the transfer, creating TNM 1.2 (see Figure 2.15).

FIGURE 2.14   Transfer Model of Rundown Flats Property Target Network Model 1.1

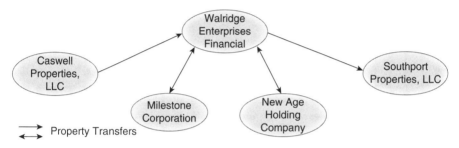

FIGURE 2.15   Ownership of Rundown Flats Property Target Network Model 1.2

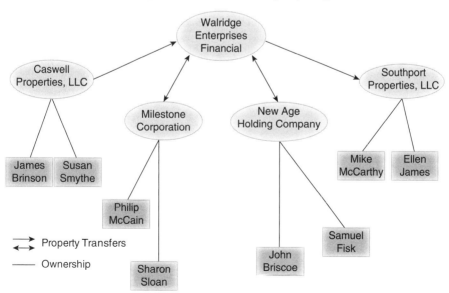

So far, the transactions all appear to be legitimate. Based on their last names, the new owners of the property in each case appear to be unrelated. But you conduct a search of public records that indicates some family, business, and social relationships exist among the transferors, as shown next.

REP #	TEXT
R1	James Brinson is married to Sharon Sloan.
R2	Susan Smythe and Philip McCain are siblings.
R3	Sharon Sloan and Philip McCain were formerly married to each other.
R4	John Briscoe and Samuel Fisk are business partners in a dry cleaning business. Briscoe originally purchased the business from a close friend, Mike McCarthy.
R5	Samuel Fisk and Ellen James are siblings.

Adding these relationships to the model results in TNM 1.3 shown in Figure 2.16.

Two of the transfers (Caswell Properties, LLC, to Milestone Corporation, and New Age Holding Company to Southport Properties, LLC) look suspicious because of the family or business relationships that exist. But one transaction, on its face,

FIGURE 2.16   Social and Family Relationships among Owners of the Rundown Flats Property Target Network Model 1.3

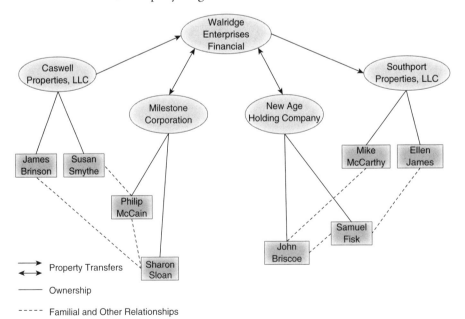

appears legitimate: There is a break in the network of relationships between transferors and transferees at the point where Milestone Corporation transfers the property and New Age Holding Company subsequently acquires it. This break deserves further investigation. So you decide to conduct another search, looking for other social or familial relationships, and come up with this additional set of relationships.

REP #	TEXT
R1	John Briscoe is Winfield Miller's stepson from a previous marriage.
R2	Sharon Sloan is Winfield Miller's sister.
R3	Elizabeth Miller is married to Winfield Miller.
R4	Elizabeth Miller is the managing partner of Walridge Enterprises Financial.
R5	Winfield Miller owns Jackson County General Contractors.

These relationships added into the network model create the next iteration—TNM 1.4, shown in Figure 2.17. The result depicts something quite different from a series of legitimate transactions. All of the participants are linked in a network of family and business relationships, with Winfield Miller as the central actor.

FIGURE 2.17   Rundown Flats Property Transactions Target Network Model 1.4

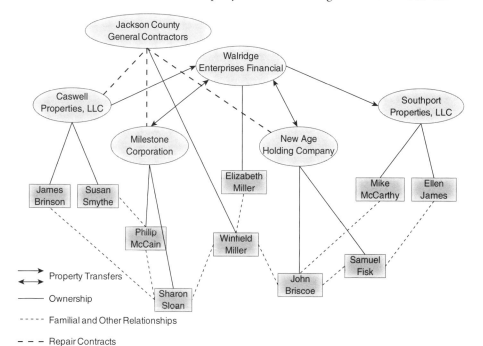

Analysis and Application of PMESII

Looking at Figure 2.17, you note that Elizabeth Miller manages Walridge Enterprises Financial, while her husband, Winfield Miller, owns Jackson County General Contractors. But didn't Jackson County General Contractors reportedly handle the building repairs to Rundown Flats three times, collecting substantial sums each time?

So the TNM is persuasive evidence that the property transfers and property repairs were not what they at first seemed. Instead, they appear to be part of a scheme to defraud HUD for the benefit of Walridge Enterprises Financial and the participants in a conspiracy. Because it is owned by Winfield Miller, Jackson County General Contractors may also have been involved in fraud concerning the repairs to the property.

Your next step would be to look at the PMESII dimensions. At first glance, PMESII might seem to have limited applicability here. This is after all simply a criminal case, primarily driven by economic gain for the participants. But consider these factors:

- **Political/Economic:** The case could stimulate policy changes that include new checks on mortgage fraud in HUD grants. So the analyst needs to determine how the perpetrators were able to stay "under the radar" for so long.
- **Military (Law Enforcement)/Social:** It is important to assess the relationships among participants in the scheme. FBI special agents will want to know the weak links in the network—specifically, which participants are most likely to testify against the rest in exchange for immunity from prosecution or a lesser sentence.
- **Infrastructure:** It is important to assess the true condition of the Rundown Flats buildings. For example, were the repairs necessary? Were they actually made?
- **Informational:** Intelligence customers within HUD will be interested in how the relationships among participants in the fraud were concealed—again, to detect future such cases.

Products Delivery

An intelligence assessment can be created directly from the Rundown Flats Property Transactions Target Network Model 1.4 (Figure 2.17). A summary of your assessment might read as follows:

> The property transfers involving Rundown Flats were not arms-length transactions. They appear to have been a series of sham deals intended to defraud HUD for the benefit of the lender, Walridge Enterprises Financial, and the participants in a conspiracy. At the center of the conspiracy are a couple, Elizabeth and Winfield Miller, who are connected by family and business

relationships with all of the purchasers. Elizabeth Miller is the managing partner of Walridge Enterprises Financial. Winfield Miller is the owner of Jackson County General Contractors, the company that handled three successive repair contracts on the property.

From the TNM (Figure 2.17) and the PMESII issues discussed previously, you can identify information gaps and prepare a collection plan to support prosecution and help HUD to avoid or uncover other such cases of fraud. Such a plan might recommend, for example, the following:

- an investigation of the claimed repairs to the property—it being likely that Jackson County General Contractors was paid for repairs that were never made
- in-depth investigation into the paper trail of the transfers, focusing especially on exchanges of funds in connection with the transfers
- background checks on the participants, to identify the ones most likely to strike a plea bargain in exchange for testimony against the key conspirators (the Millers)
- a review of HUD files and comparison with the result of the other investigations to determine how the fraud was concealed

PART II

Case Studies

3

Narcotics and the Afghan Insurgency

This case study is about Afghanistan's Ishaqzai narcotics cartel and its role in the Helmand province insurgency. A United Nations (UN) report has summarized the Afghan drug problem succinctly:

> Yet, the world over, drug money eventually trumps ideology, and becomes as addictive as the dope itself. Afghanistan is approaching this point. After years of collusion with criminal gangs and corrupt officials, some insurgents are now opportunistically moving up the value chain: not just taxing supply, but getting involved in producing, processing, stocking and exporting drugs. The impact this has on the stability of Afghanistan, and the ways and means to oppose it, require attention.[1]

The UN report also has compared the development of the Helmand insurgency to the development of the Fuerzas Armadas Revolucionarias de Colombia (FARC) as an insurgency turned narcotics cartel in Colombia.[2] The key to a flourishing drug trade in both countries, then, is limited governmental control and a violent insurgent presence.

EDUCATIONAL OBJECTIVES
This exercise provides practical experience in the following:

- introducing network modeling as an analytical technique for visualization and decomposition for the purposes of defining threat networks within an organized crime operational environment

---

[1]United Nations Office on Drugs and Crime Afghanistan Opium Survey, 2009, https://www.unodc.org/documents/crop-monitoring/Afghanistan/Afghanistan_opium_survey_2009_summary.pdf.

[2]Ibid.

- generating target network models (TNMs) based on social network analysis (SNA) supporting intelligence on an individual level as well as an organizational level
- introducing the "tear line" method of reporting and the reliability or credibility evaluations that will be encountered in succeeding exercises

ASSIGNMENT

You are an all-source[3] intelligence analyst in a coalition force (CF) anti-narcotic task force situated in your area of operations (AO): the Gereshk district of Helmand, Afghanistan. Your assignment is to develop intelligence to support operations to disrupt and influence the narcotics threat network in a manner favourable to CF operations.

To complete this assignment, each student or group should read the scenario, background readings, and intelligence tear line reporting that follows. Then complete the following tasks:

- Based on the information provided, develop problem definition models (PDMs) and TNMs as needed in order to execute the tasking.
- Use the intelligence tear lines provided to conduct basic SNA by providing an overview of the key players and their functions or roles within their own group, organization, or society as a whole.
- Using the intelligence tear lines provided, establish a timeline overview of events in the AO.
- Based on the intelligence tear lines provided, identify the intelligence gaps relative to the tasking. Create a simple intelligence collection plan (ICP) by generating twenty questions to be answered by your collection assets. (You may assume you will have access to Human Intelligence [HUMINT], Imagery Intelligence [IMINT], Measurement and Signature Intelligence [MASINT], Open Source Intelligence [OSINT], and Signals Intelligence [SIGINT].)
- Generate target sets relative to your tasking based on the intelligence provided, and indicate the desired effect on that target set; include the justification (logic) for that effect.
- Generate a high-value target list (HVTL) based on the intelligence provided.
- Generate a new ICP of ten questions to be answered by your collection process.

---

[3]An all-source analyst refers to an analyst trained to collate, integrate, and analyze information from a variety of sensors or sources with a variety of methodologies. A single-source analyst specializes in producing only products based on her particular sensor or source. For example, a HUMINT or IMINT analyst is usually single-source. It is usually the single-source products that contribute to the all-source products.

ABBREVIATIONS AND ACRONYMS

Abbreviation or Acronym	Description
AO	area of operations
ANA	Afghan National Army
ANP	Afghan National Police
ANSF	Afghan National Security Forces
CF	coalition force
COP	chief of police
FARC	Fuerzas Armadas Revolucionarias de Colombia (Revolutionary Armed Forces of Colombia) (an irregular Colombian armed force)
FOB	forward operating base
GDP	gross domestic product
GIRoA	Government of the Islamic Republic of Afghanistan
HUMINT	Human Intelligence
HVTL	high-value target list
ICP	intelligence collection plan
IED	improvised explosive device
IMINT	Imagery Intelligence
MASINT	Measurement and Signature Intelligence
NATO	North Atlantic Treaty Organization
NGO	nongovernmental organization
OSINT	Open Source Intelligence
PB	patrol base
POMLT	Police Operational Mentor and Liaison Team
RCIED	radio-controlled IED
QS	Quetta Shura
SIGINT	Signals Intelligence
SNA	social network analysis
SUPINTREP	supplemental intelligence report
UNODC	United Nations Office on Drugs and Crime

SCENARIO

This scenario is based on the actual situation in Afghanistan during 2009 and 2010 with a timeline that is within that period.

Area of Operations

Gereshk, Nahri Saraj District, Helmand Province

Area: Gereshk is the largest city in Nahri Saraj district in the Helmand province. The district includes areas of fertile farmland along both banks of the Helmand River. Gereshk is the district center.

Population: Gereshk has a population of 48,546, approximately 35,000 males and 13,000 females. The population is composed of three major tribes from four ethnic groups: Ishaqzai (48 percent), Barakzai (39 percent), Noorzai (11 percent), and Karagani (2 percent)

Religion: 97 percent of the population is Sunni Muslim; 3 percent is Shia.

Governance

Overview: The district government is led by a mayor appointed by the provincial governor. The mayor, in turn, appoints the key city administrators, who oversee tax collection, utilities (electricity and water), and local development projects. These administrators are answerable only to the mayor, with no other form of oversight. The current mayor is Mir Zafik, who has held the office for the last three years. Zafik is Barakzai and a senior elder of the tribal shura. The city administrators are Momin (tax collection), Haji Ghaffar (electricity and water), and Doth Ibrihm (local development). All three men are Barakzai and except for Momin have held office since Zafik's appointment.

Two ministries have representatives in Gereshk: Rural Rehabilitation and Development and Education. The administrators from the Ministry of Education are preoccupied with their own issues and pay little attention to the overall administration of the district and the province. As a result, the official from the Ministry of Rural Rehabilitation and Development serves as the primary liaison between the local government and the central government in Kabul.

There is no formal judicial presence in Gereshk. Disputes within and between tribes are resolved by the tribal shuras through the traditional consensus decision making. Issues involving the civil administration are resolved by the mayor, sometimes by consensus, but usually through unilateral decisions by the mayor.

Intelligence assessment: The local government is only marginally effective, handicapped by systemic corruption and intertribal friction. Mayor Zafik is outwardly cooperative with CFs, but in key leader engagements seems reluctant to provide precise details about his administration, particularly regarding the city's revenues. This reluctance seems to lend credibility to otherwise unsubstantiated reports of ties to a criminal organization allegedly run by Khan Walid, but Mayor Zafik's well-documented hatred of the Noorzai (which Khan Walid belongs to) makes such a relationship unlikely.

The city administrators appear to be capable, but at least two are possibly tainted by corruption. Momin, the administrator for taxes, has had three complaints lodged by nongovernmental organizations (NGOs) that accuse him of charging "special taxes" before allowing them to operate in Gereshk. (Chief of Police [COP] Fahran investigated all three incidents and determined that nothing improper had occurred.) Haji Ghaffar, the administrator for utilities, is reportedly selling fuel (intended for the city's generators) on the black market, which may explain the frequent fuel short-ages that lead to power outages in the city.

Even if corruption issues are discounted as cultural characteristics, Mayor Zafik's government faces legitimacy issues. The current civil government is almost completely dominated by the Barakzai tribe, which might not be a problem except that they all hold office by appointment, rather than by election. As a result, the other ethnic groups, especially the majority Ishaqzai, feel no allegiance to Mayor Zafik or his administration.

The Government of the Islamic Republic of Afghanistan (GIRoA) presence in Gereshk is also marginal. Darya, the official from the Ministry of Rural Development, is competent, progressive, and a strong supporter of CF but is limited by two key factors. First, she is a member of the minority Karagani and has no ties to any of the Barakzai or Ishaqzai power brokers. As a result, she has been marginalized by both Mayor Zafik and Police Chief Fahran. Second, she is a woman in a very conservative cultural environment, which minimizes her influence even in her own ethnic group.

The lack of a formal judicial system is not a serious hindrance as long as Mayor Zafik's government is not a party to the dispute. In meetings with the shuras of the other three ethnic groups, the elders have frequently voiced their dissatisfaction with the mayor's judgments, complaining that his unilateral decisions almost always pro-tect his officials or favor the Barakzai. When he does bother to discuss issues, he usually bullies the other party into accepting a compromise that is no better than his decisions without discussion.

Security

Overview: Gereshk has a single police station with 178 Afghan National Police (ANP) officers assigned, 105 of whom are from Gereshk or the surrounding area. Only twenty-three of the officers, including the police chief, have received formal training, either from the ANP Academy or by North Atlantic Treaty Organization (NATO) Police Operational Mentor and Liaison Teams (POMLTs). The current chief is a Noorzai named Fahran who was appointed by Mayor Zafik to ease the concerns of the Ishaqzai/Noorzai majority.

The Afghan National Army (ANA) in Gereshk consists of two platoons from A Company, 3rd Kandak under the command of Major Mohammad Ahmadi, an ethnic Tajik.

Intelligence assessment: The ANP in Gereshk are considered marginally effec-tive. Chief Fahran has turned the police force into an instrument to strengthen Noorzai power by making sure the force is dominated by ethnic Noorzais. Out of 178 officers, 109 are Noorzais, and none has formal police training. The twenty-three officers who are trained are either outsiders from other parts of Helmand or Kandahar or Barakzai, and Fahran has deliberately placed them in assignments where they cannot interfere. Fahran himself has received training from POMLT mentors but has never attended the ANP Academy.

Consequently, Fahran's relationship with CF is uneven. Although the police have been successful in providing excellent security for the provincial reconstruction teams and NGO development projects in and around Gereshk, they have done so by intimidation and extreme violence. Furthermore, while he has been supportive of CF efforts in general, Fahran has adamantly resisted any efforts to reform the police force by integrating the other ethnic groups or by increasing professionalism through formal training. Thus, the police force faces long-term issues of legitimacy and acceptance by the entirety of the local population. It has done nothing to reduce opium production; in fact, opium production and processing in the AO has increased over 30 percent since Fahran was appointed COP. There is suspicion that the number of processing facilities in the AO has increased with the full knowledge of the COP.

The ANA in Gereshk have a considerably better reputation. Major Ahmadi is considered one of the better ANA officers, and his troops are quite competent. The ANA are most effective when partnered with CF troops and tend to get sloppy when conducting independent operations.

Development

Overview
Residential: Government and provincial reconstruction team statistics have identified 4,756 private dwellings, each housing ten to twenty persons. Most of the dwellings in Gereshk are fairly modern, featuring glass windows, indoor plumbing, and a fireplace. Dwellings around the district and district government compounds, hospital, and police stations also have limited access to electricity.

Public buildings: Gereshk has two government centers (town and district), two police stations, a prison, forty mosques, five schools (including two madrassas, two boys' schools, and one mixed boys and girls school), a hospital, and the local bazaar.

The district government center is a new structure to house the offices of the district government. The building is wired for electricity and heat. Offices are spacious and capable of accommodating the district mayor's staff. The district center also has a landline phone and radio communications capability.

The current district center and government buildings are obsolete and deteriorating. The offices are small, cramped, and poorly lit. Only the district mayor's office has a telephone. Although all buildings are wired for electricity, the wiring is old and the circuits are not capable of handling large loads. As a result, electronics are not widely used, with most of the capacity used for lighting and fans in the summer.

The main police station is a medium two-story building that also serves as the ANP HQ for the district and the province. The majority of the first floor is taken up by the police station's "squad room" where the officers hang out when they are in the station. Chief Fahran has a private office in the back, adjacent to the storage room or armory. A third room serves as an interrogation room and holding area. The second floor houses the offices of the ANP district headquarters.

The Red Mosque is the largest single building in the city and is estimated to be over 300 years old. The mosque is a respected holy site.

The hospital was built last year by the Indonesian Islamic Aid Foundation. The facility staff consists of five doctors, ten nurses, and forty-five additional support personnel. The clinic can perform minor surgery and has twenty beds for in-patient stays.

Gereshk has a single school for both boys and girls, but it has been closed for the last year due to a lack of students, and the teachers have departed for lack of work. Currently, boys are sent to the madrassa run by Mullah Agir, a Ghazil tribal elder and mullah of the Red Mosque. Girls are not receiving any formal education at all.

Transportation: Gereshk currently has only one paved road leading to the market from Highway 1. The road is in poor repair and access to the main ring highway is difficult. Otherwise, all other roads are packed dirt.

A new bridge over the Helmand River is currently under construction.

Utilities: Although most residents of Gereshk have indoor plumbing and running water, there is no waste treatment facility, and sewage is dumped directly into the Helmand River. The city has several large diesel generators that are capable of providing electricity to about 40 percent of the population (in addition to the government center, hospital, and police station). The generators also power the pumps that draw water from the Helmand River. Fuel for the generators must be trucked in from Lashkar Gah, and disruptions in fuel deliveries result in frequent power outages.

Communications: The government center and police station both have landline telephone and radio communications, while the hospital has only a landline telephone. Some of the wealthier residents also have landline phone communications. There is restricted cellular service in Gereshk. There are no radio or television stations in Gereshk. Some commercial radio broadcasts are received from other parts of Afghanistan.

Economy: Gereshk's primary source of revenue comes from the opium trade. Gereshk's dependency on the opium trade has attracted several aid agency programs that have tried to transition local farmers from opium to legal cash crops. Unfortunately, all efforts to date have failed as local farmers have shown no interest in other crops.

The bazaar provides a secondary but growing source of income for the city.

The pending completion of the Helmand River Bridge has made Gereshk an attractive location for construction projects. The city has received over $10 million for projects to improve water and sewage pipes, pave roads in the residential quarters, complete the new government center, and refurbish the police stations. In anticipation of commerce-driven expansion, Gereshk is expected to receive an additional $150 million over the next year to build 300 more residential dwellings and a large indoor market and to pave all of the city's roads.

Intelligence Assessment   The current role of the Red Mosque is an enigma. As a significant historical and cultural site, it is a unifying influence on an otherwise fractured community. On the other hand, the senior religious figure, Mullah Jaweed, is a frequent and vocal critic of both CFs and Mayor Zafik's administration. However, although Mullah Jaweed is clearly a religious conservative who desires a return to religious rule under Sharia law, he has not explicitly supported the Taliban interpretation of Islam and has not advocated a return to Taliban rule.

Economy: Economic growth in Gereshk may provide an opportunity to persuade local farmers to stop cultivating opium if a more profitable crop can be found. However, sporadic and unconfirmed reports linking the mayor and the police chief to the opium trade could mean that a broader solution is required. The expected influx of development funds could also pose potential problems with the primary local contractor, BandiBak Construction. A recent investigation stemming from corruption complaints against BandiBak Construction discovered something unusual about the company: BandiBak Construction is run by members of the Barakzai tribe, but the primary labor force consists almost entirely of Noorzai tribesmen. Given the historical hostility between the two tribes, this is highly irregular.

The Insurgency-Narcotics Nexus
Taliban: The local Taliban network is long on rhetoric but short on capabilities. The Taliban has deep roots, but they seem to run mainly through the Ishaqzai and Noorzai tribes. Although the Taliban probably have supporters in the other tribes, tribal divisions probably mean that supporters are few and far between. These same divisions may hamper the ability of the local Taliban organization to coordinate efforts across tribal lines. This said, the Taliban provides a great deal of manpower and dual functionality to the narcotics industry in the AO. The bulk of narcotics revenue that the Taliban gets in Afghanistan comes from high-density poppy farming in the Gereshk district.

Despite strong rhetoric and a dedicated base of support, the Taliban have had difficulty dislodging CF—mainly because the district's geographic isolation has made it difficult for the insurgents to secure outside aid. As a result, the Taliban have had to rely on mostly local resources, and local tactics have consisted mostly of small arms and Improvised Explosive Device (IED) ambushes on CF patrols. In this regard, a certain amount of Taliban taxation is tolerated by the narcotics cartel in order to minimize the impact of Afghan National Security Forces (ANSF) efforts to control the Gereshk district and establish a judiciary presence. Figure 3.1 shows the pattern of taxation on the narcotics trade.

Criminal elements: The most significant threat in the Gereshk AO is the narcotics trafficking organization belonging to Khan Walid, a member of the Noorzai tribe. Khan Walid's forces are better equipped than the Taliban and the ANP and have demonstrated capabilities ranging from small arms ambushes and small to medium raids to complex ambushes using IEDs. Khan Walid will attack anyone that he perceives as a threat, which includes CF, ANSF, and even the Taliban.

Supplemental Intelligence Report: The Ishaqzai/Noorzai Narcotics Cartel

The objective of this supplemental intelligence report (SUPINTREP) is to highlight the relationship between the insurgency and the Ishaqzai narcotics cartel. The

FIGURE 3.1   Narcotics and Taliban Taxation

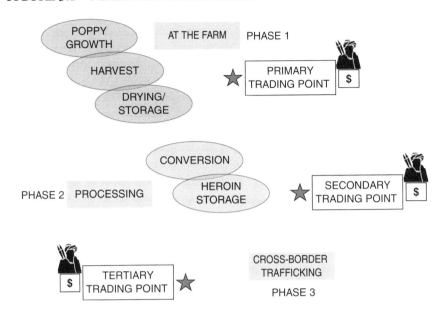

Upper Gereshk Valley region is a key opium producing area for the global opium market, worth approximately $8 billion a year. The Ishaqzai own the majority of land that produces opium; together with the Noorzai, they are political opponents of the current government and make up a majority of the insurgent leadership. In terms of vulnerabilities, the Upper Gereshk Valley is sitting on the last remaining internal/organic source of funding for the insurgents. The situation as of 2009 has been described as follows:

> Ishaqzai communities had been very influential in Helmand under the Taliban regime, at the expense of the Alizais who had dominated the province until 1994. With the fall of the Taliban, Alizai circles around Sher Mohammad Akhundzada were again elevated to the power they had been holding in 1981–94 and proceeded to marginalize and "tax" Ishaqzai communities. In 2006, a violent conflict broke out. The Taliban exploited the conflict to consolidate their influence in the Sangin district, where the Ishaqzai are the majority of the population, but this did not prevent them from maintaining their pockets of support among Alizai clans hostile to Sher Mohammad, such as in Baghran and in other parts of northern Helmand.[4]

The Ishaqzai tribe is a member of the Panjpai group of the Durrani Confederation (see Figure 3.2), and though they started as a very respected nomadic or warrior

---

[4]Giustozzi, Antonio, *Koran, Kalashnikov, and Laptop: The Neo-Taliban Insurgency in Afghanistan,* pp. 60-61.

FIGURE 3.2   Helmand Tribal Laydown

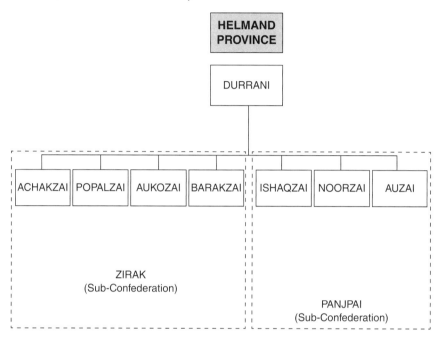

tribe for the better part of two centuries, they have been on the losing side of an internal Durrani Confederation conflict. The Ishaqzai nomads were eventually forced by circumstances to become farmers.[5] Today there are more Ishaqzai leaders affiliated with the Taliban and the narcotics industry than with the Kabul administration of Hamid Karzai, a fellow Durrani.[6]

The Ishaqzai are one of the smaller Helmand tribes but wield a tremendous amount of power through their geographic location and association with narcotics and the insurgents. Their homelands lie in the strategically important corridor of the lower Helmand valley especially within the Upper Gereshk Valley. Both the narcotics smuggling routes and routes used by the insurgents rely on passage through territory that is effectively controlled by Ishaqzai tribesmen, as Figure 3.3 shows.

Though the narcotics militia and the insurgents have acted to empower Ishaqzai—resulting in large numbers of the tribe joining the ranks of the insurgents—this could also result in the Ishaqzai influence breaking the intransigent ideology of the Ghilzai insurgents. However, on a practical level this means that

---

[5]To the other Durranis, they became "Sogzai," or the "Vegetable People."

[6]Cultural and Geographic Research Tribal Analysis Centre (TAC) Report on "Ishaqzai Tribe," Tribal Analysis Center Ltd., Williamsburg, VA, November 2009, http://www.tribalanalysiscenter .com/Home.html; note some examples of senior Ishaqzai insurgents Aktar Mohammed Monsour (Ishaqzai) and Mullah Sardar (Ishaqzai).

FIGURE 3.3   Helmand Opium Production Belt

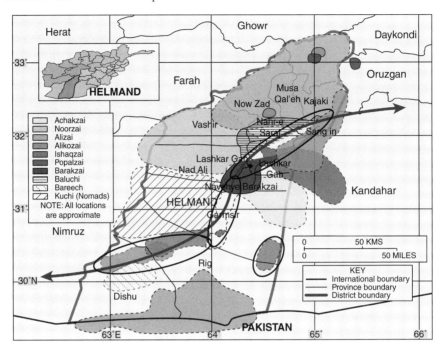

the Ishaqzai dominated areas are largely sympathetic to insurgent activity and will give succour to insurgent fighters particularly north of patrol base (PB) Greyhound in the Ishaqzai territories of the Upper Gereshk Valley. South of PB Greyhound, a subtribe of the Ishaqzai, the Sheikhanzai, act as absentee landlords and receive rent for the use of these irrigated lands from their Noorzai tenants. Due to this tribal affiliation, one can expect that insurgents will receive assistance from tenant farmers on Sheikhanzai in the Gereshk area.[7] An interesting social result of all this has been the establishment of a micro-feudal system south of PB Greyhound, to the suburbs of Gereshk, where it is often the migrant workers who manage the land.

In the past, Ishaqzai have been in violent feuds with Alikozai, Alizai, and Noorzai elements over smuggling networks and narcotics interests. However, cooperation between the Noorzai and the Ishaqzai has been an absolute necessity for the narcotics trade to continue, with the Noorzai areas linking the opium production areas that are primarily Ishaqzai territories. Furthermore, west of the Upper Gereshk Valley, the Noorzai provide for the transport of morphine paste and hashish west to Iran, and for weapons on the return leg.

---

[7]These Noorzai, a related Pashtun tribe, are linked in marriage to the Sheikhanzai.

Ishaqzai linkage into the Taliban and to insurgents is personified by Akhtar Mohammed Osmani,[8] a senior Ishaqzai tribesman and member of Quetta Shura (QS), who was key in providing Ishaqzai support to the Taliban push for Kandahar in 1996. During the tenure of Mullah Abdul Rahim, an Ishaqzai, as Helmand shadow governor until July 2008, the Ishaqzai were well represented at senior levels. The most senior Ishaqzai Taliban is now Mullah Mohammed Akhtar Mansour, joint head of the QS, who himself is entangled in a lengthy yet low intensity dispute with his Popalzai counterpart, Mullah Berader (since captured in Pakistan).

The Noorzai have had a number of senior powerbrokers from Central Helmand, including the ex and current Helmand COPs Bobby Van Dick and Pappy Losthat, respectively. The Noorzai's geographical focus around Lashkar Gar and Nad e Ali gives it significant leverage over local affairs and they are also widely involved in the narcotics industry.[9]

INTELLIGENCE REPORTS

[Note: DATE/TIME entries follow the format: day, time of day in twenty-four-hour (military time) notation, L (indicating local time), month, year. For example, 030915LFEB08 equates to 0915hrs local time on February 3, 2008.]

DATE/TIME: 071622LJUL10

SUBJECT: Khan Walid meets with the BandiBak Construction manager.

TEXT: A HUMINT source reports that on July 5, Khan Walid travelled to a storage yard that belongs to BandiBak Construction and met with BandiBak Construction's manager, a man named Pirwhal, and the company's chief of security, a man named Genghis. The source did not hear what was discussed, but Khan Walid seemed very angry and Genghis slapped Pirwhal. (Source: No previous reporting history; the report was assessed as F3 [reliability cannot be judged/possibly true])

DATE/TIME: 101421LJUL10

SUBJECT: NGOs complain of corruption in city government

TEXT: CF leadership met with representatives of two NGOs that have development projects in Gereshk. Both representatives complained bitterly about tax office administrator Momin, who was once again holding up progress until "special taxes" were paid. The NGOs had already gone to COP Fahran, but since Momin answered only to the mayor, there was nothing the ANP could do.

---

[8]However, after Osmani was likely killed in U.S. precision strike operation in late 2006, many Ishaqzai actively blamed the Taliban for his betrayal. See Reuters, "Taliban Confirm Top Commander Killed in U.S. Strike," December 27, 2006.

[9]The Taliban Ishaqzai-Noorzai Split.

DATE/TIME: 171426LJUL10

SUBJECT: Pirwhal complains about Genghis and Khan Walid to his uncle Homandi.

TEXT: A HUMINT source reports that on July 16, Pirwhal, the general manager of BandiBak Construction, met with his uncle Homandi at a tea shop in the bazaar. Pirwhal complained that "the Noorzai dog" Khan Walid had visited his office again and threatened to hurt Pirwhal if he did not stop beating his Noorzai workers. When Pirwhal retorted that he wouldn't beat them if they weren't so stupid and lazy, Genghis struck him. Pirwhal then complained that when he told his father, his father had simply shrugged and said "Inshallah." Homandi commiserated and acknowledged that Pirwhal's father was too weak to be mayor. Homandi promised that he would speak to Pirwhal's father when he saw him at the next tribal shura, but in the meantime Pirwhal had to persevere. Pirwhal agreed and departed the tea shop. (Source: No previous reporting history; the report was assessed as C2 [fairly reliable/ probably true])

DATE/TIME: 261016LJUL10

SUBJECT: The ANP report on the source of IED attacks.

TEXT: ANP sergeant Tori informed his CF patrol leader that Ishaqzai insurgent fighters were responsible for the IED attack two days earlier. Tori stated that the insurgents lacked enough men to challenge CF and the ANSF, so the commander, a man named Mansoor, had found an "engineer" to build IEDs for the insurgents until they could build their strength. Sergeant Tori did not know the name of the engineer, but based on the reports of the attack on July 24, he did not think highly of the man's abilities.

DATE/TIME: 032045LAUG10

SUBJECT: Khan Walid warns the CF of IED.

TEXT: A man with known ties to Khan Walid's opium trafficking organization approached a CF patrol and warned them of an IED attack. The man, known as Genghis, stated that the insurgents were planning to emplace an IED within the next forty-eight hours along the main route through the farmland southeast of the city. Genghis would not provide further detail nor explain how he came by the information. (Source: No previous reporting history; report assessed as F3 [reliability cannot be judged/possibly true])

DATE/TIME: 091056LAUG10

SUBJECT: There is corruption in government.

TEXT: A local farmer and member of the Noorzai shura known as Rasim spoke to a CF patrol and told them about corruption in the local government. Rasim called the mayor and his administrators "drug addicts" and "thieves" but could not provide any details. Rasim also claimed that the COP was a good man who would clean up the corruption but was blocked by the mayor. (Source: No previous reporting history; the report was assessed as F3 [reliability cannot be judged/probably true])

DATE/TIME: 151302LAUG10

SUBJECT: Khan Walid and Fahran control BandiBak Construction.

TEXT: A HUMINT source reported that Noorzai warlord Khan Walid and COP Fahran are the real power behind BandiBak Construction. Khan Walid is a co-owner of the company and often uses Fahran and the ANP to provide "legitimate" leverage over Pirwhal, the company's general manager. The source also noted that Khan Walid uses the company to advance the economic fortunes of the Noorzai by making sure the company mainly hires Noorzai workers and by using the company to "clean" money. (Analyst comment: This may be a reference to Khan Walid using BandiBak Construction to launder money from opium trafficking.) (Source: No previous reporting history; report was assessed as B2 [usually reliable/probably true])

DATE/TIME: 161403LAUG10

SUBJECT: The ANP officer is seen talking to suspected insurgent fighter.

TEXT: An ANP officer reported seeing ANP sergeant Tori talking to a suspected insurgent fighter. The ANP officer, a Karagani named Amir, stated that he was manning a checkpoint with Tori as the officer in charge. At one point, Amir went in to trees to relieve himself when he heard voices. He decided to investigate and saw Tori talking to a man known as Alamander. Alamander is an Ishaqzai, like Tori, and although it cannot be said for certain that Alamander is an insurgent, it is known that he and Mansoor have been friends since childhood. (Source: No previous reporting history; the report was assessed as C4 [fairly reliable/doubtful])

DATE/TIME: 241326LAUG10

SUBJECT: A GIRoA representative is seen arguing with the mullah.

TEXT: A joint patrol responded to a report of a disturbance at the Red Mosque. When they arrived, they found Darya, the representative of the Ministry of Rural Development, shouting at Mullah Agir while a small crowd of local residents looked on. The ANP officers in the patrol restrained Darya, who was in tears, and put her in a vehicle. After a brief conversation with the mullah, who never showed any emotion at all, the patrol departed and returned Darya to her residence with instructions to stay away from the mosque for a while.

DATE/TIME: 291622LAUG10

SUBJECT: There is a possible delivery of IED components.

TEXT: SIGINT reports intercept a conversation between a male identified as Dragam and an unidentified male (Lightfoot). Lightfoot stated that a new shipment of plates was ready for delivery. Dragam acknowledged and informed Lightfoot to arrange delivery at the usual location. (Analyst comment: Dragam is known to be a logistics facilitator for a local insurgent IED network. "Plates" may refer to ordnance.)

DATE/TIME: 041013LSEP10

SUBJECT: The bank manager provides information on Mayor Zafik and Khan Walid

TEXT: A joint patrol in the bazaar spoke with a young man named Khan, who is the assistant manager of the Bank of Afghanistan branch in Gereshk. Khan stated he was the grandson of Mayor Zafik and that he was deeply saddened by his grand-father's inability to govern effectively. Khan blamed the mayor's weakness on Khan Walid's widespread influence in Gereshk, which comes from the money he makes from narcotics, as well as from the legitimate businesses he owns. Khan stated that as long as the warlord was free, there would be no peace and no security in Gereshk.

DATE/TIME: 091318LSEP10

SUBJECT: The ANP officers beat the manager of BandiBak Construction.

TEXT: COP Fahran informed CF that one of his officers beat Pirwhal, the man-ager of BandiBak Construction. The beating occurred when ANP officers discovered Pirwhal beating one of the workers; when the officers ordered Pirwhal to stop, he ignored them; at this point, one of the police officers grabbed Pirwhal and began punching and kicking him. When the officer escalated to pistol-whipping Pirwhal, two other ANP intervened and stopped the beating. Fahran stated that Pirwhal would be fine and to disregard any complaints CF might hear from the Karagani.

DATE/TIME: 101032LSEP10

SUBJECT: Bazaar merchants voice security concerns.

TEXT: During a joint patrol in the Gereshk bazaar, several shop owners approached to voice their concerns about the security situation in Gereshk. The merchants demanded that CF do more and get the ANP under control. A merchant named Homandi was especially upset, demanding to know why CF told the ANP to beat his nephew and accusing CF of siding with the Noorzai in a tribal vendetta. The CF patrol leader assured Homandi and the other merchants that their complaints would be addressed and managed to extract his patrol without further incident.

DATE/TIME: 121143LSEP10

SUBJECT: The BandiBak manager threatens the CF contracting team.

TEXT: During a visit from the CF contracting team, Pirwhal, the BandiBak Construction manager, became extremely angry and refused to speak with them, accusing CF personnel of ordering the ANP to beat him. Pirwhal also accused CF with siding with Noorzai and told the contracting team that if they did not leave immediately, he would have them killed. The contracting team complied and left the site without further incident.

DATE/TIME: 131637LSEP10

SUBJECT: CF Muslim Chaplain meets with Mullah Agir.

TEXT: The CF commander met with CF Captain John Bec, a Muslim chaplain stationed at Camp Bastion Airfield. Bec was in Gereshk to meet with Mullah Agir as part of an outreach initiative started by the senior chaplain in Afghanistan. Bec had just left his meeting with Agir and wanted to share the results with the commander.

Captain Bec stated the meeting started poorly because as he entered the mosque, several local nationals saw his uniform and thought he was leading a raid on the mosque, so when Mullah Agir came out, he was in a hostile and defensive mood. Bec managed to defuse the situation by explaining his reason for being in the mosque, but that seemed to do little to mollify the mullah, who chastised Bec for wearing the uniform of the CF infidels. The chaplain attempted to engage Agir in a dialogue, but the mullah was very rigid in his stance. Agir refused to recognize the authority of any secular government (to include Mayor Zafik's), stating that the only true law belonged to God. He also refused offers of financial assistance from Captain Bec, explaining he would not accept aid from infidels because it would damage his standing in the eyes of God. As the chaplain prepared to leave, Mullah Agir stated that should the captain choose to shed his uniform and allegiance to secular powers, he would always be welcome at the Red Mosque as a true believer.

When asked his opinion of the mullah, Captain Bec stated that Agir was extremely conservative and rigid and would be a perpetual problem for any government in Gereshk. He also stated that the mullah was a sincerely pious man and seemed to have no other agenda than to ensure the people in Gereshk "walked a path of righteous purity." Bec specifically pointed out to the commander that while rigid and conservative, Agir's version of Islam still diverged significantly from the insurgents' interpretation.

DATE/TIME: 140937LSEP10

SUBJECT: District mayor Zafik is killed by radio-controlled IED (RCIED).

TEXT: Mayor Zafik's two-vehicle convoy with security was struck by what appears be a RCIED detonated just beside the mayor's sitting place at a tea shop owned by his friend Samir before coming to the district center this morning. (Analyst comment: No one has yet claimed responsibility, which is an indicator the insurgents might not be too keen on taking credit for this one. An investigative team from Kabul has been promised publicly, but no arrival time has been given; because of the complex politics in the area, it might never arrive.)

DATE/TIME: 162033LSEP10

SUBJECT: Homandi warns CF of hostile sentiment.

TEXT: The merchant Homandi warned CF that their personnel should not leave the Forward Operating Base (FOB), even on joint patrols with the ANA. According to the merchant, some of the city's residents would blame the mayor's death on CF—either for not protecting him or for bringing "evil" to Gereshk. Homandi expressed the opinion that it has been foolish for his brother to align himself with infidels in a holy place like Gereshk and that his death was the will of God. Homandi also informed CF that the Barakzai would need to select a new senior elder as well as a new mayor.

DATE/TIME: 171019LSEP10

SUBJECT: An interview takes place with Momin.

TEXT: CF medics assisting at the hospital spoke with Momin, the administrator of the tax office who was wounded in the explosion that killed Mayor Zafik. Momin stated that he was passing by the tea shop when Samir ran up and said the mayor wanted to see him. As they approached the shop, something inside exploded; Samir was ahead of Momin and took the brunt of the explosion, leaving Momin with only moderate wounds. Momin said he did not know who would want to kill the mayor, but he was sure it was related to Zafik's association with CF.

DATE/TIME: 181430LSEP10

SUBJECT: The contract team meets with Darya.

TEXT: During a meeting with the CF contracting team, Darya, the official from the Ministry of Rural Development, complained that the death of Mayor Zafik had caused massive confusion and that the ministry had no guidance for her. According to Darya, she had received two calls from officials in Kabul (from the ministries of Defense and the Interior) instructing her to provide assistance to Khan Walid. A third official from Kabul (from the Ministry of Commerce) and two officials from the office of the provincial mayor of Helmand directed her to provide assistance to Homandi. To add to the chaos, Homandi, COP Fahran, and Pirwhal are all demanding money the late mayor supposedly promised them but that Darya knows nothing about. Finally, Fahran has threatened to arrest Darya if she does not give him the money promised by the late mayor to purchase four new police cars.

DATE/TIME: 191011LSEP10

SUBJECT: COP Fahran presents an offer of assistance from Khan Walid.

TEXT: During a meeting between CF leaders and COP Fahran, the police chief mentioned that Khan Walid wanted to speak with CF leaders to discuss how the Noorzai tribe could assist CF. Chief Fahran emphasized the significance of the offer; Khan Walid never made such an offer to CF leaders. The additional distractions allowed the insurgents to regroup and the Barakzai to expand their influence in the local government. Fahran felt that with Khan Walid's help, CF could make a significant impact in Gereshk.

DATE/TIME: 201452LSEP10

SUBJECT: Homandi discusses the succession of power in Gereshk.

TEXT: During a joint CF and ANA patrol in the bazaar, the CF patrol leader noted a group of ANP officers arguing with Homandi. As the patrol approached the group, Homandi confronted the patrol leader and demanded to know what CF intended to do for Mayor Zafik's family. He pointed out that Zafik's relationship with CF was the most likely cause for his murder, and it would therefore be an insult for CF leaders to do nothing for Zafik's family. Homandi also wanted to know when CF planned to officially recognize him as the new mayor, considering that he had been elected as the senior elder of the Barakzai and was therefore his brother's rightful successor. At this point, the patrol leader noted that the ANP officers (all Noorzai) were becoming even angrier. The patrol leader cut the conversation short, telling Homandi he would inform the CF chain of command of Homandi's concerns. The patrol leader immediately moved both groups out of the bazaar before the ANP could cause a scene. The ANP officers complained to the patrol leader that he had emasculated them by not allowing them to respond to "that Barakzai dog." The senior ANP officer commented that it would not matter because Khan Walid would probably have Homandi killed if he became mayor.

DATE/TIME: 221110LSEP10

SUBJECT: Pirwhal believes Homandi will be the next mayor.

TEXT: During a meeting with the CF contracting team, Pirwhal stated that he was very pleased with his new job as administrator of the tax office. He was confident he would keep the job because his uncle, Homandi Zafik, would be the new mayor and would protect him. He stated that once he was appointed as mayor, Homandi would remove Fahran as COP and replace him with a Barakzai, which would allow him to cleanse Gereshk of the Noorzai influence. Pirwhal did not seem concerned with the threat posed by Khan Walid.

DATE/TIME: 220909LSEP10

SUBJECT: Homandi demands official recognition as mayor.

TEXT: During a patrol in the bazaar, the patrol leader was accosted by Homandi Zafik, who demanded to know why CF continued to insult him by refusing to officially recognize him as the mayor of Gereshk. Homandi stated that this was not how friends should treat one another and that he would remember these insults when he was appointed mayor. Homandi also wanted to know why his brother's killers had not been brought to justice. He insisted that it was obviously the Noorzai who had killed Zafik, so why hadn't CF arrested Fahran and Khan Walid? Homandi stated that it was obvious that CF favored the Noorzai, but once he was appointed mayor, the relationship between the local government and CF would change.

DATE/TIME: 221800LSEP10

SUBJECT: Haji Fahdom is appointed as new mayor of Gereshk.

TEXT: HQ CF informed CF that the governor of Helmand has appointed his nephew, Haji Fahdom (Barakzai tribe), as the new mayor of Gereshk. Fahdom was apparently selected for his loyalty to his uncle, and though he is technically an outsider, he has numerous ties to the local area; his mother is Ishaqzai and his brother studied under Mullah Agir. Although Fahdom has personal ties to individuals in the Ishaqzai and Noorzai tribes, his feelings toward the other tribes as a whole are unknown.

DATE/TIME: 231621LSEP10

SUBJECT: Khan Walid threatens to oppose new mayor.

TEXT: During a meeting with CF leaders COP Fahran informed them that he had been notified of Haji Fahdom's appointment as mayor. Fahran also stated that Khan Walid has warned the provincial governor that if Fahdom attempts to exercise his powers without Khan Walid's approval, Khan Walid would resist by any means necessary. Fahran then predicted that the situation would deteriorate in Gereshk.

BACKGROUND READING

This report on opium production in Afghanistan is taken from the United Nations Office on Drugs and Crime (UNODC) Afghanistan Opium Survey (2009): https://www.unodc.org/documents/crop-monitoring/Afghanistan/Afghanistan_opium_survey_2009_summary.pdf.

According to the UNODC Afghanistan Opium Survey (2009), the cultivation, production, workforce, prices, revenues, exports, and opium's gross domestic product (GDP) share were all down in 2009. At the same time, the number of poppy-free provinces and drug seizures rose throughout the country. Specifically where it concerns 2009 opium cultivation in Afghanistan, there was a 22 percent drop, from 157,000 hectares (ha) in 2008 to 123,000 ha in 2009. For Helmand province, cultivation declined by one-third, to less than 70,000 ha. The 2009 cultivation pattern is shown in Figure 3.4.

Despite the general decline throughout Afghanistan of the poppy yield, the country remains at the forefront of the global supply of opium, continuing to outproduce Southeast Asia and the infamous "Golden Triangle."[10]

---

[10]The Golden Triangle poppies' average yield is about 10 kg of opium per hectare. In 2010, Afghan poppies (grown in the most fertile and best irrigated part of the country) yielded a record 56 kg/ha—a 15 percent increase over last year's already high figure of 49 kg.

FIGURE 3.4 Opium Cultivation in Afghanistan during 2009

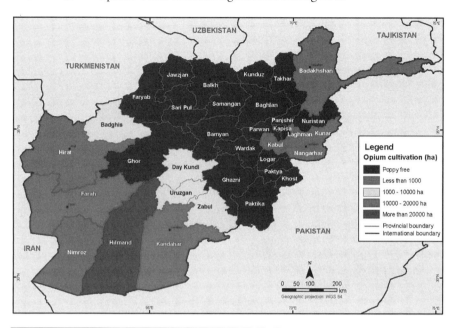

Source: Government of Afghanistan—National monitoring system implemented by UNODC

Note: The boundaries and names shown and the designations used on this map do not imply official endorsement or acceptance by the United Nations.

Helmand remains at the forefront of global poppy cultivation with over 20,000 hectares, or seventy-seven square miles, of poppy cultivation; however, oversupply at the source and lower global market demand has been pushing opium prices down. As a result, 800,000 fewer people now are involved in opium production, as compared to 2008. Prices that farmers in Afghanistan collect fell substantially during 2009, from $70/kg to $48/kg for fresh opium and from $95/kg to $64/kg for dried opium. Opium prices in the country have not been this low since the late 1990s, when the Taliban were in power and the opium harvest was half the size of today.

NATO and Afghan forces are adding to the pressure of unfavorable market forces and are attacking the link between drugs and insurgency. In the first half of 2009, joint military operations destroyed over ninety tons of precursor chemicals, 450 tons of seeds, fifty tons of opium, seven tons of morphine, 1.5 tons of heroin, nineteen tons of cannabis resin, and twenty-seven labs. Although these efforts hit only a fraction of the Afghan narcotics economy, they have increased the risks associated with drug trafficking. The UNODC Survey 2009 found that farmers are increasingly wary of retaliation, trading has become more discreet, and stocks are now buried underground. Nevertheless, Helmand remains host to some of the most productive poppy hectares in the world, as Figure 3.5 indicates, with some of the best fields located in the Upper Gereshk Valley.

FIGURE 3.5   2009 Opium Production by Province

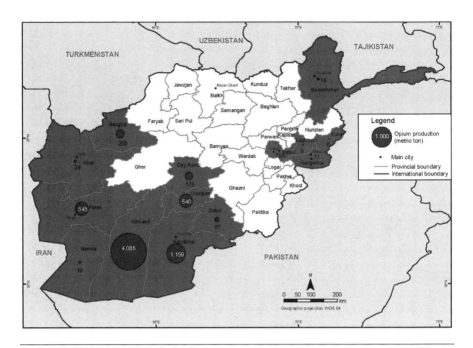

Source: Government of Afghanistan—National monitoring system implemented by UNODC

Note: The boundaries and names shown and the designations used on this map do not imply official endorsement or acceptance by the United Nations.

4

Balkans Organized Crime

This case study is set in the year 1999. Since the end of the Balkan communist regimes in the early 1990s, organized crime has taken advantage of the new freedom (and in some areas, ensuing anarchy) in this region to grow and expand. The Balkan region from its earliest history was a smuggling zone, but, after the collapse of communism, organized crime thrived as never before. Criminal groups gained an even larger freedom of movement in the conflict of 1997 and in the post-conflict environment. This growth of organized crime is well known both in and outside of the region.

EDUCATIONAL OBJECTIVES

This exercise provides practical experience in the following:

- introducing network modeling as an analytical technique for visualization and decomposition for the purposes of defining threat networks within an organized crime operational environment
- generating Target Network Models (TNMs) based on social network analysis (SNA)
- demonstrating the use of the Political, Military, Economic, Society, Infrastructure, and Information (PMESII) analytical construct in a law enforcement setting (where the *M* refers to the use of armed force by criminal and law enforcement groups, not to military use of force)
- providing an opportunity for a deeper SNA

ASSIGNMENT

In this scenario, you are the strategic all-source analyst for the newly established Europol Balkans Organized Crime Task Force that will be working out of the city of Shkodra (or Shkodër), Albania, from 1999 onward in order to assist the Albanian government with the establishment of law and order in the region.

Your assignment is to assist Europol with modeling the criminal networks associated with the Shkodra Region, including the Pattern Of Life (PoL) of the criminal organizations (i.e., their Tactics, Training, and Procedures (TTPs) related to their criminal activities). The following is based on the Intelligence Reports (INTREPs):

1. Develop TNMs as needed in order to support Europol. Start by creating TNMs illustrating the key players, their functions or roles within their own group, organization, or society as a whole. (Hint: Consider creating separate TNMs for each local and regional criminal syndicate.)

2. Establish a rough timeline overview of events in the area of operations (AO).

3. Identify the intelligence gaps relative to the tasking. Create a simple Intelligence Collection Plan (ICP) by generating ten questions to be answered by your collection assets. You may assume you will have access to Human Intelligence (HUMINT), Imagery Intelligence (IMINT), Measurement and Signature Intelligence (MASINT), Open Source Intelligence (OSINT), and Signals Intelligence (SIGINT).

4. Identify and list any early warning indicators of criminal activities that may be monitored or tracked.

5. Generate a High-Value Target List (HVTL) based on the intelligence provided. Use this to generate a new ICP of thirty questions to be answered by your collection process.

ABBREVIATIONS AND ACRONYMS

Abbreviation or Acronym	Description
AO	area of operations
DOCEX	Document Exploitation
DoS	denial of service
DP	Democratic Party (Albanian)
ECMM	European Community Monitor Mission
EU	European Union
GMTI	ground moving target indicator (a MASINT technique using airborne radar to identify moving targets)
HUMINT	Human Intelligence
HVTL	high-value target list
ICP	intelligence collection plan
IGO	intergovernmental organization
IMINT	Imagery Intelligence
INTREP	intelligence report

Abbreviation or Acronym	Description
MASINT	Measurement and Signature Intelligence
NGO	nongovernmental organization
OSCE	Organization for Security and Cooperation in Europe
OSINT	Open Source Intelligence
PMESII	political, military, economic, society, infrastructure, and information
PoL	pattern of life
SIGINT	Signals Intelligence
SNA	social network analysis
SP	Socialist Party (Albanian)
TNM	target network model
TTP	tactics, training, and procedures
UN	United Nations
UNHCR	United Nations High Commissioner for Refugees
UNICEF	United Nations Children's Fund

SCENARIO

Following is an assessment of organized crime in the Balkans as of 1999.

The types of organized crime operating out of eastern Europe through Albania can be divided into four key areas: narcotics trafficking,[1] illegal arms dealing,[2] money laundering, and human or alien smuggling.[3] The most serious criminal activities in the area include racketeering, a stolen car trade (luxury cars from the European Union [EU]), sex-slave smuggling (females from eastern Europe), and kidnapping. There are also reports of drug and human organ smuggling. Other criminal activities involve the smuggling of goods such as flour and fruit or of luxury goods such as TV sets and furniture.

The city of Shkodra is a criminal boomtown. More cars are being reported as stolen than there are registered car owners. Shkodra has one of the highest murder rates in all of Europe, averaging well over twenty-five murders per 100,000 inhabitants per year. The word *Kalash* (Russian slang for the AK-47) has been promoted from the short form of a proper noun (*Kalashnikov*) to a verb in the Albanian

---

[1]United Nations International Drug Control Programme, ODCCP Studies on Drugs & Crime Statistics, *Global Illicit Drug Trends 2000* (Vienna: United Nations, 2000).

[2]Chris Hedges, "Kosovo Rebels and Their New Friend," *New York Times,* June 6, 1999.

[3]John Follain and Edin Hamzic, "Mafia Smuggles Refugee Women into Sex Slavery," *Sunday Times,* May 16, 1999; C. B., "Crimes Committed in Italy Provide Funds for Kosovo Guerrillas," Reuters, January 19, 1999.

language. In a bloody process that kills an average of three week in a city of 100,000, irrespective of politics, religion, age, sex, intentionally, or accidentally, all are now susceptible to having their cause of death noted as *kalashed.*

Five environmental (PMESII) factors affect the development of criminal activity in Albania: the political, economic, law enforcement, social, and information environments.

Political

Albanian criminal activity is concentrated in the prefecture of Shkodra, shown in Figure 4.1. The prefecture consists of three districts: Shkodra, Hani Hotit, and Pukë. It has a population of about 320,000 people, about 100,000 of whom live in the town of Shkodra. The area shares a common border with Montenegro in the north and the northwest and Kosovo in the northeast. Well before the fall of communism, the prefecture of Shkodra was a politically sensitive area, as it was the biggest Democratic Party (DP) stronghold in Albania and was the power base of Sali Berisha (president of Albania, 1992–1997). During communist times, many Shkodrians belonged to the anticommunist "opposition" and were therefore persecuted. After the end of communism, the region was quick to embrace the democratic reforms under the Berisha government. Due to these historical developments and the political turmoil of 1997 and 1998, the political atmosphere between DP and Socialist Party (SP) supporters is confrontational. Criminal activity adds to the confrontational political climate.

Throughout the period from 1991 to 1997, there was a high degree of political abuse of the local justice system. The Western-supported government of Sali Berisha appointed untrained police and judiciary to posts throughout the region. These officials often used their authority to exact revenge on those who were known supporters of the former Hoxha regime. This lack of professionalism undermined the general confidence of the population in the police and the judiciary.[4] There was also a high degree of corruption nationally, allowing a number of pyramid schemes to flourish. The pyramid schemes collapsed in 1997, and thousands of Albanians who had enjoyed some economic growth from development aid in the early 1990s lost everything. The result was the Albanian Rebellion of 1997.

Albania consequently does not have an independent judiciary or police force, and this in itself is a serious flaw in the political system. Worse, the lack of a basic functioning law and order system permits criminal access to developing political structures. The result is that there are no restraints on corruption at any Albanian government level. Various forms of development aid have been channeled for personal use under bogus project submissions, from the smallest villages to the state level. For example, a mayor in a town outside of Shkodra used infrastructure funds, designated for the road through the centre of the town, to instead build a road and

---

[4]Human Rights Watch, *Human Rights in Post-Communist Albani,* 1996, http://www.hrw.org/reports/pdfs/a/albania/albania963.pdf.

FIGURE 4.1 General Routes Used for Criminal Activity

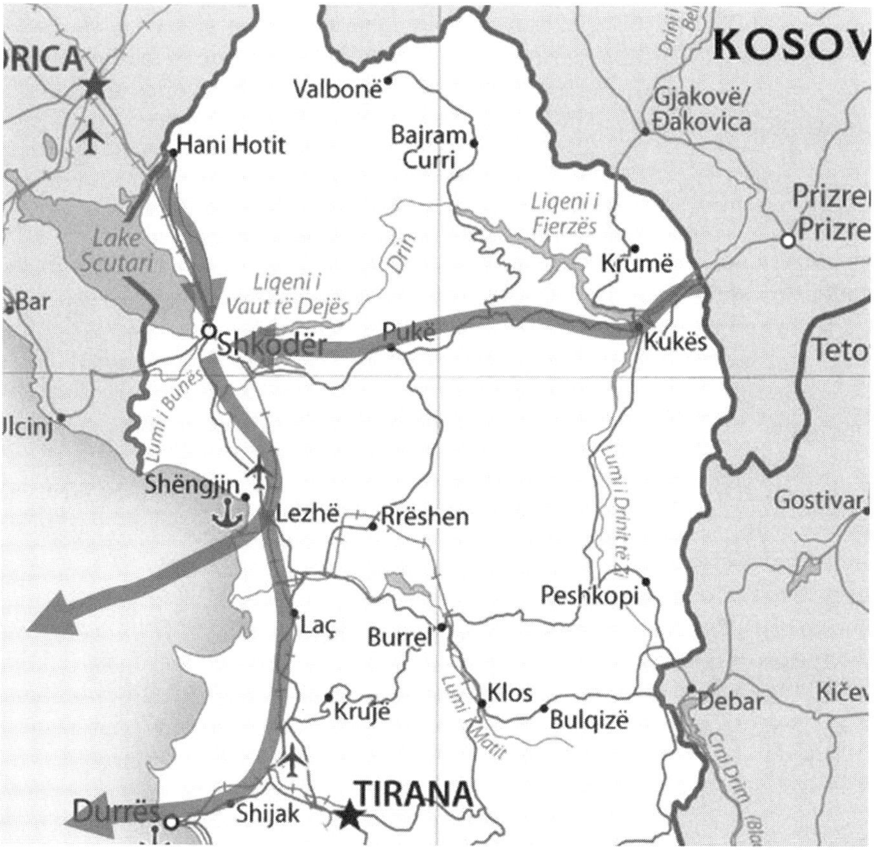

Source: Map courtesy of the University of Texas Libraries, the University of Texas at Austin.

a water system directly to his house outside of the town. More to the point, it was common in northern Albania for politicians and bureaucrats to be selling official stamps, licenses, permits, and university degrees.

Customs control is another example of an acute political problem. Individual town officials have established a customs tax on development goods that had already been taxed upon arriving in Albanian port cities. There are cases where customs must be paid three or four times before goods arrive at their end locations. Seizing the opportunity, officials imposed a 50 percent goods tax on some aid that came through the seaport of Durres during the Kosovo crisis. Taking advantage of the large amount of international development aid that has arrived in Albania since 1997, both the SP and DP use the police and judiciary to politically legitimize nondemocratic activities or to demonize political opponents.

The existing difficulties with political development were exacerbated at the national level when the West—led by the Organization for Security and Cooperation in Europe (OSCE)—decided to promote decentralization before a basic law and order system was functioning nationally in 1999. This made the establishment of a coherent law and order system more difficult by increasing the opportunities for corrupt public administration at subnational political levels.

Law Enforcement

Most Albanian police are not trained to minimum Western standards. The majority of policemen in northern Albania have no training at all. They tend to be politicized, as the government in power names the police chief, and the police chief selects the officers. Family and friends who have gained political positions in the area name most of them. In Shkodra, with one of Europe's highest murder rates, police are paid $70 to $100 per month. They have no equipment; donated equipment disappears into private use or is sold. They have no pension or disability income rights.

As a result, policemen are easily subverted to criminal activity, mainly by financial inducements. They can be seen on a regular basis extracting money or goods from cross-border traffic from Montenegro at a series of roadblocks. Stolen cars are routinely fined at these roadblocks before being permitted to pass. Cars owned by well-known dangerous criminals get free passage. Because the average person is subject to this financial coercion while major criminals walk free, the local population hates the local police. Only masked members of the special police sent up from southern Albania on a particular mission can occasionally be seen executing any serious police activity.

The judiciary is also politically appointed. They typically have no professional legal training. They make slightly more than the police and supplement their income by fining those that are brought before them, or simply allowing them to pay for their freedom. They have no protection against even small-time criminals. Therefore, dangerous criminals are rarely held or fined. So it is again the average member of the population who is fined in order to augment the judicial income, further undermining the public's faith in law and order.

In response to criticism from the international community, the Albanians have focused on the shifting around of personnel in the judiciary and the police forces. However, all that this has accomplished is to make a fundamental dilemma much more apparent. The police, if under a new leadership that did try to pick up some of the more dangerous criminals, are undercut by the judiciary. Because of bribes, the same dangerous criminals return to the streets within days. Conversely, new judges that attempt to enforce some sort of punishment on dangerous criminals quickly change their mind; police will not pick up the criminals' associates, so the judges have no protection from retaliation.

Ironically, cooperation between the police and the judiciary occurs only when minor lawbreakers with a little money are arrested and then freed by the judiciary after paying a fine. The proceeds are then redistributed among those police and judiciary who contributed to the action.

The weakness of the law and order system in Albania, if it were not for the often deadly results, would border on the comical. For example, in one joint Italian-Albanian operation on the Strait of Otranto, six Albanian smuggling boats and numerous people were arrested and handed over to Albanian custody. The boats and people were back in operation within twenty-four hours after armed criminals simply cordoned off the Albanian town where the boats were impounded and demanded their return.[5]

Economic

The prefecture of Shkodra is an economically underdeveloped area with little industry and high unemployment. All economic life is concentrated in Shkodra, whereas the rural areas of Pukë and Malësi e Madhe depend on self-sufficient agriculture. Industrial plants and factories—especially the communist-era large state enterprises—are in bad shape. Although investment is badly needed, no credits are available and there is no bank in Shkodra. Private capital was largely invested in pyramid schemes during the mid-1990s and was lost. The precarious security situation, the unclear business and ownership laws, the lack of managerial skills, the inefficient bureaucracy, and widespread corruption all further hamper economic development.

The number of people on welfare has been rising since 1996, even though measures have been taken to train and educate people, or to employ them in state public service projects. Welfare payments are very low (2600 lekë or $50/month) in Shkodra and less in the villages. Residents must look for additional income in order to make ends meet.

Furthermore, the area has seen some migration from the even poorer mountainous region northeast of the country, which adds to the economic problems. As a result, the main sources of employment and income in the region are smuggling and organized criminal activities.

Similar to the corruption that undermines political development, the lack of a basic functioning law enforcement system undermines economic development in the region. The main economic problem concerns contract awards and contract enforcement. Contracts for work often are not fulfilled, and the result is a "money for nothing" economic development philosophy that destroys legitimate investor confidence. This philosophy limits the money going into economic development from aid funds that are not as tightly monitored and are easily derailed by corruption.

A second major economic factor is that Albanian organized crime has easy access to hard currencies such as the U.S. dollar. Much of this access is an indirect result of international aid programs. In Albania, there are few banks

---

[5]Frank Viviano, "Migrants Offered Package Deal to Freedom," *National Post,* March 1, 1999; Reuters, "Albanian Gang Recaptures Boats Seized by Police," January 23, 1999.

where international currency can be officially exchanged and many towns have no bank at all. Most international currencies brought in by InterGovernmental Organizations (IGOs) and NonGovernmental Organizations (NGOs) are changed on the street from the trunk of a Mercedes, where the exchange rate on Albanian currency (the lekë) is much better than the official exchange rate and no receipts are issued. Consider that just one OSCE Field Office with all transport, communication, utilities, and salaries where five internationals are stationed can easily change over $25,000 per month. There are eight OSCE offices that must do this, along with the European Community Monitor Mission (ECMM), EU, the United Nations (UN), United Nations High Commissioner for Refugees (UNHCR), United Nations Children's Fund (UNICEF), and other international NGOs and their respective personnel. The result is that millions of dollars per month of hard currency are being made available to fund criminal organizations' international operations.

Social

Exploitation of NGO aid efforts has become an attractive work option in Northern Albania. Over three months during the Kosovo refugee crisis, more than 125 local NGOs were formed in Shkodra, a city of 100,000, in order to compete for lucrative subcontracts from the UNHCR or the Red Cross. The competition for contracts was sometimes violent and opened a whole new economic area for criminal exploitation.

Absent a functioning criminal justice system, the weaker elements of society have no protection. Orphans are particularly vulnerable. Children are kidnapped and sent to Greece to work in factories. Females without family attachments are forced to become sex slaves. Some reports indicate that orphaned children are victimized to support an organ trade.

Information

Without a functioning legal framework, the media is constantly exposed to politicization and abuse. In an environment where the judges are constantly under threat, media personnel face serious consequences if they take a stand against organized crime.

INTELLIGENCE REPORTS

Rep #	Date	Text
R1	April 1, 1999	**HUMINT—011-C3:** The leader of the Albanian international human smuggling syndicate is Isuf Bardhi, and the whole of the DP is involved in the trafficking of sex slaves.
R2	April 1, 1999	**DOCEX:** Accounting documents recovered by special police from Tirana banker Tori Lokaj indicate that several international currency transactions involve known human sex slave traders from Moldova.

Rep #	Date	Text
R3	April 1, 1999	**OSINT:** Four people connected to the Aldonis Mafia were gunned down in an Aldonis restaurant (Shafari Palms, in the west end of Shkodra) at around 2000 hours.
R4	April 1, 1999	**HUMINT—023-B2:** The Ristani family has the monopoly on the cigarette market in Northern Albania.
R5	April 2, 1999	**HUMINT—011-C4:** At least three Mafia hit men currently are in the Shkodra region. They are Lumtri Gashi mob.042576847,[6] Murat Haxhi mob.042989475, and Gjon Celaj mob.042393878.
R6	April 2, 1999	**DOCEX:** Documents retrieved from a local brothel bust in Shkodra indicate that each sex slave was purchased for $30,000.
R7	April 2, 1999	**INTREP:** A typical sex slave can bring $200,000 per year gross in income to the criminal organization, while the overhead cost to the brothel owners are often the absolute minimum.
R8	April 2, 1999	**INTREP:** It is assessed that there are significant links between the DP and the Nesimi Crime syndicate, which operates in the mountain border areas with Montenegro.
R9	April 3, 1999	**SIGINT:** Saban Lokaj, a suspected member of an international crime syndicate, called Edi Jasari, who is the police chief, and reported that the flowers Jasari ordered were going to be delivered within three days.
R10	April 3, 1999	**SIGINT:** Emir Dosti called suspected mafia financer Edon Lokaj, asking if Lokaj had received the funds.
R 11	April 4, 1999	**Cyber:** Several servers belonging to the known members of the Nesimi crime syndicate were attacked with distributed denial of service (DDoS) packets. The origin of the attack could not be determined, as the source Internet protocol (IP) addresses appear to have been hijacked.
R 12	April 4, 1999	**OSINT:** Police corruption complaints in the Shkodra region have increased by 68 percent during the last year.
R 13	April 4, 1999	**HUMINT—050-F6:** Smugglers are using a tunnel to transport goods to and from Montenegro. The tunnel is 3 km long and is located on the south end of Lake Scutari. It is working twenty-four hours a day and is guarded at each end with at least two men armed with AK-47s.
R 14	April 4, 1999	**SIGINT:** Azem Pojani, reported head of a regional crime syndicate, told "Kristi" to pick up "Fatmir," take him to the "Fisherman" for a meeting, wait for him, and drive him back to Shkodra.
R15	April 4, 1999	**HUMINT—050-F6:** Cars at the stolen car market located outside of Shkodra primarily come from Austria, Switzerland, Montenegro, and Serbia. A stolen Mercedes sells for $5,000 to $10,000 at the market. Sales are conducted every third Saturday of each month.
R16	April 5, 1999	**SIGINT:** Traffic analysis indicates there has been an increase of calls made between two international criminal syndicates located in Moldova and Albania.

(Continued)

[6]Albanian telephone numbers: 2### ### used from inside the Capital, Tirana; 04 2### ### used from within Albania); +355 4 2### ### used from outside Albania.

(Continued)

Rep #	Date	Text
R17	April 5, 1999	**SIGINT:** Leka Penaska called an unidentified car dealer in Italy from his location at the stolen car market on the outskirts of Shkodra. Penaska told the Italian that each Mercedes would cost $11,000.
R18	April 5, 1999	**INTREP:** Assets recently purchased by DP member Daradana Krizi cannot have been paid for by her salary alone. The assets include two Mercedes, a luxurious villa outside of Shkodra with a large swimming pool, and several hectares of private ground.
R19	April 5, 1999	**SIGINT:** DP member Gjon Meksi has originated numerous late night (0100–0400) international telephone calls.
R20	April 5, 1999	**HUMINT—011-C4:** The top three small-time local criminal families in Shkodra are the Ristani, the Thika, and the Duka.
R21	April 5, 1999	**SIGINT:** Ardi Lokaj, head of the local Shkodra car boot (trunk) currency changers, called Edon Lokaj and asked how much currency Edon Lokaj would have to move next month.
R22	April 5, 1999	**HUMINT—023-B2:** Alban Lokaj has ordered boat captain Ardit Jasari to make the boats ready for a crossing and that Jasari should coordinate with Ditmir Berishaj on the Albanian side.
R23	April 5, 1999	**Cyber:** Attempts to hijack local business servers by IP addresses belonging to DP offices in Shkodra have been monitored. The offices are registered to DP Party member Daradana Krizi, wife of DP Party member Valbon Krizi.
R24	April 5, 1999	**INTREP:** Shkodra ranks as the leading city in Europe for murder rate, currently averaging forty murders per month in a city of approximately 100,000.
R25	April 6, 1999	**OSINT:** A fund-raiser was held at the DP Headquarters in Shkodra last night. In attendance from the DP were Prek Alia, Roza Topalli, Ledion Krizi, and Isuf Bardhi. Prominent Shkodra citizens attending including Mentor Murati and Ardi Lokj.
R26	April 6, 1999	**OSINT:** Local Shkodra news has reported that the SP politician Fatmir Berishaj has direct connections to the Pojani crime syndicate.
R27	April 6, 1999	**INTREP:** The movement of sex slaves from Moldova to Italy is a convoluted process, characterized by moving the victims from one holding brothel to another. The victims have already worked in these waypoint brothels before they reach a brothel inside the destination European countries. A group of slaves can stay at the same waypoint brothel for a very long time.
R28	April 7, 1999	**OSINT:** Local Shkodra TV interviewed SP Fatmir Berishaj on his reported connections to the Mafia; Fatmir insists these are stories planted by the DP and it is in fact their members who are "in bed" with the Mafia.
R29	April 7, 1999	**IMINT:** An imagery search of the Adriatic coast south of Shkodra identified the port of Shengjin as a likely candidate port for smugglers moving goods to Italy.

Rep #	Date	Text
R30	April 7, 1999	**SIGINT:** Ardit Jasari called Qerim Jasari and told him to get two more boats ready for "the crossing" and that Jasari should "be ready to be captain of one of them."
R31	April 7, 1999	**SIGINT:** A scatter plot analysis of six months of COMINT traffic indicates that the preferred smuggler route across the Adriatic is between Shengjin, Albania, and Bari, Italy.
R32	April 7, 1999	**HUMINT—014-C3:** The regional crime syndicate leader along the Adriatic coast met with Fatmir Kaleci and gave him the name of a hit man his boss could possibly use for an upcoming job. The hit man's name is Xhon Rama.
R33	April 7, 1999	**DOCEX:** Analysis of documents seized during a brothel raid by Albanian special police suggests that several well-known Shkodra politicians have used these facilities.
R34	April 7, 1999	**OSINT:** A content analysis of local news in Shkodra province indicates that the population is opposed to international crime syndicates and the sex slave trade. However, small-time smuggling is not frowned upon but seen rather as a tradition.
R35	April 7, 1999	**OSINT:** A content analysis of local news in Shkodra province indicates that residents have little or no confidence in the local police but a high degree of confidence in the special police forces from Tirana.
R36	April 7, 1999	**INTREP:** Historical reporting along with current all-source reporting indicates that local crime is driven by smuggling from Montenegro over Lake Shkodra to Albania. The smuggling is controlled by three families that respectively have the stolen car market, the stolen electronics market, and the cigarette market.
R37	April 7, 1999	**INTREP:** Italian Carabinieri intelligence combined with a variety of all-source reporting indicates that Alban Lokaj is the dominant figure in the international sex slave syndicate in Italy.
R38	April 7, 1999	**SIGINT:** Fatmir Kaleci called Pal Vulaj to ask if Vulaj owned a transport bus with air conditioning.
R39	April 7, 1999	**OSINT:** National media focus is on Albania being seen by the EU as a major source and facilitator of sex slavery. A number of Albanian politicians from both ends of the political spectrum voiced their calls for more action to halt the trade.
R40	April 7, 1999	**SIGINT:** Edi Jasari told policeman Burim Krizi to be ready to provide an escort for one or two buses with approximately thirty packages.
R41	April 7, 1999	**HUMINT—024-B2:** Known drivers for the three regional crime syndicate leaders are Luan Zagreda, Loran Simaku, and Kristi Shala.
R42	April 7, 1999	**OSINT:** In an interview with local Shkodra TV, the mayor of Shkodra says he will soon be asking for the permanent presence of the federal special police.

(Continued)

(Continued)

Rep #	Date	Text
R43	April 7, 1999	**SIGINT:** Analysis of cell phone traffic over the last four months indicates the presence of a stolen car market in the vicinity of Zus, Albania.
R44	April 8, 1999	**OSINT:** A large funeral was held recently for Luan Ristani, the cousin of Fatos Ristani. Local media speculates that Luan was killed in a dispute with rival gang members.
R45	April 8, 1999	**DOCEX:** Documents retrieved from a brothel in London, United Kingdom, indicate that the resident sex slaves were recruited or snatched from Moldova, then smuggled into Albania; from there, they were smuggled over water to Italy.
R46	April 9, 1999	**IMINT:** Report on the results of a periodic broad area imagery search of the Shkodra region: On the third Saturday of the previous two months, approximately twenty to thirty late model automobiles were observed to be present in the town of Zus (N42° 01″ 58,′ E019° 28″ 33′), south of Shkodra. (Analyst comment: This search was conducted in response to collateral intelligence reporting the general location of a stolen automobile market near Shkodra.)
R47	April 9, 1999	**OSINT:** Albanian media outlets in Tirana are suggesting that DP politician Gjon Meksi might be indicted for corruption in the near future.
R48	April 9, 1999	**HUMINT—049-C3:** The leaders of the regional criminal organizations in Northern Albania include Kristi Rama mob.042980905 and Azem Thika mob.042459475.
R49	April 9, 1999	**OSINT:** A restaurant belonging to Azem Pojani was reportedly raided by four armed men; one person was reported beaten badly and sent to the hospital.
R50	April 10, 1999	**HUMINT—031-F6:** In the near future, a shipment of about twenty women is scheduled to transit from Moldova to Italy. The person responsible for them during transit has the first name Rezart.
R51	April 11, 1999	**SIGINT:** Begir Thika called Ardi Lokaj and said after the recent two extra shipments of computers and phones that he has a lot of cash that needs to be changed.
R52	April 11, 1999	**Cyber:** A series of hacking attempts on DP sites and servers have occurred in the last three months. The origin of these attacks could not be traced due to IP address hijacking.
R53	April 11, 1999	**OSINT:** National news reports that the special police have arrested several senior members of the national police. Many of those arrested originally came from the Shkodra region.
R54	April 11, 1999	**INTREP:** All-source reporting generally indicates a strong connection between the DP and several international crime syndicates. There are also indicators that Fatmir Berishaj (SP) is involved in facilitating slave smuggling.

Rep #	Date	Text
R55	April 11, 1999	**HUMINT—024-B2:** Pal Vulaj runs the coastal region crime syndicate and controls casinos in Velipojë and Shëngjin.
R56	April 11, 1999	**IMINT:** Sokol Nesimi's compound headquarters has been identified at N32° 35′ 20″ E19° 41′ 33″ near Vermosh, in the mountains.
R57	April 12, 1999	**IMINT:** Detailed tactical analysis is now available on Sokol Nesimi's compound HQ imagery.
R58	April 12, 1999	**OSINT:** A young couple was shot to death yesterday at a main intersection in Shkodra. After the traffic police signaled their car to stop, an unidentified man emptied two magazines into their idling Mercedes.
R59	April 12, 1999	**HUMINT—031-F6:** The boats used for smuggling slaves across the Adriatic are supercharged and can outrun any other boat on the water.
R60	April 12, 1999	**HUMINT—014-C3:** Fatmir Berishaj has personally invested heavily in the slave trade but he has no operational role.
R61	April 13, 1999	**SIGINT:** Zamir Marku called Sokol Nesimi and agreed that he would "ring to Pal Vulaj with the offer."
R62	April 13, 1999	**OSINT:** Local newspapers report that a special police task force could arrive to set up a long-term base at any time.
R63	April 13, 1999	**OSINT:** DP members Daradana and Valbon Krizi held their tenth wedding anniversary at the Palma restaurant in Shkodra. Many local celebrities attended the event.
R64	April 13, 1999	**Cyber:** SP Party servers were hit with denial of service (DoS) attacks from an unidentified source.
R65	April 13, 1999	**OSINT:** Local advertising in Shkodra papers suggest that the Thika family has a great deal of electronics to sell extremely cheap.
R66	April 13, 1999	**INTREP:** Three small-time smuggling families operate in Shkodra; there are usually no problems among them as they have their defined markets—cars, cigarettes, and electronics.
R67	April 14, 1999	**OSINT:** Residents in the vicinity of South Shtoj, a village on the road from Koplik to Shkodra, are complaining about all the activity around the local brothel.
R68	April 14, 1999	**MASINT:** A ground moving target indicator (GMTI) has observed a considerable amount of boat traffic on Lake Scutari between Shkodra and the opposite shore during the hours between 0200–0300 daily.
R69	April 15, 1999	**OSINT:** National news reports suggest that the special police will be given new powers of detention without trial for anyone considered capable of assisting with an investigation.
R70	April 15, 1999	**SIGINT:** Daradina Krizi called Ledion Krizi to assure him that the money was not an issue between family members. She closed by calling him "brother-in-law."

(Continued)

(Continued)

Rep #	Date	Text
R71	April 15, 1999	**SIGINT:** Police Chief Edi Jasari called policeman Burim Krizi and told him to expect a shooting, as Xhon Rama has been seen in the town.
R72	April 15, 1999	**HUMINT—024-B2:** Fatos Ristani loads his contraband at a little cove east of the village of Besa along the south coast of Lake Shkodra.
R73	April 15, 1999	**DOCEX:** Documents exploited from a special police raid indicate that a black market American passport and driver's license cost $10,000, while similar Canadian and Australian documentation costs $8,000.
R74	April 15, 1999	**MASINT:** GMTI shows a high degree of abnormal cross-border traffic on a dirt road west of Shkodra, Albania, and just a short distance from the official border crossing point.
R75	April 15, 1999	**OSINT:** Local Shkodra media reports that NGO Red Barnet was robbed by five masked gunmen.
R76	April 16, 1999	**OSINT:** National SP leader stated on national television that the recent spate of cyber attacks on both SP and DP servers could be due to an overexcited youth movement in both parties.
R77	April 16, 1999	**Cyber:** Special police headquarters servers suffered a six-hour long DoS attack originating outside of Albania.
R78	April 16, 1999	**SIGINT:** Saban Lokaj called Ditmir Berishaj and told Berishaj that there would be eight more security personnel on the payroll.
R79	April 16, 1999	**OSINT:** National media suggests that parliament will approve the establishment of a long-term special police unit in Shkodra.
R80	April 16, 1999	**SIGINT:** Traffic analysis shows a spike in communications between Northern Albania and Moldova just before a group of sex slaves are set in transit.

BACKGROUND READING

In 1990 and 1991, as the Hoxha regime collapsed in Albania, so did border enforcement. It became even easier than before to smuggle foodstuffs and luxury goods from Kosovo or Montenegro, and the permissive environment facilitated the start of the stolen Mercedes trade from the EU. Wholesale beer and cigarette smuggling became common and accepted forms of income supplements for the locals. Still, with the exception of some mountainous regions that had always had a high level of violent crime, the main centers of population enjoyed a relative peace and local banks were able to function normally. Businesses in the region had to deal with a relatively modest level of racketeering. Before 1997, the majority of the population was not armed, and household firearms were not seen as essential. Violent crimes such as armed robbery and hijacking were not sufficiently widespread to create an atmosphere of fear amongst the general population.

The Albanian Rebellion of 1997 dramatically changed the country's organized crime landscape. Government, law enforcement, and the military were seen by many to have sanctioned the pyramid schemes that had bankrupted an already poor populace, sparking the unrest. Rebels and angry civilians ransacked military bases, and suddenly the general population was armed with everything from 9mm pistols to 14.5mm anti-aircraft weapons. The AK-47 became a household item along with grenades and other pyrotechnics. Factories and successful businesses were looted. Citizens anxious to make up for personal losses became involved in serious criminal activities such as armed robbery and hijacking. The police and judiciary were rendered completely ineffective. During the unrest, many dangerous criminals were freed from prisons. These criminals robbed local banks and undertook racketeering on a wide scale. A sense of anarchy spread over the land, and a self-imposed curfew took place as soon as it became dark. Criminals could behave with impunity; known murderers were able to walk in public, drink at cafés, and conduct business. With the police and judiciary deemed ineffective, businessmen refused to pay taxes an d instead supported racketeering as the most promising method of securing protection for their small businesses.

Albanian criminal activity expanded internationally after 1997 by establishing a better distribution network and better bilateral criminal cooperation with criminal networks in the former Soviet Union. Especially noteworthy is the cooperation that developed between the Russian and Balkan Mafias, and between the Albanian and Italian Mafias. Working together with foreign organized crime, the Albanian organized crime groups were able to use Albania as a safe haven and grew far stronger in the post-1997 lawless environment.

The Albanians also began acting more and more as the *camels*—couriers—for eastern European sex slaves and drugs, and Albania became a hub for the sex-slave trade. In that trade, women were kept in holding centers across Albania waiting for travel arrangements into Europe or the Americas via Italy or Greece. The criminal syndicates used the same system for refugee smuggling into the West from Africa and the Middle East, with the Albanians supplying the needed false documentation. Logistical connections, established internationally with former Albanian refugees accepted into European countries and the Americas since 1991, were refined to maximize international criminal efficiency. This efficiency depended on family connections, which are traditionally strong in Albania. An example of this efficiency was the fact that you could buy your way to New Zealand, the United States, or Canada for $8,000 to $10,000 using contacts in those countries. This package included all necessary documentation including a bank card, being picked up at the airport, and a construction job. Criminal activity could be seen as divided into two mutually supportive categories: the continuing criminal activity with local implications that had dominated the early part of the 1990s, and the criminal activities beginning with the 1997 rebellion that became transnational with major international ramifications particularly between Albania and the EU.

In this environment, Albania became the topographical center of eastern European and Balkans organized crime. Post-conflict situations along its northern and northeastern borders provided smugglers with easy land access to Albanian Adriatic ports such as Durrës or Vlora. The Strait of Otranto then provided a water gateway to Italy and from there to the rest of the EU and the Americas.

In 1998, the G8 summit in the United Kingdom labeled transnational organized crime as one of the three major challenges facing the world, with the Balkans noted as a primary source. The Italian, Swiss, Austrian, and German police, being acutely aware of the organized crime originating from the Balkans region, have written numerous reports concerning it.[7] Inside the Balkan region, there is also recognition of the problem. The ex-president of Macedonia, for example, named organized crime in the region as the major roadblock to democratic development.

---

[7]Bruce Johnston, "Crisis Talks as Milan Is Hit by Wave of Killings," *Daily Telegraph,* January 13, 1999.

5

Democratic Republic of Congo Baseline

This is the baseline scenario for a series of four separate but interrelated case studies that follow. Each one makes use of the basic fact situation presented here. Successful completion of the assignments for all four cases requires the reader to be familiar with the baseline information and be aware of the collection capabilities available that are documented in the "Intelligence Support" section. These collection assets are referred to frequently in each case. Scientific and technical (S&T) issues are involved in a few of the exercises, but a background in S&T is not needed to complete the assignments.

The scenario is set in June 2017. It reflects actual events up until 2014; the events described from 2014 to 2017 are notional.

ABBREVIATIONS AND ACRONYMS

Abbreviation or Acronym	Description
APC	armored personnel carrier
CNDP	National Congress for the Defense of the People (Tutsi rebel group)
COMINT	Communications Intelligence (a subset of Signals Intelligence [SIGINT])
DGSE	General Directorate for External Security (France)
DRC	Democratic Republic of Congo
ELINT	Electronic Intelligence (a subset of SIGINT)
FLDR	Democratic Forces for the Liberation of Rwanda
GMTI	ground moving target indicator
HUMINT	Human Intelligence
JIC	Joint Intelligence Center
MMKK	Mai Mai Kata Katanga
LWIR	long wavelength infrared

(Continued)

(Continued)

Abbreviation or Acronym	Description
MASINT	Measurement and Signature Intelligence
MONUC	United Nations Organization Mission in the Democratic Republic of Congo
MONUSCO	United Nations Organization Stabilization Mission in the Democratic Republic of the Congo
NGO	nongovernmental organization
OOB	order of battle
SAM	surface-to-air missile
SAR	synthetic-aperture radar
SIGINT	Signals Intelligence (includes COMINT and ELINT)
S&T	scientific and technical
UAV	unmanned aerial vehicle
UN	United Nations
UNITA	Union for the Total Independence of Angola

SCENARIO

The Democratic Republic of Congo (DRC) has vast resources and potential, but it also has a tragic past that continues to shape events. The Second Congo War (1998–2003) was one of the bloodiest conflicts since WWII, and it laid the foundations for the 2017 insecurity. The war involved eight African nations and twenty-five armed groups. Killing over 5 million people, the war disrupted communities, devastated the economy, made guns and ammunition readily available, and traumatized entire populations. In consequence, the United Nations (UN) deployed its largest-ever peacekeeping mission to the DRC, with the assignment to protect civilians and consolidate peace.

In July and August 1999, when six heads of state and over fifty rebel leaders signed a cease-fire in Lusaka, Zambia, it appeared that the DRC might actually see an end to what had become a continental scale war. In 2000, the UN Security Council sent a peacekeeping force to monitor the ceasefire. In fact, the accord only temporarily froze armies, and after a brief respite, the hostilities resumed on all fronts. Other rebel forces had refused to sign. Former allies Uganda and Rwanda began to fight over the future of the Kisangani region in northeast Congo.

A Window of Opportunity: 2001–2002

2001   The national wars of the DRC neighbors continued to spill over onto Congolese soil, and ethnic feuds and bloodletting in the eastern part of the country continued unabated. A UN panel concluded that the conflict was being prolonged by the plundering of gold, diamonds, timber, and coltan (a metallic ore containing the elements niobium and tantalum used in electronics worldwide).

Most Western observers soon concluded that the principal obstacle to the implementation of the Lusaka Agreement was the DRC President Laurent Kabila, who understood that he was unlikely to retain power should the country ever be at peace. Kabila suspended the Lusaka agreement on August 23, 2000, and the country continued to fragment. His assassination in January 2001 and the ascension to power of his son, Joseph, provided a window of opportunity for the pursuit of peace. Joseph, originally viewed as a lightweight interim leader (and referred to in Western diplomatic circles as "the pale shadow of a pale shadow of a man"), responded well to his new responsibilities and emerged as an effective leader. He began to travel to Western capitals seeking support for his vision of peace in the DRC. The new U.S. administration greeted President Joseph Kabila warmly and began to take a harder line toward Rwanda and Uganda—both of which had continued to support rebels within the DRC. The newly installed president Kabila managed to revitalize the Lusaka process. Progress in negotiations was helped by the decaying alliances between belligerents, the increasing realization that the destruction of the war had exceeded all participants' expectations, and the impact upon the national economies of the countries involved. None of the major protagonists had achieved any of the strategic objectives they had sought when they entered the war, and the costs of the protracted, tenuous stalemate were becoming staggering.

2002   With all participants exercising uncommon restraint, the belligerents (Rwanda, Uganda, Burundi, Angola, Zimbabwe, Namibia, and DRC) began to search for a diplomatic escape from the quagmire. The first step was a series of bilateral consultations between the warring parties. The presidents of Congo and Rwanda signed a peace agreement. Steps such as this kept tensions under control but served only to preserve the status quo. Measurable progress was negligible. Remarkably, however, a self-imposed cease-fire held up as diplomatic maneuvering continued.

Though there were cracks visible in the peace agreements from the start, most noticeably that the belligerents themselves were largely responsible for policing the agreements, open hostilities ceased and the principal parties began to withdraw their conventional forces. While the geopolitical situation appeared more stable than it had been for a decade and full-scale war had been averted, the corrosive effects of forty-two years of interconnected political, military, economic, and social instability in the DRC remained. Up to 2 million Congolese had been displaced. The Congolese government and its armed forces controlled only 40 percent of the country—a country roughly the size of western Europe. The DRC had been reduced to a fragmented set of fiefdoms, especially in the east where tribal leaders ruled. There was no sense of nationhood and little more than a subsistence barter economy. For a decade, the Congolese economy had been the world's fastest shrinking; survival had become the primary focus of the citizenry.

It was against this backdrop that, in the summer of 2002, Joseph Kabila initiated the "National Dialogue" designed to organize democratic elections, the formation of a new national army, which included the integration of former rebels into the armed forces, and the reestablishment of state administration throughout the country.

In October 2002, Kabila negotiated the withdrawal of Rwandan forces occupying the eastern DRC. Two months later, all remaining warring parties signed the Pretoria Accord, temporarily ending the fighting and establishing a government of national unity.

The Democratic Republic of Congo Consolidates and Stabilizes: 2003–2013

2003   Though progress was slow, the belligerents incrementally withdrew during the year, and the Second Congo War officially ended. Rwandan and Ugandan conventional forces returned home, and by mid-2003 the rebel forces supported by Rwanda had dispersed and ceased fighting. But these rebel groups did not disband, nor were they disarmed. Shortly thereafter, Angola, Zimbabwe, and Namibia withdrew the forces they had committed to supporting the DRC. Over time, the Congolese government, whose territorial control had been reduced to the provinces of Bas-Congo, Kinshasa, and Bandundu, reasserted control of Equateur, both Kasai provinces and most of the Katanga province. In the area of the Kivus, over 1 million displaced persons continued to present an overwhelming humanitarian problem. As stability increased and the DRC government forces were able to guarantee security over most of the western two-thirds of the country, UN and U.S. disaster relief contributions increased, and nongovernmental organizations (NGOs) mobilized to confront the persistent refugee, disease, and famine problems in the eastern DRC. In June, French soldiers arrived in Bunia, spearheading a UN-mandated rapid-reaction force.

Progress also was made in the political situation during the year. In April, President Kabila signed a transitional constitution, under which an interim government would rule pending elections. The president named a transitional government to lead until elections were held. In July, leaders of the main former rebel groups were sworn in as vice presidents, and an interim parliament was inaugurated in August.

Nevertheless, fighting continued in the eastern Congo throughout 2003, driven by trade in conflict minerals such as coltan. The eastern regions of the DRC also continued to be plagued by interethnic fighting and the persistence of Congolese "Mai-Mai" militias in addition to the staggering number of displaced persons.

2004   The United Nations Organization Mission in the Democratic Republic of Congo, or MONUC, had grown to 4,200 by April 2004 and had established strongholds and logistics nodes in Mbandaka, Kisangani, and Kananga. But the Congo's vast size, its remoteness, and the existence of very few passable roads made it impossible for MONUC to deploy to many locations. The MONUC forces avoided dangerous and remote locations and focused instead on the achievable mission of policing the cessation of hostilities and monitoring logistical choke points in the areas where conventional troops and rebels had been active. MONUC forces assisted by reporting cease-fire violations and ensuring that the belligerents did not reintroduce armed forces. MONUC forces were also responsible for overseeing humanitarian aid transshipment points and the protection of civilians.

The envisioned peacekeeping and enforcement mission did not progress as planned. Political squabbling over the details of the deployment slowed implementation. Moreover, the logistics proved to be a nightmare. Virtually all UN troops and equipment had to be brought in by air because Congo's only ocean port (Matadi) has an extremely limited capability. There was also the poor condition of most of the country's roads. Complicating matters, the country's airports were in terrible condition, lacking air traffic control, radars, night lighting, and unloading equipment. In 2003, when the second phase of UN presence was to begin, a UN planner had estimated that it would take nine to twelve months to deploy 20,000 troops with the necessary equipment. By late 2004, consensus behind this deployment of armed troops evaporated; Joseph Kabila began to resist such a high-profile deployment of troops and reminded anyone who would listen of the unhappy memories his people had of the UN mission's blue helmet army that had participated in Congo's civil war from 1960 to 1964.

Nevertheless, all key participants agreed that the success of the disengagement and disarmament resulting from the UN Military Observer Force had exceeded their expectations. By the close of 2004, the second-phase deployment of UN peacekeeping and peace enforcement troops was put on indefinite hold. The cease-fire and a tenuous "peace" held up for the entire year, much to the surprise of almost everyone concerned.

2005 In May, the DRC parliament adopted a new constitution, with text agreed to by former warring factions. The voters approved the new constitution in December, paving the way for elections in 2006.

2006 This year saw the first free elections in the DRC in four decades. The new constitution came into effect in February. In July, presidential and parliamentary polls were held. With no clear winner in the presidential vote, incumbent leader Joseph Kabila and opposition candidate Jean-Pierre Bemba prepared for a runoff poll. Forces loyal to the two candidates clashed in the capital. Kabila was declared winner of October's runoff presidential election. The poll had the general approval of international monitors.

Unfortunately, the relative peace that had existed in the east ended during 2006. Thousands became refugees in the northeast as the army and UN peacekeepers stepped up their drive to disarm irregular forces ahead of the elections. Renegade DRC general Laurent Nkunda established the National Congress for the Defense of the People (CNDP), an armed militia in the Kivu region. Nkunda was a Tutsi rebel leader, formerly a senior officer in the Congolese Rally for Democracy, Goma faction. In December, Nkunda's forces clashed with the UN-backed DRC army in

North Kivu province, causing over 50,000 people to flee. The UN Security Council expressed concern about the fighting.

2007   By 2007, the deaths attributable to the Congo conflicts numbered 5.4 million people, including those who had died from starvation, violence, or disease. Deaths were estimated to be continuing at the rate of 45,000 per month.

In May, the UN opened an investigation into allegations that UN peacekeepers in the Ituri region were engaged in gold and arms trafficking. Aid agencies reported a large increase in refugees in North Kivu, blaming the CNDP and general Nkunda.

In September, a major outbreak of the Ebola virus occurred in Kasai Occidental province. Seventy-one percent of the 264 victims who contracted the disease died.

2008   In April, DRC army troops clashed with their former allies, the Rwandan Hutu militias in the eastern Congo, and thousands of people were displaced. During August, the violence erupted in the east between the DRC army, supported by UN troops, and rebels loyal to Laurent Nkunda. In October, Nkunda's primarily Tutsi rebel group, the CNDP, captured the major army base of Rumangabo and took control of the area surrounding Goma, the regional capital. Thousands more people, including Congolese troops, fled as clashes in the eastern DRC intensified. Chaos gripped the provincial capital Goma as rebel forces advanced. MONUC engaged the rebels in an attempt to protect Goma. The Congolese government accused Rwanda of backing General Nkunda, a claim Rwanda denied. During November, a campaign by general Nkunda to consolidate control over the eastern DRC prompted a new wave of refugees. The UN Security Council approved a temporary increase of troops to bolster the strained UN peacekeeping effort.

2009   In January, Rwandan troops removed Laurent Nkunda as leader of the CNDP. Nkunda was replaced by Bosco Ntaganda and arrested in Rwanda. Rwandan troops began a joint campaign with the Congolese army against the CNDP in North Kivu province. The campaign lasted five weeks. The government then signed a peace agreement with the CNDP. President Kabila approved a law giving amnesty to armed groups as part of a deal meant to end fighting in east.

In April, after the CNDP campaign had ended, Hutu militia reemerged in the east as the Democratic Forces for the Liberation of Rwanda (FLDR). The Congolese and Rwandan forces then began a campaign against the FDLR. The fighting cost the FDLR its control of several mining areas and other strategic locations, which came under the control of Congolese army units and former CNDP fighters that had integrated into the Congolese army.

2010   On July 1, 2010, the United Nations Organization Stabilization Mission in the Democratic Republic of the Congo (MONUSCO) took over from MONUC. The reorganization of the mission was done in accordance with Security Council resolution 1925. MONUSCO was authorized to use all necessary means to carry out its mandate relating, among other things, to the protection of civilians, humanitarian personnel, and human rights defenders under imminent threat of physical violence and to support the government of the DRC in its stabilization and peace consolidation efforts.

From June through August, the DRC army conducted an offensive, Operation Rwenzori, against Ugandan rebel groups. The conflict prompted 90,000 to flee their homes in North Kivu province. Mass rapes were reported in North Kivu province and the UN envoy blamed both the rebels and the DRC army. Rape and murder of civilians by government troops, rebels, and militias continued through the remainder of 2010. The UN peacekeepers were unable to stop the violence. A UN report accused networks within the DRC army of promoting violence in the east to profit from mining, smuggling, and poaching.

2011 Events in 2011 strengthened Kabila's hold on power. In January, the DRC constitution was changed, boosting President Kabila's reelection chances. In November's presidential and parliamentary elections, Kabila gained another term. The vote was criticized abroad, and the opposition disputed the result.

The year saw a number of incarcerations for human rights offenses—and one person escaping incarceration who would later bedevil the DRC.

- In February, a court sentenced Lieutenant Colonel Kibibi Mutware to twenty years in jail in a mass rape case in eastern Congo. This was the first conviction of a commanding officer for rape in eastern DRC.
- In May, Rwandan Hutu rebel Ignace Murwanashyaka went on trial in Germany for alleged crimes against humanity in the DRC.
- In July, Colonel Nyiragire Kulimushi, who was accused of ordering the mass rape of women in eastern DRC, surrendered to authorities.
- In September, Mai Mai Kata Katanga (MMKK) rebel leader Gédéon Kyungu Mutanga escaped from a Lubumbashi prison during a mass prison breakout by almost 1,000 inmates. He subsequently formed the MMKK militia, with the goal of securing independence for the province.

2012 The attempt to integrate CNDP members into the Congolese military had failed, prompting the CNDP to defect in 2012 and form the M23 rebel group (named after the March 23, 2009, peace agreements). M23 began a violent campaign that displaced large numbers of people in North Kivu.

In October, the UN Security Council approved a resolution imposing sanctions against leaders of the M23 rebel movement and violators of the DRC arms embargo. A UN panel accused Rwanda and Uganda of supplying M23 with weapons and support. Both countries denied the accusation.

In November, M23 troops briefly entered Goma, the main city in the resource-rich east, and then withdrew after being promised that the DRC government would release some of their supporters.

2013 In February, representatives of eleven African countries signed an accord in Ethiopia pledging to help end the conflict in the DRC. The M23 rebel group declared a cease-fire ahead of the talks. In March, M23 founder Bosco Ntaganda surrendered at the U.S. embassy in Rwanda and was transferred to the International Criminal Court in The Hague to face war crimes charges. But the DRC continued to be the scene of violence committed by other armed groups including the FLDR and MMKK groups.

In July, a UN Intervention Brigade was deployed to neutralize the armed groups and rebels in the eastern Congo. The brigade included Malawian, South African, and Tanzanian peacekeepers, supported by attack helicopters (AHs). The UN authorized the brigade to use unmanned aerial vehicles (UAVs) for reconnaissance of militia activity. With the brigade's backing, the DRC army captured the last M23 strongholds in the east. In December, M23 signed a peace deal with the government.

The Democratic Republic of Congo Fragments: 2014–2017

The Material in the Remainder of This Scenario Is Notional   In the last three years, the DRC government and MONUSCO have had to face two new challenges to central government authority: the MMKK and the resurgent M23. Currently, these two groups control the regions of the DRC shown in Figure 5.1.

The Mai Mai Kata Katanga   The MMKK is a DRC rebel group that claims to fight for the independence of Katanga province. ("Kata Katanga" is Swahili for "secede Katanga.") The group was founded by Gédéon Kyungu Mutanga, known as Commander Gédéon, after he escaped from prison in September 2011 with assistance from members of his militia.

During 2014, Angola's relations with the Kabila government had become strained. Originally, Angola had entered the Congolese wars to save President Laurent Kabila's regime—principally to prevent a vacuum that might be filled by forces friendly to Union for the Total Independence of Angola (UNITA) rebels. In return for its assistance to the DRC through 2012, Angola reaped considerable economic spoils. The Angolan government gained control of much of the DRC petroleum distribution and production network as well as a controlling interest in future exploration in Kinshasa's offshore territorial Congo basin. The result was strategic control of a 1,000 km stretch of the Atlantic Seaboard. With the shift of UNITA from an insurgent force to a political opposition party, the Angola military commitment to the DRC became minimal, though Angola's financial interests in the DRC and in particular in the diamond business continued. The success of Joseph Kabila in establishing a relatively stable and increasingly strong government in the DRC began to cause Luanda concern and threatened Angola's emergence as a regional power. Fortified by the increasing price of oil and the disappearance of the UNITA irritant, Angola's appetite for the huge untapped mineral, timber, and agricultural resources of the DRC increased.

In April 2015, a senior officer of the Congolese army, Major General Gabriel Mala, defected from the government and took charge of the MMKK after the death of Commander Gédéon. Luanda saw an opportunity in the new commander of the MMKK. General Mala, raised in Angola and the son of a revolutionary leader of the

FIGURE 5.1   Territory Controlled by the Mai Mai Kata Katanga and M23

Source: CIA world Factbook.

Congo in the 1970s, had risen through a series of high positions in the Congolese armed forces. Even though he was disliked by both Kabila regimes, he had been able to keep his positions because of his close ties to Angola—a needed ally during the 1998 to 2006 time frame. With the Angolan relationship souring, he had been arrested and humiliated by Joseph Kabila. Viewed as a threat to Kabila, he has been vocal in his distrust of Western and UN involvement in Congolese affairs. He has managed to survive several assassination attempts. After the most recent assassination attempt, he fled and took charge of the MMKK stronghold in Katanga. The number of supporters rallying to his cause multiplied quickly and by the end of 2015 numbered 25,000. Most of the DRC forces in the province deserted to the MMKK or simply went home. By 2016, Katanga had slipped from Kinshasa's control. Angola, recognizing an opening, provided financial support to the MMKK, applauding its anti-Kabila, anti-Western philosophy. The MMKK quickly established control of Katanga province.

The MMKK today effectively governs most of the Katanga province, funding its operations with income from diamonds, uranium, and—most recently—coffinite mining.[1] It has a rapidly modernizing and effective army that receives support and training from mercenaries and Angolan army elements. It reportedly has received modern arms from many sources. The leadership is antagonistic toward the West because of U.S. and European support for the DRC government.

Since Mala's rebellion, European and U.S. policymakers have been sharply divided over how best to deal with the MMKK. Some see the MMKK as a threat to the DRC and believe the MMKK wishes to make the DRC into a rogue state, inimical to Western interests; they argue that forceful action against the MMKK is needed. Others contend that UN-backed diplomacy and the promise of foreign investment and assistance will work; their goal is to influence the MMKK leadership and its backers, the Angolan government, to constrain the activities of the MMKK. They also argue that the Angolan government and the MMKK are potential allies against M23, which they regard as much more dangerous.

M23   During 2013, the UN had secured a regional agreement to end the M23 rebellion in eastern areas. Early in 2014, Rwanda remobilized the dispirited M23 elements in the DRC and encouraged their affiliation with the charismatic Tiba Besebo. In the summer of 2014, Besebo became the leader of M23, which consisted largely of Congolese members of the Tutsi ethnic group. The group has a long history of murder, rape, and pillaging. It has always been anti-Western and strongly anti-United States.

Rwanda began providing sufficient funding to Besebo for him to pay and care for his troops, thus temporarily reducing the pillaging and abuse of civilians in the areas in which he operated. This was so rare in the eastern DRC that Besebo and M23 were soon extremely popular. By the end of 2016, M23 forces numbered 17,000 and appeared to have no factional friction. The rebels were operating along the eastern borders of the country from Fizi north to Beni and threatening to move westward toward Kindu and Kisangani.

In April 2017, M23 forces were responsible for the massacre of thousands of refugees in the Mugunga refugee camp, 80 km northwest of Lake Kivu (Goma area). The Mugunga camp was supposedly protected by a unit of the DRC army, but the army unit apparently fled when the M23 rebels appeared. At least seven NGO workers were reportedly murdered, including two U.S. citizens. There were at least a dozen American citizens associated with NGOs in the region. The reaction from European and African capitals and the UN was for swift action, given that the

---

[1]Coffinite is a uranium-bearing mineral and is highly radioactive. It was first identified in 1954 at a mine in Mesa County, Colorado.

camp was established under Organization of African Unity and UN Security Council resolutions.

Besebo is believed to receive arms and manpower support from Rwanda, but details on this relationship are unclear. The relationship between M23 and the MMKK is also unclear. Conflicting evidence suggests that (1) the MMKK and M23 may be cooperating against a common enemy (the DRC government) and (2) the two groups are competing for the same territory and will eventually wind up fighting each other.

Funding for M23 also is not understood aside from the support that it gets from Rwanda. Originally most of the group's funding came from mineral mining using slave labor, but UN embargos on minerals from the region have dried up this source of Besebo's funds.

M23 also may be getting substantial funding from an extraterritorial narcotics business. The group has also been accused of being an offshoot of the former al-Qaeda network and of receiving some funding from the same sources. However, Besebo hotly denies ever having any relationship with al-Qaida, though during the 1990s he visited Osama bin Laden in the Sudan.

Besebo reportedly has the objective of removing "foreign influences" from all of Africa but especially from the DRC. He occasionally threatens to use terrorist tactics against European and U.S. interests. His strategy appears to be to keep U.S. and European governments off balance through constantly changing asymmetric attacks. He has so far refrained from extending his terrorist activities outside Africa.

Current Situation: June 2017

The period of relative stability and the progress toward restoring the territorial sovereignty of the DRC are now threatened by two rebellions. In spite of the tremendous natural resources within the DRC, the country still has no economy. Commerce is informal and corrupt. Two decades of refugees and refugee migration have resulted in deforestation and soil erosion throughout the Great Lakes region in the east. Excessive mortality due to AIDS, periodic epidemic outbreaks, and starvation continues. Kabila's rhetoric about nationhood, constitutional reform, and democratic elections cannot excite a starving, exhausted population. Political opposition has grown especially among students who have been exposed to Western culture and universities. The reemergence of well-organized rebel groups supported by external states, persistent and violent militias, and ethnic and civil strife do not bode well for the DRC or regional stability. The newly emerged MMKK and M23 appear well funded and well organized and may present more of a threat to Kabila and regional security than the uncoordinated rabble that made up rebel movements of the not too distant past. The MMKK has consolidated its control of Katanga province; current force disposition and recent intelligence indicates that an assault on Mbuji-Mayi and the diamond mines is likely.

In the east, ethnic fighting, ethnic killings, and human rights violations continue. The three principal concentrations of refugees are vicinity of Goma

(800,000), vicinity of Bukavu (240,000), and vicinity of Uvira (perhaps as many as 150,000, exact locations unknown). The Goma area has the most organized camps and is the focus of current UN and NGO relief efforts—when M23 allows such operations.

While the two rebel forces have gained strength, the DRC armed forces, never terribly reliable, have clustered in the capital and in strongholds within the central region—in essence within or west of the triangle patrolled by the MONUSCO forces. One DRC unit continues to guard the refugee camps in the Goma region and is subject to frequent M23 harassment. Once numbering nearly 55,000, with desertions and defections the DRC armed forces have shrunk to fewer than 40,000.

United Nations Organization Stabilization Mission in the Democratic Republic of the Congo and Allied Forces

Special envoy: The UN DRC policy is, according to a variety of sources, largely that of UN special envoy Philip Smythe. He has the UN General Secretary's ear and respect. Smythe is negotiating with the Congo, Rwanda, Uganda, Angola, and Zimbabwe to find a solution to the problem of rebel group occupation, the refugee problem, and support to the two major rebel groups in the area: the M23 faction, in the eastern DRC, and the MMKK, located in the southeast and probably supported by Angola. Smythe is more of an activist than most special envoys and appears to be willing to move away from a strict "African solutions to African problems" doctrine especially in view of the deteriorating regional situation.

Military: The bulk of MONUSCO forces consists of units from Belgium, France, Canada, South Africa, Pakistan, Namibia, Morocco, and Tunisia. At present, as a result of a Smythe brokered deal, the United States is providing air traffic control, logistics, command and control, limited intelligence, and military police support to the MONUSCO forces who are currently stationed in the cities of Kisangani, Mbandaka, and Kananga. MONUSCO forces have been guaranteed free movement in this area by the DRC while they serve in their blue helmet "peacekeeping" role, but the DRC troops are present throughout this area and sometimes obstruct MONUSCO operations. Most such incidents of obstruction occur when DRC officers attempt to conceal illicit activities from discovery.

MONUSCO has about 4,000 troops in Kisangani and 3,000 troops deployed from Kisangani to the Goma camps. The remaining forces are consolidated in the area defined by Mbandaka, Lusambo, Mbuji-Mayi, Kananga, and the capital.

Almost all MONUSCO forces are stationed in the cities, and their patrols usually only extend out 25 km from those metropolitan areas. At least 10,000 of at most a 40,000 person Congolese Armed Forces are in the Kinshasa region. In essence MONUSCO, originally in-country to monitor the cease-fire, is now serving as a wedge between the belligerents and the capital. They still have the mission of overseeing humanitarian aid.

Current Order of Battle

[From MONUSCO Intelligence assessment, April 7, 2017] Current order of battle (OOB) information on combatant forces operating in DRC is illustrated in Table 5.1. Specific locations and force dispositions are not available. Estimates of force dispositions are as follows:

Table 5.1 Democratic Republic of Congo Forces Order of Battle

	M23 Forces	Mai Mai Kata Katanga Forces	DRC Forces Forces Armées Congolaises
MANPOWER	17,000 (est.)	25,000 (est.)	40,000
Organization	Unknown	Unknown	10 + Infantry Brigades (~30,000 men)
			1 X Presidential Guard Brigade (3,200 men)
			1 X Mechanized Infantry Brigade (3,200)
			1 X Commando Brigade (3,000 est.)
EQUIPMENT			
Main battle tanks	None	None	20 X Chinese Type 59
			42 X Chinese Type 62
Armored fighting vehicles	20 X BTR-60 APC	25 X BMP-1 2 X BMP-2	30 X Panhard AML 60
			30 X Panhard AML 90
			60 X Panhard M-3
Artillery	None	25 X 81mm mortars	30 X M116 75mm Pack Howitzers
			20 X Chinese Type 56 85 mm
			15 X Chinese Type 60 122 mm
			20 X Chinese Type 63 107 mm multiple rocket launchers (MRLs)
			81 mm mortars (quantity unknown)
			107 mm M30 mortars (quantity unknown)
Anti-tank	57mm anti-tank gun (quantity unknown)	AT-3 Sagger (quantity unknown); 2 X 85mm D-44	57 mm M18 recoilless rifles
			75 mm M20 recoilless rifles
			106 mm M40A1 recoilless rifles
Air defense	20+ X 14.5mm	10 X ZSU-23–2	14.5 mm ZPU-4
			40 X 37 mm M1939/Type 63
			40 mm L-60

(Continued)

(Continued)

	M23 Forces	Mai Mai Kata Katanga Forces	DRC Forces Forces Armées Congolaises
Surface-to-air missile (SAM) systems	Types and quantities unknown	Types and quantities unknown	SA-7 (quantity unknown)
Combat aircraft	None	None	15 Su-25
Counterinsurgency reconnaissance aircraft	None	2 X Cessna 172	1 X Learjet 36
Transport aircraft	None	2 X AN-2	1 X 707–320, 1 X 727–30 5 X C-130, 8 X C-47
Combat helicopter	None	5 X MI-25	6 X SA-319 Alouette helicopter
Transport helicopters	None	2 X MI-8	
Naval ships	None	None	4 X Chinese Shanghai II PCC

DRC forces: At least three brigades are in Kinshasa. One brigade, assigned to refugee camp security, is believed to be operating in the vicinity of Goma. A less than full-strength brigade is operating in Kisangani. The remainder of the DRC army is operating in the polygon defined by Kinshasa, Mbandaka, Lusambo, Mbuji-Mayi, and Tshikapa. Very few forces operate outside of major population centers.

MMKK forces: The HQ has been established in Kamina. MONUSCO currently assesses the MMKK to be in control of most of Katanga province. A majority of artillery, armored vehicles, and air defense equipment are dedicated to the area between Kamina and Mbuji-Mayi.

M23: Units and activities are believed to be confined to Nord and Sud-Kivu provinces. MONUSCO has limited knowledge of the organizational structure or strength of this group.

Table 5.2 shows the composition of MONUSCO forces.

INTELLIGENCE SUPPORT

MONUSCO has established a Joint Intelligence Center (JIC) at Kisangani, staffed by French, Belgian, Canadian, and South African Intelligence Officers. It receives both raw and finished intelligence primarily from French and German Intelligence Services.

Open Source

Open source comes from local newspapers and the Internet; the JIC team is experienced in exploiting Internet social media.

Table 5.2 United Nations Organization Stabilization Mission in the Democratic Republic of Congo Forces Order of Battle

	MONUSCO Forces
MANPOWER	20,688
Organization	On March 28, 2013, the Security Council decided by resolution 2098 that MONUSCO shall, for an initial period of one year and within the authorized troop ceiling of 19,815, include an "Intervention Brigade" consisting inter alia of three infantry battalions, one artillery, and one Special force and Reconnaissance company. The authorized strength was increased to 21,244 in March 2016.

Current strength

- 20,688 total uniformed personnel
  - 18,766 military personnel
  - 504 military observers
  - 1,418 police (including formed units)
- 994 international civilian personnel
- 561 UN volunteers
- 2,974 local civilian staff

Military personnel are from Algeria, Bangladesh, Belgium, Benin, Bolivia, Bosnia and Herzegovina, Burkina Faso, Cameroon, Canada, China, Czech Republic, Egypt, France, Ghana, Guatemala, Guinea, India, Indonesia, Ireland, Jordan, Kenya, Malawi, Malaysia, Mali, Mongolia, Morocco, Nepal, Niger, Nigeria, Pakistan, Paraguay, Peru, Poland, Romania, Russian Federation, Senegal, Serbia, South Africa, Sri Lanka, Sweden, Switzerland, Tunisia, Ukraine, United Kingdom, United Republic of Tanzania, United States, Uruguay, Yemen, and Zambia.

HQ	Kinshasa

Human Intelligence

Human Intelligence (HUMINT) support to MONUSCO comes from several sources. Much of the HUMINT reporting comes from MONUSCO forces in the field and from refugee interrogation at field debriefing centers. MONUSCO also maintains a network of informants that includes DRC officers, NGOs, and civilians.

Liaison reporting comes into the JIC from intelligence services of MONUSCO participants. The United Kingdom, Dutch, Belgian, French, German, and Portuguese services have all provided reporting in the past. The International Criminal Police Organization (INTERPOL) also is a source of liaison reporting. Some liaison exists with DRC police and the DRC intelligence service, but these DRC sources often shape the information they provide, in an attempt to influence MONUSCO decision making.

External Imagery Support

France provides daily imaging of selected DRC targets from its commercial imaging satellites. The primary source is the Pleiades satellite, which provides both visible and multispectral imagery. Visible imagery is very good quality (40 cm resolution), and multispectral imaging is at 1 m resolution. The satellite can acquire imagery anywhere within an 800-km-wide ground strip. It does strip mapping with a 20-km-wide swath and can produce stereo imagery.

Upon request, Germany will provide imagery from its hyperspectral imaging satellite. The EnMAP satellite images in approximately 250 narrow spectral channels, 136 of which are in the SWIR band and 96 in the NIR band. The satellite, launched in 2015, uses push broom imaging spectrometers having a spatial resolution of 30 m within a 30 km wide swath.

Synthetic Aperture Radar (SAR) imagery is provided by Germany. The SAR-Lupe has performance characteristics that make it an excellent intelligence collection sensor. It provides a resolution of about a 0.5 m over a frame size of 5.5 km on a side in the spotlight mode. Resolution is about 1 m over a frame size of 8 km × 60 km in the strip map mode. The radar is able to image a given area of the earth once every 10 hours or less.

In-Country Imagery and Measurement and Signature Intelligence Support

In-country, the MONUSCO JIC has available three long-range UAVs that can provide imaging. The three are Israeli-produced Hermes 900 all-weather UAVs capable of auto-landing on non-instrumented runways. The Hermes 900 has a payload capacity of 300 kg and can operate for up to 30 hours at 18,000 feet altitude with an airspeed of 105 knots. These UAVs operate from a Kisangani airfield and are capable of carrying one of three imaging packages:

- A high-resolution video camera capable of imaging at 20 cm resolution. The video is downlinked via satellite to the MONUSCO command center at Kisangani.
- An experimental high-resolution hyperspectral imager, the RAPHIDE hyperspectral sensor, operates in 244 spectral bands, including the long wavelength infrared (LWIR) band, with resolution that varies from 30 cm to 70 cm, depending on the spectral band. The imagery must be sent to a French laboratory for Measurement and Signature Intelligence (MASINT) processing. RAPHIDE imagery can be processed to identify the existence of many chemical compounds of intelligence interest.
- The Israeli-produced ELM-2054, a lightweight SAR/ground moving target indicator (GMTI) sensor designed to be carried on small tactical UAVs for all-weather, air-to-surface intelligence, surveillance, targeting, and reconnaissance applications. The ELM-2054 can produce strip map images of 15 cm resolution and can map moving targets in an 80 ×100 km swath. The imagery is processed at the MONUSCO JIC.

All UAV missions carry the reporting tag RHINO. Video camera missions are tagged RHINO RED. Hyperspectral imaging missions are tagged RHINO BLUE. SAR missions are tagged RHINO GREEN.

Signals Intelligence Support

Tactical Communications Intelligence (COMINT) collection in-country is handled by French and Canadian assets. Sanitized strategic COMINT is provided by France's General Directorate for External Security (DGSE).

Daily Electronic Intelligence (ELINT) reports on the locations and types of radars in the DRC are provided by the DGSE to the MONUSCO JIC. The source of the reporting is France's Electronic Intelligence Satellite (ELISA). ELISA comprises a constellation of four satellites, located a few kilometers apart in space. Each satellite receives and records incoming radar pulses and transmits the pulse data to a French ground station. The ground station then combines the received signals to geolocate radars.

Cyber Collection Support

Cyber collection for high-priority collection is handled remotely by the DGSE. A local capability exists to conduct HUMINT-enabled collection against wireless communications, including wireless Internet service. Most such collection is targeted on MicroNet, the leading wireless Internet access service provider in the DRC and Congo Brazzaville.

MONUSCO is prohibited by agreement with the DRC government from conducting offensive cyber operations.

6

Democratic Republic of Congo: Gray Arms Traffic

This case study is set in June 2017 and is based on the Democratic Republic of Congo (DRC) baseline that is described in Chapter 5.

In the decade following the end of the Cold War, Central Africa received tons of small arms from outside the continent. By 2005, this era had passed, because regional supply was able to satisfy local demand. The small arms trafficked during the 1990s did not evaporate and continued to be recirculated throughout the region, especially in the DRC.

Criminal and insurgent groups therefore do not need international traffickers to obtain light weapons such as AK-47s. Such firearms have flowed into the region over the years, and many stockpiles remain. The situation with heavier and more sophisticated weapons in the DRC is considerably less clear and is the focus of this case study.

EDUCATIONAL OBJECTIVES

This exercise provides practical experience in the following:

- defining the intelligence problem and creating a problem definition model (PDM)
- creating alternative process models and target network models (TNMs)
- making judgments based on incomplete information
- developing and supporting conclusions and explaining assumptions
- conveying uncertainty to customers in intelligence assessments

ASSIGNMENT

You are the United Nations Organization Stabilization Mission in the Democratic Republic of the Congo (MONUSCO) Joint Intelligence Center (JIC) analyst responsible for assessing arms flow into and within the DRC. When you reported for duty, the MONUSCO commander gave you the following general guidance:

> We are not attempting to assess small arms traffic. Our primary concern is MMKK acquisition of heavy weaponry, either directly or through Angola. Significant quantities of heavy weapons in MMKK hands would alter the balance of power in the DRC and likely embolden General Mala to attack the disorganized government forces. Also of concern is possible M23 acquisition of heavy weaponry to support terrorist activity.

Today, the MONUSCO commander has followed up that guidance by asking you for an intelligence assessment that answers the following questions about heavy weapons[1] traffic:

- What are the sources and supply routes for weaponry flowing to the Mai Mai Kata Katanga (MMKK)?
- What are the sources and supply routes for weaponry flowing to M23?
- What weaponry is being provided, to which groups, and in what quantities?
- What entities are facilitating the transfer of these weapons? How are the weapons being paid for?

To achieve the goals laid out by the MONUSCO commander, individuals or teams should do the following:

1. Create a PDM. (Hint: Refer to Chapter 2, Figure 2.6, as a starting point.)

2. Prepare process models to show the flow of heavy armaments to the MMKK and M23 (including equipment types and quantities) and the financing involved. Include in the model points of origin, means of transport, and final destinations of the equipment. This task calls for making judgments in the absence of credible intelligence.

3. Create two TNMs—one showing the network (people, organizations, and financing) that supports the flow of weaponry to the MMKK and one showing the network that supports the flow of weaponry to M23. (Hint: Refer to Chapter 2, Figure 2.9, for a starting template.)

4. Prepare a brief (two to four paragraphs) intelligence assessment that addresses the questions posed (to the extent that you can). Support your conclusions using the models you have created.

---

[1]"Heavy weapons" in this context includes tanks and armored personnel carriers (APCs), aircraft and helicopters, rocket and missile launchers, surface-to-air missiles (SAMs), mortars and field artillery, and the ammunition for them all.

ABBREVIATIONS AND ACRONYMS

Abbreviation or Acronym	Description
CNDP	National Congress for the Defense of the People
COMINT	Communications Intelligence
DGSE	General Directorate for External Security (France)
DRC	Democratic Republic of Congo
EFT	Electronic Funds Transfer
ELINT	Electronic Intelligence
ELISA	Electronic Intelligence Satellite
HUMINT	Human Intelligence
IMINT	Imagery Intelligence
INTERPOL	International Criminal Police Organization
JIC	Joint Intelligence Center
MASINT	Measurement and Signature Intelligence
MMKK	Mai Mai Kata Katanga
MONUSCO	United Nations Organization Stabilization Mission in the Democratic Republic of the Congo
MV	Motor Vessel
NATO	North Atlantic Treaty Organization
NFI	No Further Information
OSINT	Open Source Intelligence
PDM	Problem Definition Model
SAM	Surface-to-Air Missile
TNM	Target Network Model
UAE	United Arab Emirates
UAV	Unmanned Aerial Vehicle

SCENARIO

Democratic Republic of Congo Arms Traffic—Background

The following contains excerpts from "Organized Crime and Instability in Central Africa: A Threat Assessment," produced by the United Nations Office on Drugs and Crime (UNODC), Vienna, October 2011.

The primary source of new weaponry in the DRC appears to be official state stocks, legitimately procured but diverted to the illicit market. Thousands of weapons came into the DRC during the decades of rebellions, the Hutu flight from Rwanda, and the two Congolese wars. In consequence, criminals and rebel groups can obtain almost any of the weapons possessed by local security forces. Some imports continue to be made through commercial channels; when the arms arrive, they are funneled through corrupt officials to the end users. These transfers often are the result of sympathy for the rebels' cause or because of informal obligations and family or ethnic ties.

Also, in the 2010 to 2017 time period, large numbers of rebels were "integrated" into the military and police. This has allowed an easy transfer of weapons between the military and the rebels. There have been numerous reports of arms caches being placed under the control of former National Congress for the Defense of the People (CNDP) officers who now are part of the DRC military.

Air transport has long been the primary method for illegal deliveries of arms and ammunition to the DRC. Only aircraft were able to make such deliveries in the remote eastern areas. The most popular aircraft for such missions were single- and twin-engine *Antonov* transports because of their ability to land on primitive runways. The pilots used several techniques to defeat attempts to monitor illicit arms traffic. They never flew directly to their destinations, instead taking circuitous routes, frequently changing call signs, and making multiple landings and refueling stops. Many of these aircraft were leased at major regional airports in Burundi, Rwanda, and Uganda.

Such aircraft cannot carry heavy vehicles such as tanks, of course. But light aircraft can readily transport man-portable air defense systems (MANPADS), mortars, antitank weapons, and ammunition for all heavy weapons. Heavy vehicles can be brought into the DRC overland from neighboring countries.

Democratic Republic of Congo Arms Traffic—2017 Situation

The remainder of this scenario and the intelligence reporting that follows are notional.

More sophisticated and heavier weaponry may be flowing to both the MMKK and M23 from a number of sources. Such weaponry could pose a serious threat to both the DRC government and MONUSCO forces. MONUSCO has a priority requirement to identify types and numbers of such weaponry that are currently in the DRC or expected to arrive in-country in the near term.

A requirement also exists to identify the sources and means of transport of the weaponry. Angola is suspected of being a transit point for MMKK weapons because of Angolan government sympathy for MMKK objectives, but MONUSCO has no proof that weapons transfers have occurred. If Angola is in fact the transit point, the most likely route for heavy weaponry would be from Luanda port via the recently completed Luanda-to-Luena railroad and thence by rail to Kolwezi, Katanga province (see Figure 6.1).

FIGURE 6.1   Possible Arms Flow Route through Angola

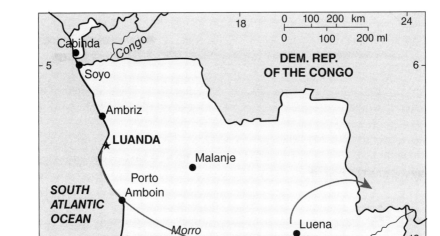

Source: CIA world Factbook.

M23 may be receiving heavy weapons from international arms dealers through several sources, but only fragmentary evidence exists for such transfers.

INTELLIGENCE REPORTS

Source/Date-Time Group	Text
Communications Intelligence (COMINT) October 14, 2016	The North Korean motor vessel (MV) *Ku Wol San,* originating from Namp'o, 50 km southwest of Pyongyang, onloaded cargo at Qingdao, China, on October 3 enroute to Luanda, Angola. (Comment: The *Ku Wol San* has a previous history of transporting missile parts between Pakistan and North Korea.) (Source: French General Directorate for External Security [DGSE] liaison)

Source/Date-Time Group	Text
Imagery Intelligence (IMINT) November 26, 2016	Imagery of Luanda port on November 22 showed six ships in the port. The North Korean MV *Ku Wol San* was in the process of offloading military cargo that included an unidentified type of mobile (tracked) surface-to-air missile (SAM) system. (Source: French Pleiades satellite imagery) *Port / Luanda*
Analysis December 18, 2016	Sergei Anatolyevich Bout (successor to the Viktor Bout arms trafficking operation) currently controls six air cargo companies that are suspected of handling illicit arms shipments in Africa. The six are Bukavu Aviation Transport, DRC; Abidjan Freight, Ivory Coast; Centrafrican Airlines, Central African Republic; Transavia and Santa Cruz Imperial Airlines, United Arab Emirates (UAE); and Air Zory, Sofia, Bulgaria. (Source: International Criminal Police Organization [INTERPOL] Report, December 18, 2016) *X*
COMINT January 21, 2017	Angolan army general Pancho Mutumbe has been linked in communications with Sergei Anatolyevich Bout, who succeeded to control of the Bout arms smuggling enterprise after his brother Viktor was imprisoned in the United States in 2011. General Mutumbe's brother, Eduardo Mutumbe, is a member of the board of the People's National Bank of Angola. (Source: German liaison) *Mutumbe Bout Angola + Bank*
Open Source Intelligence (OSINT) February 2, 2017	The MV *Antigone*, of Greek registry, loaded military cargo at Odessa, Ukraine, on January 13, 2017. The cargo consisted of 200 9K38 Igla (SA-18) man-portable missile systems, ten Russian 9A52–4 Tornado multiple launch rocket systems with 800 rockets, and twelve Ukrainian-made T-80UD tanks. The end user certificate designated South Africa as the recipient of the cargo. (Comment: The South African military analyst assigned to the JIC believes that the end user certificate must have been forged. South Africa has not ordered this equipment, and it is inferior to that in the existing South African inventory.) (Source: Lloyds of London) *Port / Ukraine BOUT*
Cyber February 14, 2017	During December 2016, the People's National Bank of Angola transferred $23 million to an unidentified account in the Bank of China Xi'an Branch. The transfer was ordered by Eduardo Mutumbe, a member of the board of the People's National Bank of Angola. (Source: French DGSE liaison) *Bank Mutumbe*
COMINT February 14, 2017	On February 6, an MMKK officer in Lubumbashi, DRC, contacted a Chinese official requesting maintenance manuals and technical support for "the HQ 17 system." The Chinese speaker, who was located at an unidentified factory in Xi'an, China, argued that the manuals had been supplied with "the initial shipment." *MMKK China*

(Continued)

(Continued)

Source/Date-Time Group	Text
	He then agreed to ship additional manuals with "the next shipment" and promised to check on the status of technical support. (Comment: The term *HQ-17* may refer to a Chinese mobile [SAM] system that is a copy of Russia's SA-15 SAM. The HQ-17 SAM is believed to be produced at a factory in Xi'an.) (Source: French DGSE liaison)
COMINT February 21, 2017 *Port/ Luanda*	The MV *Antigone* was in communication with port authorities in Luanda, Angola, on February 17 regarding the availability of equipment for unloading heavy cargo. When queried about what the *Antigone*'s captain meant by "heavy," he replied, "At least 53 metric tons." The port authority replied that it would require special offloading equipment, which the authority agreed to provide. (Source: French DGSE liaison)
Cyber February 21, 2017 *Mutumbe & Bank*	Monitoring of electronic funds transfers (EFTs) between banks in Angola, Luxembourg, Zambia, and Tanzania suggests that large transfers of funds are occurring. The increased EFTs also include several offshore banking institutions known to be havens for money laundering. Several of the accounts in question have been tied to Eduardo Mutumbe, a member of the board of the People's National Bank of Angola. (Source: French DGSE liaison)
COMINT February 25, 2017 *Bout/ Port/ Dubai*	On February 22, the captain of the MV *Antigone* contacted "Valeriy" in Dubai to report that "the goods have been delivered" and asked for further instructions. "Valeriy" replied "Proceed to Port 6 as planned. My man will meet you there with the payment." (Comment: "Valeriy" may refer to Valeriy Naydo, a member of the Sergei Bout arms trafficking network. Naydo is believed to have an office in Dubai. The location of "Port 6" is unknown.) (Source: French DGSE liaison)
Analysis March 3, 2017 *Angola/ DRC govt*	Relations between Angola and the DRC, already poor, have deteriorated sharply during this year. The DRC government is suspected of supporting the independence movement for Cabinda, an Angolan enclave separated from the rest of the country by DRC territory. The DRC is probably motivated by the potential for acquiring access to Cabinda's extensive offshore petroleum reserves. (Source: MONUSCO JIC assessment, March 3, 2017)
Human Intelligence (HUMINT) March 24, 2017 *M23*	Source reports that M23 rebel leaders are hiring mercenaries to provide security to ensure that drugs destined for sale in Europe and the United States safely cross the DRC. The rebels are reportedly using the money from drug sales to finance the purchase of weapons (NFI). (Source: MONUSCO clandestine source, usually reliable)

Source/Date-Time Group	Text
OSINT March 25, 2017 *Angola* *MMKK*	Angola: President Eduardo Vicente held a news conference at the conclusion of his four-day unofficial visit to Lubumbashi, DRC. In response to one question about the aspirations of the MMKK, President Vicente responded with this: "All Africans who love freedom and independence support General Mala and the Mai Mai Kata Katanga. They are fighting oppression from the forces of colonial subjugation, which today comes with a black face. Kabila is a corrupt thief, stealing from his own people, and supported by the former colonial powers, which use the United Nations as their surrogate. I support the liberation of the Congo and will work for it diligently." In response to another question, President Vicente stated, "We fought a long struggle against the forces that tried to subjugate Africa. We were victorious, and those who support the oppressors should note that we will continue this struggle throughout the continent until the final vestiges of colonial oppression are destroyed." (Source: Angola in English over Angolan government radio)
HUMINT March 25, 2017 *Bout/* *Air/* *Luanda*	At 1230L on Friday, March 10, 2017, a two-engine aircraft loaded unidentified crates at Quatro de Fevereiro Airport, Luanda. The aircraft bore the markings of Bukavu Aviation Transport, an airline reportedly controlled by the Bout arms trafficking network. The aircraft took off at 1330 L. (Source: Portuguese liaison)
IMINT March 26, 2017 *Port/ Luanda*	Imagery of Luanda port on March 22 indicated the presence of eight T-80 tanks next to a warehouse at S 08° 48′ 16″ E 13° 15′ 10.″ Ten unidentified vehicles were parked in the compound with the tanks. (Source: French Pleiades satellite imagery)
HUMINT April 1, 2017 *Bout*	During November and December 2016, suspected arms trafficker Valeriy Naydo made six trips to Rwanda, meeting with unidentified government officials in Kigali each time. Naydo arrived by air from Dubai and departed by air for Luanda, Angola, each time. (Source: INTERPOL reporting)
COMINT April 3, 2017 *Port/* *Luanda*	The North Korean cargo vessel MV *Ku Wol San,* originating from Namp'o, 50 km southwest of Pyongyang, has made three port calls at Luanda, Angola, in the last year, unloading unspecified cargo. (Comment: The *Ku Wol San* has a previous history of transporting missile parts between Pakistan and North Korea.) (Source: French DGSE liaison)
OSINT April 15, 2017 *Civilian* *Massacre* *(m23?)*	Kinshasa, DRC: Nairobi KTN television reported today on a massacre near Goma. A KTN video of the Mugunga refugee camp confirms that casualties from the massacre of refugees on April 13 and 14 number at least several thousand. Nongovernmental

(Continued)

(Continued)

Source/Date-Time Group	Text
	organization (NGO) reports estimate the number in the "tens of thousands." M23 rebels appear responsible, from eyewitness accounts. Reuters reports from Kampala that the Ugandan government is concerned with the rapid rise of refugees crossing its border with the DRC in the past two days. Border control officials have been overwhelmed and unable to estimate the numbers of refugees. Rumors of the Mugunga massacre appear to have motivated the flight from the DRC. The Ugandan foreign minister said he intends to raise the refugee crisis with the special UN envoy, Philip Smythe, when he visits Kampala on Wednesday. (Source: Nairobi KTN Television in English— independent Nairobi TV station with respected news coverage; majority of audience is in Nairobi; Reuters news service)
HUMINT April 21, 2017	Interrogation of refugees from the Mugunga refugee camp indicates that the attack on the camp was preceded by an intense bombardment from artillery or mortar fire that caused widespread panic and sent refugees fleeing from the camp. Many refugees then were killed by small arms fire in the surrounding region. The refugees claim that the attackers wore M23 rebel uniforms. (Field comment: This is the first evidence of artillery or mortar weaponry being used by M23 rebel units.) (Source: Refugee interrogation by MONUSCO field unit; reliability not known)
HUMINT May 2, 2017	During the past year, a two-engine airplane has landed at Kavumu Airport, South Kivu province, at a time just before dusk every other Friday. The side of the aircraft is marked "Bukavu Aviation Transport." Armed men in trucks wait for the aircraft's arrival. At night, the men offload boxes from the aircraft onto the trucks and load boxes from the trucks onto the aircraft. The boxes being loaded onto the aircraft are unmarked. The source observed markings on the offloaded boxes but did not understand the language, which contained strange letters. In one case, the source was able to observe the markings "9K38" on several crates that were about 2 m long. After the offloading and loading is complete, the aircraft takes off at about midnight. (Source: MONUSCO informant with a history of reliable reporting)
IMINT May 2, 2017	RHINO RED Mission 7321 on May 1 imaged a MMKK military depot located west of Kamina, DRC at S 08° 43′ 15″ E 24° 58′ 03.″ Imagery analysis has identified the presence of four T-80 tanks and three 9A52–4 Tornado multiple launch rocket systems at the depot that were not present in previous imagery on April 6.

Source/Date-Time Group	Text
COMINT May 2, 2017 *Bout* *Bank* *Angola*	Over the past four months, suspected arms trafficker Valeriy Naydo has received numerous funds transfers into several UAE bank accounts from the East African Trust Company, Rwanda; the Rwandan Commercial Bank; and Angolan Banks Banco de Comércio e Indústria and Banco de Poupança e Crédito S.A.R.L. The amounts involved could not be determined. (Comment: Naydo is a key lieutenant of arms trafficker Sergei Bout. The two Angolan banks involved in the transfers are state-owned.) (Source: French DGSE liaison)
HUMINT May 3, 2017 *Angola* *Bank* *MMKK*	During the early part of 2017, the People's National Bank of Angola received diamonds valued at approximately $55 million from a MMKK source in Lubumbashi, DRC. The bank subsequently resold the diamonds on the Antwerp, Belgium, diamond market. (Source: INTERPOL)
COMINT May 7, 2017 *DRC → M23*	A partial intercept of a cell phone call suggests a high-ranking DRC official is in contact with M23 representatives. The call indicated foreknowledge of upcoming meetings between President Kabila and UN representatives. It also referenced "movement of goods" in the area controlled by the M23 rebels and the need to avoid police patrols. In the intercept, the M23 speaker referred to the other as "Jean." No further information is available. (Source: French DGSE liaison)
HUMINT May 9, 2017 *M23* *Rwanda*	On or about April 2, source observed a weapons transfer between men dressed in civilian clothes and M23 soldiers just east of Bukavu, near the Rwandan border. The civilians transferred crates from their trucks (which had canvas-covered markings on the sides) to M23 trucks. One of the canvas covers had torn off, displaying Rwandan army markings. (Source believes that about six truckloads of crates were transferred.) Some crates had the markings "2B11" on the sides. (MONUSCO comment: This may refer to the 2B11 *Sani*, a 120 mm mortar that was produced in the Soviet Union and proliferated to other countries after the USSR collapsed.) After the transfer was complete, the M23 leader handed one of the civilians a large envelope. The civilians then departed in the direction of the Rwandan border. (Source: Refugee interrogation by MONUSCO field unit; reliability not known)
Electronic Intelligence (ELINT) May 11, 2017 *MMKK* *Control*	ELINT intercepts have identified the presence of a target acquisition radar usually associated with the Russian "Tor" SAM system (North Atlantic Treaty Organization [NATO] code name: SA-15) at Kamina Airfield, DRC. Coordinates of the intercept are S 08° 43' 48" E 24° 59' 28." (Source French electronic intelligence satellite [ELISA] intercept)

(Continued)

(Continued)

Source/Date-Time Group	Text
OSINT May 15, 2017 *[handwritten: MZ3 Control]*	Kinshasa, DRC: Radio Okapi reported on May 8 that it had received reports that an *Antonov* transport aircraft, possibly an AN-12, had been shot down near Goma. The aircraft crashed in Gisenyi. Rwandan forces have sealed off the area around the wreckage. Radio Opaki disclosed that a Doctors without Borders team that was in Uganda at the time originated the reports and intercepted distress calls on their radios. (Comment: Kinshasa Radio Okapi in French-independent radio station was jointly funded by the UN Observer Mission in Congo and the Geneva-based NGO Foundation Hirondelle.)
Analysis May 15, 2017 *[handwritten: SAM System]*	The Tor missile system (North Atlantic Treaty Organization [NATO] code name SA-15) (see Figure 6.2) is an all-weather low to medium altitude, short-range SAM system designed for engaging airplanes, helicopters, cruise missiles, and unmanned aerial vehicles (UAVs). It is a mobile, self-propelled SAM similar to the British Rapier or French Crotale. After the Cold War, Russia sold or transferred SA-15s to Egypt, Iran, Belarus, the Ukraine, and Iran. (Source: MONUSCO analysis)
HUMINT May 17, 2017 *[handwritten: Angola - MMKK]*	Reportedly, the Angolan government is using Air Zory to import arms from Bulgaria for further transfer to the MMKK. Angola plans to use the same company to import more arms from Slovakia. The types of weapons imported were not known. (Source: INTERPOL liaison)
Measurement and Signature Intelligence (MASINT) May 18, 2017 *[handwritten: MZ3]*	Preliminary analysis of radar data indicates that an aircraft in the eastern DRC was struck by a SAM on May 7 at 0345L. The aircraft subsequently disappeared from the radar display. The aircraft is believed to be the *Antonov* transport that was reportedly shot down near Goma, DRC, on May 7.
COMINT May 22, 2017 *[handwritten: DRC gov't]*	A telephone conversation between the DRC minister of finance, Philippe Adawawon, and an unknown party indicates the finance minister has interest in a "special shipment." The shipment apparently is to go by air to an unknown location "up north." The finance minister at one point asked whether "all of the shipment could be made." The other party indicated that there was "sufficient room . . . on the flight." (Source: French DGSE liaison)

BACKGROUND READING

The following section is an excerpt from "International Crime Threat Assessment," Chapter 2, 2000.[2]

---

[2]"International Crime Threat Assessment," December 2000, www.fas.org/irp/threat/pub45270 chap2.html.

FIGURE 6.2   Tor (SA-15) Surface-to-Air Missile System

Source: Vitaly V. Kuzmin, http://en.wikipedia.org/wiki/Tor_missile_system.

Illicit gray- and black-market arms sales became an increasing problem worldwide during the 1990s. The end of the Cold War and the winding down of several regional conflicts, such as those in Lebanon and Central America, increased the availability of both newly produced and used weapons. The items typically sold on the illegal arms market include spare parts for large weapons systems, particularly for clients under UN embargoes or sanctioned by the original seller; small arms, including assault rifles, and man-portable antitank and antiaircraft weapons; and ammunition for both small arms and larger artillery and armor systems. In some cases, however, larger military systems also are sold.

The U.S. Government in 2000 estimated that military equipment worth several hundred million dollars was sold annually on the illegal arms market to countries under UN arms embargoes. Insurgents, terrorists, and organized criminal groups acquire smaller quantities of small arms and other light infantry weapons on the illegal arms market.

Most illegal arms sales are through the *gray arms market,* which has been dominated by individual brokers—and their arms brokering firms—during the past decade. Gray-market arms transfers exploit legitimate export licensing processes, usually by using false paperwork to disguise the recipient, the military nature of the goods involved, or—more rarely—the supplier. Obtaining licenses, however fraudulent, allows gray-market players to make deals appear legitimate, helping them to arrange payment and international transportation for transactions that can be valued at millions of dollars and involve hundreds of tons of weapons.

In some cases, however, large illegal arms shipments arranged by arms brokers will be smuggled as contraband. Illicit arms sold or transferred to combatants in Afghanistan and the former republics of Yugoslavia were often provided by foreign suppliers donating and transporting tens of millions of dollars' worth of weapons disguised as "humanitarian aid."

The end of the Cold War has made the bloated defense industry and large inventory of weapons in Russia and other former Warsaw Pact countries an easy mark for arms brokers. Since 1992, for example, combatants in civil conflicts in Afghanistan and the republics of the former Yugoslavia have purchased dozens of complete helicopters and fighter aircraft from gray arms suppliers. Brokers also acquire military equipment from U.S. and other Western suppliers.

Black-market arms transfers do not go through an export licensing process. Rather, smugglers rely exclusively on hiding contraband arms from government officials. Black-market transfers usually involve smaller quantities of weapons, often pilfered from military stocks or gun shops. The theft and illegal sales of weapons and other military stocks has become a significant problem in Russia.

Organized crime groups have become increasingly involved in arms trafficking since the end of the Cold War, taking advantage of both the availability of large numbers of infantry weapons from the former Soviet Bloc countries and regional conflicts.

7

Democratic Republic of Congo: Narcotics Traffic

This case study is set in 2017 and is based on the Democratic Republic of Congo (DRC) baseline that is described in Chapter 5.

In the past twenty years, Nigeria has become a major corridor for illicit drug movement from South America and Asia to Europe. Drugs like cocaine and heroin pass freely through the country. West African—primarily Nigerian—drug smugglers now have control over about $1.6 billion worth of cocaine that transits through the region yearly. Most of this cocaine comes from Latin American cartels. Previously, the Latin American cartels had exclusive control over this traffic; they have been displaced by Nigerian trafficking groups who now own the drug transport and distribution systems. The Nigerians have even taken control of exports in São Paulo, Brazil, where most cocaine leaves South America for Nigeria.

The Nigerian drug cartels do not follow the mafia-type model that is typical of most criminal organizations. They instead are organized along familial and ethnic lines. Their organizational structure provides a formidable defense against law enforcement efforts to infiltrate the cartels.

For decades, air transport was the preferred means of delivering drugs from Nigeria. The cartels now are shipping narcotics by sea. The cartels have found seaborne smuggling to be safer than high-risk smuggling on commercial aircraft, which can more easily be interdicted at airport checkpoints.

The drug traffic through Nigeria has become a major issue for the Nigerian government, the International Criminal Police Organization (INTERPOL), and the U.S. Drug Enforcement Administration (DEA) for two reasons:

- Until 2010, not many Nigerians consumed cocaine and heroin. But in addition to Nigeria being a major drug route, Nigerians are becoming major consumers also.
- A significant part of the funding of terrorism in Nigeria and in other parts of the world comes from money earned through drug trafficking.

EDUCATIONAL OBJECTIVES

This exercise provides practical experience in the following:

- creating a target network model (TNM)
- performing Geospatial Intelligence (GEOINT) analysis
- making judgments based on incomplete information
- developing and supporting conclusions and explaining assumptions
- conveying uncertainty to customers in intelligence assessments

ASSIGNMENT

You are on special assignment from the DEA to the United Nations Organization Stabilization Mission in the Democratic Republic of the Congo (MONUSCO) Joint Intelligence center (JIC). The guidance given to you by DEA is as follows:

> West African drug smuggling groups have long been involved in smuggling Southwest Asian heroin into Europe and the U.S. We have unconfirmed reports that these groups now are involved in heroin production as well. You are to work through MONUSCO to investigate possible heroin production and distribution in the DRC or transiting the DRC. Your assignment has been vetted with the UN authorities, and MONUSCO has agreed to share their intelligence with you.

Your first task is to determine whether heroin production, distribution, or both are occurring in the DRC. If that is the case, you are to assess the sources of heroin production or distribution in the region. This second task involves these subtasks:

- Prepare a geospatial model of the narcotics production and/or distribution network that is responsible for supplying the heroin. Include the transport mechanisms. (Hint: This subtask can be done on a map of the region or on a diagram with geographical identifiers.)
- Create a TNM showing the network (people, organizations, and financing) involved in the drug trade. Identify the key players in the network and locations involved in production and distribution.
- Prepare an intelligence assessment (five to eight paragraphs) based on the models you have created, indicating the confidence levels in your judgments. Conclude the assessment with an intelligence gap analysis identifying at least six knowledge gaps.

ABBREVIATIONS AND ACRONYMS

Abbreviation or Acronym	Description
BBC	British Broadcasting Service
COMINT	Communications Intelligence

Abbreviation or Acronym	Description
DEA	Drug Enforcement Administration (United States)
DGSE	General Directorate for External Security (France)
DRC	Democratic Republic of Congo
GEOINT	Geospatial Intelligence
HUMINT	Human Intelligence
INTERPOL	International Criminal Police Organization
JIC	Joint Intelligence Center
MASINT	Measurement and Signature Intelligence
MONUSCO	United Nations Organization Stabilization Mission in the Democratic Republic of the Congo
NFI	No Further Information
NGO	Nongovernmental Organization
OSINT	Open Source Intelligence
SIGINT	Signals Intelligence
UN	United Nations
UNICEF	United Nations Children's Fund

SCENARIO

The following material in this chapter is notional.

During 2015, the Afghan government, with U.S. assistance, was successful in identifying and shutting down the major heroin production laboratories in Afghanistan. The labs could be readily identified because the effluents of processing were visible in spectral imaging. The shutdown caused a dramatic reduction in the amount of heroin flowing into Europe and the United States from Southwest Asia. The Nigerian drug trafficking networks handling this traffic largely were shut down but only temporarily.

Beginning in late 2016, a few Nigerian drug trafficking networks began shipments of white heroin (which is high in quality and commands a premium price) to Europe. Heroin analysis programs have in the past distinguished three main types of heroin, according to area of origin: Southwest Asian heroin, found in samples from Afghanistan and other countries in that subregion; Southeast Asian heroin, found in samples from the Golden Triangle (the Lao People's Democratic Republic, Myanmar, and Thailand) and other countries in that subregion; and South American heroin. It appears that a new source exists. Chemical analysis of samples indicates that the heroin is very high in purity and did not originate in any of the three existing catalogued regions. INTERPOL suspects that the heroin is coming from a new source, possibly in Africa.

INTELLIGENCE REPORTS

Source/Date-Time Group	Text
Communications Intelligence (COMINT) July 20, 2016	An unidentified person (believed to be Tutsi) in Goma, DRC, queried several European firms about contracts for shipments of acetic anhydride. (Analyst comment: Because of its use for the synthesis of heroin by the diacetylation of morphine, acetic anhydride is listed as a U.S. DEA List II precursor.) (Source: French General Directorate for External Security [DGSE] liaison)
Open Source Intelligence (OSINT) March 4, 2017	Local Goma radio is reporting that rebel forces are suspected of being behind the murder of a regional official in Goma whom the rebels believe was supporting the DRC government.
Human Intelligence (HUMINT) March 6, 2017	An officer of the DRC military (a lieutenant) assigned to MONUSCO indicated to MONUSCO officials that he had information on Nigerian organized crime, including criminal activity of an organization known as Trojan Enterprises, a foreign corporation with U.S. subsidiaries. The lieutenant stated that he felt it was necessary to tell MONUSCO about this because of suspicions within his organization that Kazadi Nyembwe, his superior in the DRC intelligence service, the Agence Nationale de Renseignements, is corrupt. The lieutenant is afraid for his life because he did not bribe local officials to protect drug traffic as he was supposed to do (he used the money instead to buy food and other goods for his family) and that if this information on Trojan Enterprises gets out, he will be killed.
HUMINT March 23, 2017	Rumors persist that large-scale heroin operations are underway in the eastern DRC. The M23 rebels have reportedly set up a high-quality heroin production lab that relies on raw opium imported from South Asia. We have no information about how the heroin is getting out of the country. (Source: DRC law enforcement liaison)
HUMINT March 24, 2017	The source reports that M23 rebel leaders are hiring mercenaries to provide security to ensure that drugs destined for sale in Europe and the United States safely cross the DRC. The rebels are reportedly using the money from drug sales to finance the purchase of weapons (NFI). (Source: MONUSCO clandestine source, usually reliable)
COMINT March 27, 2017	Communications intercepts indicate that Hamza Okonkwo, a suspected Nigerian drug figure, has been in regular contact with a DRC customs official who runs the customs facility at the Kinshasa Ndjili Airport. No details are available on the information passed in these contacts. Okonkwo is believed to be a lieutenant of Nigerian drug kingpin Joseph Nwafor. (Source: MONUSCO Special Signals Intelligence [SIGINT] Service)

Source/Date-Time Group	Text
HUMINT March 28, 2017	On March 16, presidential household Chief of Staff Jean Larroche visited Finance Minister Phillipe Adawavon at the minister's home in Kinshasa. The meeting was observed personally by source. The meeting was unusual, as the source has never known Larroche, a more junior official, to visit the finance minister at his home. (Source: Belgian liaison service, from a usually reliable source)
HUMINT April 3, 2017	In response to your query regarding Kazadi Nyembwe, deputy chief of intelligence, Agence Nationale de Renseignements, DRC, the following is provided. We have long believed that Nyembwe has been accepting bribes and kickbacks from drug organizations in return for turning a blind eye to drug related activities in the DRC. (Source: Belgian liaison)
OSINT April 3, 2017	In an effort to control information both within their expanding "zone" and that disseminated to the world outside, M23 authorities have mounted an aggressive campaign to censor or ban publications and radio programs. We have received increasing reports of journalists being threatened, detained, and harassed. Communications equipment has been seized. (Source: Social network analysis)
HUMINT April 3, 2017	A Mormon nongovernmental organization (NGO), working outside Mbandaka, told a MONUSCO official that despite a government edict banning traffic on the Congo River after dark, unknown groups are moving heroin via riverboats at night into Brazzaville and Kinshasa, having bribed local authorities. The NGO further stated that he believes the heroin is originating much farther upriver. (Source: MONUSCO internal)
OSINT April 10, 2017	M23 rebels "arrested" two British Broadcasting Service (BBC) "stringers" in Bukavu on April 8. These contracted native journalists were accused of listening to "secrets" on their walkie-talkies. They were detained in the Central Bukavu Prison. (Source: Reuters)
HUMINT April 14, 2017	Drug couriers arrested in the United States on April 10 and 11 (one heading south on I-95 near Richmond and one headed north on I-95 near Philadelphia) were carrying bags of heroin that appear to be of very high purity. The couriers carried the tattoo markings of the Washington, DC-based MS-13 gang. Samples of the heroin have been sent to a forensics laboratory for detailed analysis. (Source: U.S. law enforcement reporting)
OSINT April 15, 2017	On April 11, Egyptian authorities seized approximately 800 kilograms of acetic anhydride concealed in a shipment supposedly originating with Suez Chemical Company, Cairo, and destined for the Sanru Hospital in Goma, DRC. The acetic anhydride was packed into steel canisters labelled "hydrogen peroxide." (DEA comment: Because of its use for the synthesis of heroin by the diacetylation of morphine, acetic anhydride is listed as a U.S. DEA List II precursor.) (Source: *Daily News Egypt*)

(Continued)

(Continued)

Source/Date-Time Group	Text
OSINT April 15, 2017	Kinshasa, DRC: Village authorities in the Kinshasa region are speculating that the massacre of thousands of men, women, and children over the weekend may have been the result of government bombing of the refugee camp. The government was responsible for the indiscriminate bombing of refugees in 1998. In addition, they think that NGO members are being murdered because the rebels believe they are reporting information about the rebels to the DRC government. (Source: Various local newspapers)
OSINT April 15, 2017	Kinshasa, DRC: Nairobi KTN television reported today on a massacre near Goma. A KTN video of the Mugunga refugee camp confirms that casualties from the massacre of refugees on April 13 and 14 number at least several thousand. NGO reports estimate the number in the "tens of thousands." M23 rebels appear responsible, from eyewitness accounts. Reuters reports from Kampala that the Ugandan government is concerned with the rapid rise of refugees crossing its border with the DRC in the past two days. Border control officials have been overwhelmed and unable to estimate the numbers of refugees. Rumors of the Mugunga massacre appear to have motivated the flight from the DRC. The Ugandan foreign minister said he intends to raise the refugee crisis with the special UN envoy, Philip Smythe, when he visits Kampala on Wednesday. (Source: Nairobi KTN Television in English—independent Nairobi TV station with respected news coverage; majority of audience is in Nairobi; Reuters news service)
OSINT April 15, 2017	M23 rebel forces have reportedly seized hundreds of refugees who fled the massacre at the Mugunga camp. The rebels are holding the hostages in a remote forested area of northeastern Orientale province. (Source: Paris AFP [World Service] in English—world news service of the independent French news agency Agence France Presse)
OSINT April 15, 2017	Rwanda: A Rwandan radio station is reporting that the massacre of thousands of men, women, and children over the weekend in the Mugunga Camp was the result of government bombing of the refugee camp. (Source: Kigali Radio Rwanda in English)
OSINT April 15, 2017	Uganda: Renewed fighting in the eastern DRC by rebel forces has resulted in an escalation of unlawful killings and other human rights abuses by the combatants against unarmed civilians. Thousands of civilians are reportedly fleeing to neighboring countries. The Ugandan government, expressing concern that refugees fleeing renewed fighting in the northeastern DRC may be carrying the Ebola virus, has closed the border. (Source: Reuters)
OSINT April 15, 2017	Kigali radio reports that residents of Gisenyi, Rwanda, took in hundreds of refugees who fled from the Mugunga camp on the day of the massacre. These refugees are said to have observed DRC forces

Source/Date-Time Group	Text
	killing, raping, and looting in the camps. The M23 rebel forces allegedly drove the DRC forces out of the camps. (Source: Kigali Radio Rwanda in English)
OSINT April 15, 2017	Radio Maendeleo, the only independent radio station in South Kivu, which has a tradition of producing features on human rights (assisted by NGOs), reported today that it had been ordered to stop developing its own reports and to report only that information fed to it by the M23 minister of information, press, and cultural affairs. In the same broadcast, Radio Maendeleo announced it would disregard the order.
OSINT April 15, 2017	A local opposition newspaper is accusing the DRC finance minister of corruption. The article accuses Philippe Adawavon of looting $10 million from the national treasury. Adawavon is known to have purchased a villa on Tortola (British Virgin Islands). In addition, Adawavon and his family have taken several vacations to expensive resort areas in Switzerland, Brazil, and the United States. The article goes on to report that Adawavon's two children attend private schools in Belgium and cites the numerous parties given by Adawavon for businessmen, foreign nationals, and local government officials as evidence of his wrongdoing.
OSINT April 20, 2017	In South Kivu, several Radio Maendeleo personnel, who had been asked to stop developing reports on human rights abuses, have been threatened with physical harm if they continue to disregard the order to report only that information fed to them by the M23 minister of information, press, and cultural affairs.
Analysis April 22, 2017	DEA analysis of heroin seized along U.S. I-95 on April 10 and 11 indicates the existence of a new source of highly pure heroin. Chemical analysis indicates that the source is the same as that of heroin seized in Amsterdam and Naples early in 2017. The heroin samples do not match any existing samples from South America or South Asia. (Source: DEA analysis)
HUMINT April 30, 2017	The city of Mbandaka, just four days upriver from Kinshasa, has become an important transshipment point for heroin. From Mbandaka, the heroin is shipped down the Congo River on boats. The source did not know the origin or final destination of the shipments. (Source: MONUSCO informant who has limited reporting history)
OSINT May 2, 2017	A local Kinshasa opposition newspaper is running a story accusing DRC soldiers of having escorted a drug shipment "bound for the United States."
OSINT May 2, 2017	The bodies of the two Belgian BBC "stringers" who had been captured by M23 rebels last month and had been detained in an unknown location since then, were found in the center of Bukavu

(Continued)

Source/Date-Time Group	Text
	today. They had been brutally murdered and had been decapitated. Their ears had been cut off and their tongues cut out as an apparent warning to others who may be thinking of reporting on events in the M23 controlled parts of the DRC. (Source: Reuters)
HUMINT May 2, 2017	Dutch authorities seized 1.1 metric tons of heroin hidden in a concealed compartment on the private yacht *Xanthe Mist* off the coast of Denhelder. The heroin had reportedly been transferred to the *Xanthe Mist* from a barge at the mouth of the Congo River in the vicinity of Kinshasa. The follow-on investigation revealed that the Bishop Company owns the 300-foot yacht. In addition, passports under a series of aliases were found on the yacht. (Source: Dutch law enforcement)
HUMINT May 4, 2017	The following is in response to a MONUSCO request: Bishop Company is a UK subsidiary of Trojan Enterprises, owned by Joseph Nwafor, a Nigerian. Intelligence has linked him to drug running in the past. Trojan Enterprises is currently under investigation for drug running and money laundering. (Source: UK MI-6 liaison)
HUMINT May 4, 2017	A sensitive source reports that drug smuggling out of Ndjili is controlled by the chief of airport customs, Ohidi Matumba. Matumba has close ties to Minister of Finance Philippe Adawawon. (Source: MONUSCO informant with a history of reliable reporting)
HUMINT May 6, 2017	The Liberian registered cargo ship *Callisto Lyrae* departed Banana, DRC, two weeks ago bound for an unknown port. Rumors in Banana are that the *Callisto Lyrae* is carrying unspecified "drugs." (Source: Belgian liaison, from a port official in Banana who has a history of reliable reporting)
HUMINT May 6, 2017	HUMINT sources report that a customs official is involved in drug trafficking in the DRC. Reporting indicates that luggage containing large quantities of drugs (NFI) is checked in at the luggage facility at the airport. A customs official then discreetly checks it onto a specific European-bound flight where a passenger, eventually enroute to the United States, picks it up. (Source: Belgian liaison)
COMINT May 7, 2017	A partial intercept of a cell phone call suggests a high-ranking DRC official is in contact with M23 representatives. The call indicated foreknowledge of upcoming meetings between President Kabila and United Nations (UN) representatives. It also referenced "movement of goods" in the area controlled by the M23 rebels and the need to avoid police patrols. In the intercept, the M23 speaker referred to the other as "Jean." No further information is available. (Source: French DGSE liaison)
COMINT May 7, 2017	DRC: Despite its pledge to cooperate in antidrug efforts, communications intercepts indicate that Rwandan army elements are assisting the M23 rebels in the movement of heroin out of the DRC. (Source: Canadian SIGINT unit deployed East of Kisangani)

Source/Date-Time Group	Text
HUMINT May 8, 2017	A review of manifests for Compagnie Africaine d'Aviation Flights 1038 and 1039 for the past eight months show that passenger Mbeki Kingombe frequently comes in to Kinshasa from Goma on Flight 1038 and departs two hours later on return Flight 1039. Mbeki Kingombe is a known associate of drug kingpin Joseph Nwafor. (Source: DRC liaison)
OSINT May 8, 2017	Tele Congo reported on May 8 that an unknown group moving down the Congo River just 3 km south of Yumbi overwhelmed government soldiers who had challenged them for defying government orders banning travel on the river at night. At least eight armed individuals and seventeen soldiers were killed or injured. There is speculation in the local police department that the armed individuals were drug traffickers. (Source: Brazzaville Tele Congo in French—state-owned, government-controlled television)
OSINT May 9, 2017	DRC: A small aircraft makes weekly cargo flights out of a dirt airstrip on the Mora Mora plantation in the North Kivu province. At the airstrip, the aircraft is loaded with boxes of unknown material. Workers on the plantation described the boxes as containing "drugs." (Source: Social media)
OSINT May 12, 2017	Water in a tributary of Lake Kivu that runs through the village of Shasha, North Kivu province has been contaminated. In addition to a large fish kill, villagers are finding extensive animal kills in the area near the tributary. Some villagers are also exhibiting symptoms of poisoning. (Source: Doctors without Borders report via social media)
HUMINT May 12, 2017	Italian police seized a large shipment of heroin from the Liberian registered ship *Callisto Lyrae* in Naples. A Libyan on board was arrested. The ship's last port of call was Algiers, but the Italian police suspect an unrecorded stop because of the long elapsed time between the ship's call at Algiers and Naples. Several of the ship's crew reported that they had signed on because the ship was ultimately destined to make a port call in Baltimore. (Source: Italian liaison)
OSINT May 14, 2017	DRC: The website of the Kigali *New Times* carried a report by Philip Munyane on May 8 that included the following paragraph: "Unconfirmed reports have been received that a caravan carrying ten members of a Doctors without Borders team is missing. Five members of the team are U.S. citizens; three are French, one each Swiss and Moroccan. The caravan was headed northwest from the Bukavu refugee camp in the Eastern DRC. The doctors were fleeing after hearing of the slaughter at the Mugunga camp. Their last confirmed location was east of Lubutu; the caravan was enroute to safety in Kisangani."
OSINT May 15, 2017	Kinshasa, DRC: Radio Okapi reported on May 8 that it had received reports that an *Antonov* transport aircraft, possibly an AN-12, has been shot down over Goma. The aircraft crashed in Gisenyi.

(Continued)

(Continued)

Source/Date- Time Group	Text
	Rwandan forces have sealed off the area around the wreckage. Radio Opaki disclosed that a Doctors without Borders team that was in Uganda at the time originated the reports and intercepted distress calls on their radios. (Comment: Kinshasa Radio Okapi in French-independent radio station jointly funded by the UN Observer Mission in Congo and the Geneva-based NGO Foundation Hirondelle)
OSINT May 15, 2017	Brazzaville, DRC: The French newspaper *Le Monde* reported on May 8 that a passenger died onboard a South African-bound flight that originated in Brazzaville. The autopsy report on the male Congolese passenger indicates that the man had swallowed ten bags of heroin and that one of the bags had broken. An investigation into the incident by the gendarmerie indicates that the man was flying on a false passport and that three other passengers on the flight were also traveling with false papers. These men, ultimately en route to Atlanta, Georgia, were also found carrying heroin. When questioned by the gendarmerie, the other men admitted that they had been paid $2,000 apiece by a Nigerian to carry the heroin into the United States.
Measurement and Signature Intelligence (MASINT) May 18, 2017	RHINO BLUE Mission 7633 was conducted over North Kivu on May 14, 2017. The airborne spectral imaging sensor detected a ground spill containing signatures of lime, ammonium chloride, hydrochloric acid, and acetic anhydride at coordinates E29° 00′ 54″ S01° 37′ 30″ near the town of Shasha, North Kivu province. (MASINT analyst comment: This signature combination is normally associated with the effluent mix of a heroin production laboratory.)
Analysis May 17, 2017	The UN Office for the Coordination of Humanitarian Affairs reports that all NGOs are withdrawing their personnel due to the out-of-control violence and disease outbreaks in the Kivu provinces. Massacres, extortion, and forced displacements are said to be occurring throughout the region. Most NGO personnel have fled to the relative safety of Uganda or Rwanda. Relief agencies continue to maintain HQ elements in Kinshasa. The United Nations Children's Fund (UNICEF) continues operations in Orientale, Kasa, and Equateur. (MONUSCO comment: The departure of UN and relief agencies, as well as the few remaining journalists, leaves the camps without any semblance of law and order.) (Source: MONUSCO analysis)
HUMINT May 18, 2017	In a follow-up report on the Liberian-registered ship *Callisto Lyrae* seized in Naples last week, the Italian police report that the chief engineer has admitted that the ship had stopped in Nigeria where it took on the heroin.
OSINT May 19, 2017	Regarding the refugee situation in the eastern DRC, solid information appears to be elusive. There are many rumors and anecdotal accounts, mostly coming from NGO personnel who have exited the area. What

Source/Date-Time Group	Text
	little reporting that there is comes from NGOs who report that the rebels left the camp areas following the massacre last week, taking some refugees as prisoners. (Source: Social media)
HUMINT May 19, 2017	Tiba Besebo, leader of M23 operating in the eastern DRC, held a meeting with his staff and senior commanders in April 2017. The purpose of the meeting was to reveal the group's strategy for expelling Western influence from Africa. Besebo told the group that the narcotics trade with the United States not only provides funds to keep his operation going but also weakens the U.S. resolve. He claimed that they have found ways to get large quantities of heroin into the United States and western Europe "with the help of friends around the world who sympathize with our objective of getting imperialist influences out of Africa." He also said that the group would use "dramatic and unusual" means in the near future to induce panic and disorganization directly within the United States. His senior lieutenant, Adrien Biruta, was given the honor of carrying out the task, along with a selected group of "volunteers." No details were given about the nature of the "dramatic and unusual" means. Biruta and fifteen "volunteers" left the area in early May on travel to Kigali, Rwanda, and have not returned. (Source: Defector, a former lieutenant in M23 who surrendered to MONUSCO authorities in Kisangani on May 17, 2017)
OSINT May 22, 2017	In a follow-up piece, a local opposition newspaper ran an article criticizing the government for its inability to respond to drug trafficking on the Congo River. The article also provides additional information about a skirmish on the river that Tele Congo reported on May 8. The opposition forces had far superior weapons (including automatic machine guns) than those used by the government forces; the government forces were armed with M-1 rifles and shotguns. The paper also reports on rumors that many of the government forces fled the area immediately after the first shots were fired.
COMINT May 22, 2017	The office of DRC finance minister Phillipe Adawavon has been in frequent communications over the past six months with New Age Caribbean Bank, headquartered in Barbados. Texts of the communications were encrypted and are not available. (Comment: New Age Caribbean Bank has a history of money laundering.) (Source: French DGSE liaison)
OSINT May 22, 2017	The Ugandan government is reporting that its efforts to suppress illegal drug trafficking through its country are proving successful. The Ugandans are reporting a decrease in drug seizures and certain drug related crimes in their country.
COMINT May 22, 2017	A telephone conversation between the DRC minister of finance, Philippe Adawawon, and an unknown party indicates the finance

(Continued)

(Continued)

Source/Date-Time Group	Text
	minister has interest in a "special shipment." The shipment apparently is to go by air to an unknown location "up north." The finance minister at one point asked whether "all of the shipment could be made." The other party indicated that there was "sufficient room . . . on the flight." (Source: French DGSE liaison)
COMINT May 22, 2017	Fragmentary telephone intercepts indicate that some Rwandan government officials are assisting M23 rebels by providing false documentation for unidentified individuals who are leaving the region for destinations in the United States and western Europe. (Source: French DGSE liaison)
HUMINT June 1, 2017	Dutch authorities, who seized 11 kg of heroin found on the private yacht *Xanthe Mist* off the coast of Denhelder last week, reported that tests on the heroin conducted by Scotland Yard have revealed an unusual chemical marker which is also present in the heroin seized by Italian police from the Liberian ship *Callisto Lyrae* in the port of Naples. This chemical marker is different from those associated with heroin produced in Southeast and Southwest Asia and in Mexico, suggesting a new country of origin. (Source: Dutch liaison)
HUMINT June 4, 2017	Local authorities in Kinshasa have noted an increase in drug abuse. While abuse of marijuana continues, authorities have noted an increase in the use of more potent drugs, especially heroin, and believe this is a spillover effect of the increase in drug trafficking within the country. (Source: DRC law enforcement liaison)

BACKGROUND READING

The following is taken from a DEA report titled "Heroin Production Process."[1]

In the spring or fall, the illicit opium farmer plants his crop. About three months later, the plants have matured and brightly colored flowers appear. After fertilization, the petals drop from the flower exposing the seedpod (usually about the size of a walnut). Opium is produced in the root system and distributed to all parts of the plant, with the majority collecting in the seedpod. To release the opium, the farmer makes a series of shallow, vertical or horizontal incisions across one or two sides of the seedpod with a small cutting tool. Milky opium slowly bleeds from the incisions, turning from white to brown as it dries. The pods may be incised up to five or six times before the opium is depleted.

Because the incising and harvesting of opium is very labor intensive, most opium poppy is grown in small plots, usually not more than one acre and usually along with

[1]DEA Report, "Opium Poppy Cultivation and Heroin Processing in Southeast Asia," http://www.drugs-forum.com/forum/showthread.php?t=40013#ixzz2iwzYGH46.

several acres of a legitimate crop. In choosing a field to grow opium poppies, soil quality, access to sunlight, and acidity are critical factors, so experienced poppy farmers choose their fields carefully. Westerly orientations are typically preferred to optimize sun exposure. Most fields are on mountain slopes at elevations of 1,000 m (3,000 feet) or more above sea level. Slope gradients of between 20 to 40 degrees are considered best for drainage of rainwater.

Once the opium is collected, the farmer sells it to a processor who sets up a crude laboratory near the poppy fields.

The following process is generally used to extract morphine from opium in the field laboratories: Opium is placed in boiling water and the mixture is stirred thoroughly. Opium is not soluble in water. Lime is added to the mixture, reacting with the morphine to form water-soluble calcium morphenate. The water, which now contains the soluble calcium morphenate, is filtered into another container. Ammonium chloride is added, causing the morphine base to settle out of the solution. The mixture of water and morphine base is filtered to recover the morphine base. The morphine base is purified further by using activated charcoal and hydrochloric acid, producing morphine hydrochloride. The morphine hydrochloride is dried and pressed into bricks for transport to a heroin lab.

After the morphine hydrochloride bricks are delivered to the heroin lab, they are pulverized and the process of making heroin is started. The pulverized morphine hydrochloride is mixed with acetic anhydride. The mixture is heated for several hours, producing an impure form of heroin. Water is added to the mixture, along with activated charcoal. The mixture is filtered and sodium carbonate is added, causing the heroin base to precipitate out of the solution. The mixture is filtered to recover the heroin base.

Heroin comes in both white and brown forms, white being purer, more potent, and more expensive. White heroin is far more difficult to manufacture than brown heroin. It requires additional processing with special chemicals and equipment to turn it into a very pure form. The last stage of this processing is especially risky. It requires the use of ether, a dangerous chemical which must be handled with care. Explosions caused by careless use of ether have destroyed entire drug laboratories in the past.

8

Democratic Republic of Congo: Disease Outbreak

This case study is set in June 2017 and is based on the Democratic Republic of Congo (DRC) baseline that is described in Chapter 5. While the case study refers to actual organizations, the fact situations and persons' names are all notional.

The case concerns a disease outbreak in the DRC that has spread to Germany and the United States, killing dozens of people and causing widespread panic in the affected countries. Adding to the panic is that public health organizations so far have been unable to agree on the source and nature of the virus causing the disease.

Note: This case study was originally drafted several years prior to the 2014 Ebola outbreak in West Africa.

EDUCATIONAL OBJECTIVES

This exercise provides practical experience in the following:

- formulating alternative hypotheses to explain observed events
- developing network and alternative process models
- evaluating sources of intelligence when populating target models
- conveying uncertainty to customers in intelligence assessments

ASSIGNMENT

You are the senior analyst with the United Nations Organization Stabilization Mission in the Democratic Republic of the Congo (MONUSCO) Joint Intelligence center (JIC). The MONUSCO commander, the United Nations (UN) World Health Organization (WHO) and the Centers for Disease Control and Prevention (CDC) have queried you about the source and nature of a virulent disease outbreak that may have originated within the DRC and subsequently has spread to New York and Frankfurt. A composite of the questions that have been posed to you by these organizations is as follows:

- Are the New York and Frankfurt outbreaks the result of deliberate biological warfare (BW) attacks or the unintentional spread of a highly contagious disease?

- Are BW agents being deliberately produced in the DRC? If so, where, by whom, and for what purpose?
- If the outbreak is a deliberate BW attack, who are the intended targets, and what is the delivery mechanism? Who are the likely perpetrators, and where are they?

You understand exactly what needs to be done and immediately get to work on these tasks:

1. Create a problem breakdown model.

2. Evaluate the source of each item of raw intelligence (Hint: Refer to Chapter 2 for a starting point).

3. Create at least two process models explaining alternative hypotheses about the sources of the disease outbreak.

4. Even if you believe the disease is naturally occurring, your customer will want to see how you eliminated the other possibilities. Create two network models. One should show the relationships among Iranian scientists and doctors described in the intelligence reporting. The second model should show the relationships among M23 members.

5. Prepare an intelligence assessment (five to eight paragraphs) that addresses the questions posed (to the extent that you can). Support your conclusions using the models you have created, and explain the uncertainties in your conclusions.

ABBREVIATIONS AND ACRONYMS

Abbreviation or Acronym	Description
BBC	British Broadcasting Service
BW	biological warfare
CDC	Centers for Disease Control and Prevention (United States)
COMINT	Communications Intelligence
DGSE	General Directorate for External Security (France)
DRC	Democratic Republic of Congo
HIV/AIDS	human immunodeficiency virus/acquired immunodeficiency syndrome
HUMINT	Human Intelligence
JIC	Joint Intelligence Center
MONUSCO	United Nations Organization Stabilization Mission in the Democratic Republic of the Congo

(Continued)

(Continued)

NGO	nongovernmental organization
TGEBRC	Tehran Genetic Engineering and Biotechnology Research Center (Iran)
UN	United Nations
UNICEF	United Nations Children's Fund
WHO	World Health Organization (United Nations)

SCENARIO

In early 2017, fragmentary reporting from the DRC and neighboring countries indicates a new type of disease outbreak in the eastern DRC. Most of the reported incidents are occurring in North and South Kivu provinces (see Figure 8.1). The nature of the disease has not been identified, but early indications are that it is some form of viral hemorrhagic fever.

To further complicate the situation, at the same time, the M23 rebel organization is carrying out attacks on civilians, primarily refugees, in the areas controlled by the rebels.

INTELLIGENCE REPORTS

The intelligence reporting is listed in chronological order. However, the reporting prior to November 2016 is the result of Open Source Intelligence (OSINT) research

FIGURE 8.1   Map of the Kivu Provinces

Source: Map courtesy of the University of Texas Libraries, the University of Texas at Austin.

followed by a request to Dutch law enforcement authorities, prompted by your review of the 2016–2017 material.

Source/Date-Time Group	Text
OSINT December 12, 2011	At a meeting of the European Scientific Working Group on Influenza, Dr. J. F. M. Braun told the scientists in Malta that his Dutch group, the Infectious Disease Research Center in Utrecht, had mutated the virus H5N1, turning the bird flu into something that could infect monkeys. And then, Dr. Braun continued that he had done "something really stupid," swabbing the noses of the infected monkeys and using the gathered viruses to infect another round of animals, repeating the process until he had a form of H5N1 that could spread through the air from one mammal to another. (Source: *Proceedings of the ESWI Influenza Conference,* December 2011)
Liaison March 23, 2012	On March 7, 2012, a warrant was issued for the arrest of Dr. Farbod Jafar, an Iranian national who was employed as a researcher at the Infectious Disease Research Center in Utrecht. His immediate supervisor, Dr. J. F. M. Braun, reported to police that Jafar was removing sensitive medical research records from the center. Before he could be arrested, Dr. Jafar fled to Switzerland and subsequently flew from there to Tehran. Subsequently, it was discovered that Jafar had bypassed the center's information technology security system and downloaded a number of sensitive and proprietary electronic files. A warrant was issued for Jafar's arrest, but Iranian authorities refused the request for extradition. (Source: Dutch law enforcement)
OSINT February 13, 2013	In 2012, the Great Lakes Restoration project, a nonprofit organization, sponsored the import of pigs from Malaysia to support the Pigs for Peace program in South Kivu province. The Malaysian pigs were selected because of their high resistance to the diseases that plague African pigs. (Source: Great Lakes Restoration website, http://www .glrbtp.org)
OSINT December 12, 2013	The Tehran Genetic Engineering and Biotechnology Research Center (TGEBRC) in Iran was founded in 1994 under the Ministry of Culture and Higher Education. The TGEBRC is the lead research institute for genetic engineering in Iran. D. N. Atyabi is the director. In 2011, the British government identified TGEBRC as an entity of concern because of suspected weapons of mass destruction-related procurement, and the United Kingdom has denied

(Continued)

(Continued)

Source/Date-Time Group	Text
	its request for export licenses. In 2009, the Japanese government listed TGEBRC as an entity of concern for biological and chemical weapons proliferation. In 2008, the German government warned industry that TGEBRC was involved in procurement of dual-use biotechnology equipment. (Source: Various)
HUMINT November 2, 2016	DRC: A field hospital was set up in 2015 near the town of Lubutu, Maniema province, and staffed by doctors from some Middle Eastern country. The hospital compound was a complex of tin-roofed buildings. The doctors treated local people who were sick. The compound was guarded by Tutsi soldiers who locals believed to be members of Tiba Besebo's militia. Rumors say that Besebo visited the compound sometime in 2016. (Source: MONUSCO field interrogation unit, Kisangani, from an NGO member fleeing the violence in North Kivu)
HUMINT December 12, 2016	Iran: Atash Fanaei heads a special department at TGEBRC that conducts classified research on biotechnology. The purpose of the research is unknown, but the TGEBRC has not in the past been known to conduct classified research. (Source: German liaison reporting)
HUMINT January 7, 2017	In mid-2015, a group of Iranian doctors set up a field hospital near Lubutu in Maniema province, specializing in treating victims of diseases. The doctors refused to treat injuries, claiming that they specialized in local diseases. Over the past year, they have treated several hundred patients. Many locals refused to be treated at the hospital, because a lot of patients died while being treated there. The source did not know what diseases were treated. (Source: MONUSCO field interrogation unit, Kisangani, from a refugee fleeing the violence in North Kivu)
COMINT March 9, 2017	A Persian speaker identified only as "Khajeh" communicated from the Goma, DRC, area with Farbod Jafar at TGEBRC about Khajeh's continued progress on an unidentified medical experiment. Khajeh reported that "results to date are code green three. What shall we do now?" Jafar replied to Khajeh, "I'll check with Dr. Fanaei. He'll have to approve the next phase." (Source: French General Directorate for External Security [DGSE] intercept of satellite telecom between Goma and Tehran)
HUMINT March 28, 2017	On March 16, presidential household chief of staff Jean Larroche visited Finance Minister Phillipe Adawavon at the minister's home in Kinshasa. The meeting was

Source/Date-Time Group	Text
	observed personally by source. The meeting was unusual as the source has never known Larroche, a more junior official, to visit the finance minister at his home. (Source: Belgian liaison service, from a usually reliable source)
OSINT April 3, 2017	In an effort to control information both within their expanding "zone" and that disseminated to the world outside, M23 rebel authorities have mounted an aggressive campaign to censor or ban publications and radio programs. We have received increasing reports of journalists being threatened, detained, and harassed. Communications equipment has been seized. (Source: JIC social network analysis [SNA])
OSINT April 15, 2017	Uganda: Renewed fighting in the eastern DRC by rebel forces has resulted in an escalation of unlawful killings and other human rights abuses by the combatants against unarmed civilians. Thousands of civilians are reportedly fleeing to neighboring countries. The Ugandan government, expressing concern that refugees fleeing renewed fighting in the northeastern DRC may be carrying the Ebola virus, has closed its borders. (Source: Reuters news service)
OSINT April 15, 2017	Radio Maendeleo, the only independent radio station in South Kivu, which has a tradition of producing features on human rights (assisted by nongovernmental organizations [NGOs]), reported today that it had been ordered to stop developing its own reports and to report only that information fed to it by M23 minister of information, press, and cultural affairs. In the same broadcast, Radio Maendeleo announced it would disregard the order. (Source: Radio Maendeleo)
OSINT April 20, 2017	In South Kivu, several Radio Maendeleo personnel, who had been asked to stop developing reports on human rights abuses, have been threatened with physical harm if they continue to disregard the order to report only that information fed to them by the M23 minister of information, press, and cultural affairs. (Source: JIC SNA)
OSINT April 20, 2017	During 2014 and 2015, a series of epidemics in North and South Kivu provinces almost completely wiped out the chicken and pig populations in the region. The diminished populations started to recover in late 2016. (Source: United Kingdom/European Union [EU] Save The Children Project report, April 2017)

(Continued)

(Continued)

Source/Date-Time Group	Text
OSINT April 20, 2017	Rwandan newspapers, TV, and radio stations are reporting a new outbreak of Ebola virus in the eastern DRC. At least twenty people have already died. There is growing panic among local residents because of the swiftness with which so many have succumbed, some within twenty-four hours of exhibiting symptoms. Many local officials and elders are blaming the NGOs, calling them witch doctors. Doctors throughout Europe are being mobilized to respond to the new outbreak. (Sources: Kigali Radio and TV Rwanda in English and the Kigali *New Times*)
OSINT April 21, 2017	Local DRC radio and TV stations are reporting news of a threat made by the M23 rebels to contaminate the Kinshasa water supply with a deadly virus. (Source: Kinshasa Radio-Television Nationale Congolaise TV in French—state owned, government-controlled television)
OSINT April 22, 2017	Radio-Television Nationale Congolaise TV is reporting that local doctors have asserted that there is no medical crisis and that the reports coming in from field medical facilities regarding a new outbreak of the Ebola virus are an overreaction on the part of NGO health officials and merely reflect normal manifestations of human immunodeficiency virus/acquired immunodeficiency syndrome (HIV/AIDS) and the side effects of malnutrition. The minister of health is reported as saying he believes there is a new strain of HIV appearing and is blaming the NGOs. (Source: Kinshasa Radio-Television Nationale Congolaise TV in French—state-owned, government controlled television)
Analysis April 23, 2017	Passenger manifests show that a team of six Iranians traveled from Tehran, Iran, to Goma, DRC, in March 2015. The team consisted of Jahanshahi Amir, Mousavi Ali Hatef, Seyedi Bijan, Ranjbar Saeed, Allameh Kambiz, and Khajeh Reza. Seyedi Bijan returned to Tehran on April 4, 2016; there is no evidence of any others returning. (Source: Review of airline passenger manifests)
OSINT May 2, 2017	The bodies of the two Belgian British Broadcasting Service (BBC) "stringers" who had been captured by M23 rebels last month—and had been detained in an unknown location since then—were found in the center of Bukavu today. They had been brutally murdered and had been decapitated. Their ears had been cut off and their tongues cut out as an apparent warning to others who may be thinking of reporting on events in the M23 controlled parts of the DRC. (Source: Reuters)

Source/Date-Time Group	Text
OSINT May 2, 2017	NGOs report panic in the refugee camps as word spreads of a new highly contagious and deadly virus that refugees claim is contracted through the water supply. Doctors without Borders working in the Uele River area between Titule and Bondo are reporting a significant number of villagers arriving at their medical facilities who have symptoms, suggesting they have been poisoned. The villagers are telling the medical personnel that their water tastes peculiar. (Source: Paris AFP [World Service] in English—world news service of the independent French news agency Agence France Presse)
OSINT May 2, 2017	In a May 1 interview, a M23 spokesman accused the DRC government of deliberately spreading the Ebola virus in the eastern DRC and blaming it on M23. (Source: Kigali, Rwanda, newspaper *New Times*)
Analysis May 11, 2017	E-mail report: "You asked what others here knew of the refugee situation in the eastern DRC. Solid information appears to be elusive. Lots of rumors and anecdotal accounts, mostly coming from contacts with NGO personnel who have exited the area. From what I can tell most of the camps have been deserted after the massacre. UNHCR office has no good estimate of the number of displaced refugees but believes it could number as many as 400,000, with most of them having sought the sanctuary of the forest. Sorry for the delay in getting back to you. The local panic over a new disease outbreak here has consumed my time." (Source: Copy of e-mail between UN field representative in Kinshasa and UN HQ, shared with MONUSCO)
Diplomatic Cable May 14, 2017	A new and more virulent strain of the Ebola virus is reported in the eastern region, and large numbers of Hutu villagers near Rutshuru, northwest of Goma, appear to be infected. The WHO is warning local health workers to initiate an active surveillance system to monitor the extent and magnitude of the new outbreak, as there is a high risk that the virus could spread to the refugee camps and health workers. WHO has not ruled out the potential that what we are observing is a never before observed type of virus. All African stations should remain alert. (Source: Diplomatic cable from Belgian Ministry of Foreign Affairs)
OSINT May 14, 2017	DRC: The website of the Kigali *New Times* carried a report by Philip Munyane on May 8 that included the following paragraph: "Unconfirmed reports have been received that a caravan carrying ten members of a Doctors without

(Continued)

(Continued)

Source/Date-Time Group	Text
	Borders team is missing. Five members of the team are U.S. citizens; three are French, one each Swiss and Moroccan. The caravan was headed northwest from the Bukavu refugee camp in the Eastern DRC. The Doctors were fleeing after hearing of the slaughter at the Mugunga camp. Their last confirmed location was East of Lubutu; the caravan was enroute to safety in Kisangani." (Source: Kigali *New Times*)
OSINT May 15, 2017	Kenya: The website of the Nairobi *Daily Nation* reported on May 9 that it has acquired sensitive information via WHO sources that the CDC is investigating the possibility of a new viral epidemic which may have originated in Africa, possibly the DRC. Numerous medical facilities worldwide are reporting several cases of patients, recently returned from African countries (mostly Rwanda and the DRC), who exhibit similar symptoms. The main presenting features were fever, headache, dizziness, and vomiting. Many had a reduced level of consciousness and prominent brain-stem dysfunction. Of the ninety-four cases reported, seventy-eight patients died after rapid deterioration in their condition, usually within forty-eight hours of entering a medical facility. (Source: Nairobi *Daily Nation* [Internet-Version-WWW] in English—independent newspaper with respected news coverage; Kenya's largest circulation newspaper; published by the Nation Media Group; www.nationaudio.com)
HUMINT May 15, 2017	A Western doctor in Rwanda (a retired British army officer) retrieved a blood sample from a dying refugee near Mwenga and determined that the virus currently afflicting the population of the DRC is the Nipah virus, which he had dealt with while stationed in the Philippines. A sample was sent to the British Health Organization for analysis. (Source: British liaison)
Analysis May 17, 2017	The UN Office for the Coordination of Humanitarian Affairs reports that all NGOs are withdrawing their personnel due to the out-of-control violence and disease outbreaks in the Kivus. Massacres, extortion, and forced displacements are said to be occurring throughout the region. Most NGO personnel have fled to the relative safety of Uganda or Rwanda. Relief agencies continue to maintain HQ elements in Kinshasa. The United Nations Children's Fund (UNICEF) continues operations in Orientale, Kasa, and Equateur. (MONUSCO comment: The departure of UN and relief agencies, as well as the few remaining journalists, leaves the camps without any semblance of law and order.) (Source: MONUSCO analysis)

Source/Date-Time Group	Text
HUMINT May 19, 2017	Tiba Besebo, leader of M23 operating in the eastern DRC, held a meeting with his staff and senior commanders in April 2017. The purpose of the meeting was to reveal the group's strategy for expelling Western influence from Africa. Besebo told the group that the narcotics trade with the United States not only provides funds to keep his operation going but also weakens the U.S. resolve. He claimed that they have found ways to get large quantities of heroin into the United States and western Europe "with the help of friends around the world who sympathize with our objective of getting imperialist influences out of Africa." He also said that the group would use "dramatic and unusual" means in the near future to induce panic and disorganization directly within the United States. His senior lieutenant, Adrien Biruta, was given the honor of carrying out the task, along with a selected group of "volunteers." No details were given about the nature of the "dramatic and unusual" means. Biruta and fifteen "volunteers" left the area in early May on travel to Kigali, Rwanda, and have not returned. (Source: Defector, a former lieutenant in M23 who surrendered to MONUSCO authorities in Kisangani on May 17, 2017)
OSINT May 20, 2017	Local newspapers and other news media continue to report on the conflicting stories concerning the possibility of a medical crisis in the DRC. Conflicting stories identify the virus as an AIDS variant; as nothing new; as an unknown virulent, highly contagious virus that is a threat worldwide; or as a new strain of Ebola. The reporting suggests increasing tensions between local health officials (who do not believe there is a crisis) and Doctors without Borders and other NGO health officials (who believe there is a new virus in the DRC). (Source: Various newspapers in the eastern DRC and Rwanda)
CDC Analysis May 21, 2017	The Department of Health, Social Services and Public Safety, London reports on a zoonotic virus based on samples taken from victims in the region near Mwenga. The virus has caused disease in animals and, via contact with infected animals, in humans. In a cautionary report to Doctors without Borders, the British Health Organization is cautioning health care providers in the DRC that the outbreak in the DRC currently thought to be Ebola may in fact be a new strain of the Nipah virus first detected in 1999 in Malaysia. The virus is contracted by contact with infected pigs. Because of reports that the virus is being transmitted via water supplies, the

(Continued)

(Continued)

Source/Date-Time Group	Text
	department conducted diagnostic tests that determined that the virus was in fact capable of surviving in a water supply for up to thirty-six hours. (CDC comment: Neither the Ebola virus nor the Nipah virus are known to survive extended immersion in water. Further investigation of the nature of the virus is recommended.)
COMINT May 22, 2017	Fragmentary telephone intercepts indicate that some Rwandan government officials are assisting the rebels by providing false documentation for unidentified individuals who are leaving the region for destinations in the United States and western Europe. (Source: French DGSE liaison)
HUMINT May 30, 2017	On May 27, Adrien Biruta arrived at JFK airport on KLM Flight 6107 from Frankfurt. Biruta was traveling on a Rwandan tourist visa and Rwandan passport. Four individuals also traveling on the flight carried Rwandan passports and may have been traveling with Biruta: Milton Museveni, William Obote, Paul Rwigyema, and Richard Murekatete. The five are believed to still be in the United States, but their whereabouts are unknown. (Source: Response to MONUSCO query of U.S. immigration authorities)
OSINT June 9, 2017	Fourteen people have been hospitalized so far in New York in what some medical personnel fear could be an outbreak of Ebola hemorrhagic fever. The disease was first observed among customs officials and personnel who work in JFK airport. Doctors report that the symptoms are similar but not identical to those caused by the Ebola virus. New York hospitals have implemented viral hemorrhagic fever barrier precautions to prevent the spread of the disease. (Source: *New York Times*)
OSINT June 13, 2017	There have been eight deaths so far of JFK airport personnel infected with what appears to be a hemorrhagic fever virus. Six more patients are in critical condition, and twenty-five new cases of the disease have been identified. Doctors are still uncertain about the nature of the disease, describing it only as "an apparent variant of Ebola virus." The newspaper also reports widespread panic among the public in the New York City area. More than 19,000 people have shown up at New York hospital emergency rooms claiming to have Ebola symptoms and demanding medical treatment. (Source: *New York Times*)
OSINT June 14, 2017	Hospitals in Frankfurt, Germany, are dealing with an influx of patients having the symptoms characteristic of

Source/Date-Time Group	Text
	viral hemorrhagic fever. Preliminary reports suggest that the disease may be identical to the one that struck New York ten days ago and was observed earlier this year in the eastern part of the DRC. (Source: Frankfurter Allgemeine Zeitung)
OSINT June 16, 2017	A CDC official reports that two passengers arriving on May 27 aboard KLM Flight 6107 from Frankfurt appear to have been carriers of the viral hemorrhagic fever disease that has caused panic in New York City. William Obote and Paul Rwigyema traveled on the flight under Rwandan passports. Obote and Rwigyema both succumbed to the disease on June 13. Authorities have asked all passengers who traveled on the May 27 flight to immediately report for a health screening. (Source: New York Times)

Note: HUMINT = Human Intelligence; COMINT = communications intelligence.

BACKGROUND READING

The following is a summary of reports produced by the CDC.

Nipah Virus

Nipah virus[1] was first identified during an outbreak of disease that took place in Kampung Sungai Nipah, Malaysia, in 1998. In 1998 and 1999 during the disease outbreak, 257 patients were infected with the virus. About 40 percent of those patients who entered hospitals with the disease died from the illness. On this occasion, pigs were the intermediate hosts. In Malaysia and Singapore, humans were infected with Nipah virus through close contact with infected pigs. The Malaysian outbreaks were controlled in both domesticated animals and humans by culling more than 1 million pigs. In addition, pig farming was permanently banned in some high-risk areas.

Since 2001, human outbreaks and clusters of cases have been reported periodically in Bangladesh and a neighboring region of northern India. In some of these outbreaks, Nipah virus seems to have been transmitted directly from bats to humans, with person-to-person transmission the most significant means of spread. Why Nipah virus periodically emerges into humans and domesticated animals is not known; however, fruit bat populations in southeast Asia are being disrupted by various factors that may alter their foraging patterns and behavior and bring them into closer contact with domesticated animals and humans.

---

[1]Centers for Disease Control and Prevention, "Nipah Virus (NiV)," March 20, 2014, http://www.cdc.gov/vhf/nipah.

Illness with Nipah virus begins with three to fourteen days of fever and headache. This is followed by drowsiness and disorientation characterized by mental confusion. These signs and symptoms can progress to coma within twenty-four to forty-eight hours. Some patients have had a respiratory illness during the early part of their infections. There is no vaccine for either humans or animals. The primary treatment for human cases is intensive supportive care.

Ebola Virus

Ebola hemorrhagic fever is a severe, often fatal disease in humans and nonhuman primates (monkeys, gorillas, and chimpanzees) that has appeared sporadically since its initial recognition in 1976. The disease is caused by infection with Ebola virus,[2] named after a river in the DRC in Africa where it was first recognized.

The exact origin, locations, and the natural reservoir of Ebola virus remain unknown. However, on the basis of available evidence and the nature of similar viruses, researchers believe that the virus is zoonotic (animal-borne), occurring in an animal host native to Africa. A similar host, most likely in the Philippines, is probably associated with the Ebola-Reston subtype, which was isolated from infected monkeys that were imported to the United States and Italy from the Philippines.

Because the natural reservoir of the virus is unknown, the manner in which the virus first appears in a human at the start of an outbreak has not been determined. However, researchers have hypothesized that the first patient becomes infected through contact with an infected animal. After the first case-patient in an outbreak setting is infected, the virus can be transmitted in several ways. People can be exposed to Ebola virus from direct contact with the blood and/or secretions of an infected person.

The incubation period for Ebola hemorrhagic fever ranges from two to twenty-one days. The onset of illness is abrupt and is characterized by fever, headache, joint and muscle aches, sore throat, and weakness, followed by diarrhea, vomiting, and stomach pain. A rash, red eyes, hiccups, and internal and external bleeding may be seen in some patients. The fatality rate can be as high as 90 percent.

---

[2]Centers for Disease Control and Prevention, "Ebola (Ebola Virus Disease)," November 4, 2014, http://www.cdc.gov/vhf/ebola.

9

Democratic Republic of Congo: Likasi Chemical Plant

This case study is set in 2017 and is based on the Democratic Republic of Congo (DRC) baseline that is described in Chapter 5. The fact situation in this case study is notional.

The case concerns a recently completed chemical plant located in the Mai Mai Kata Katanga (MMKK)-controlled part of the DRC. Conflicting reporting about the purpose of the plant indicates that it could be designed to produce chemical warfare (CW) agents, pesticides, or both.

EDUCATIONAL OBJECTIVES

This case study is designed for maximum assignment flexibility. It is also an optimal opportunity for collaboration, either working as a team and/or through verbal and/or written peer reviews. The intelligence herein lends itself to three possible hypotheses regarding a particular manufacturing plant's function: (1) the plant is intended for CW production, (2) the plant is intended for pesticide production, or (3) the plant is intended for dual use. Following are a few assignment configurations that work especially well in this context:

A. Form three teams (up to eight to ten members each). Assign each team a position to develop and defend, using supporting evidence (CW, pesticide, or dual use). Each team, in turn, will present its position and defense, leading to a classroom critique or discussion of the team's findings. A whole-class discussion wrap-up is encouraged.

B. Divide the students into three segments (CW, pesticide, or dual use). Individual students in each segment will *independently* develop and defend their assigned position, using supporting evidence. This can lead to different types of written peer review activities. Students in each segment can be responsible for a peer review of the products of others who have their same assignment.

Or students from all segments can be assigned to peer review the work of those who are *not* in their own segment.

C. Assign an individual project where each student is instructed to develop all three positions, and in the end, determine which one to defend, using supporting evidence. Written peer reviews (where two students exchange models and assessments) work particularly well with this scenario.

This exercise provides practical experience in the following:

- making and defending intelligence judgments in the absence of raw intelligence
- developing and defending a position on an issue, including the presentation of supporting evidence
- creating alternative target models
- collaborating with other analysts in developing assessments and/or by providing incisive peer review
- conveying uncertainty to customers in intelligence assessments

ASSIGNMENT

You are a CW specialist on temporary assignment to the United Nations Organization Stabilization Mission in the Democratic Republic of the Congo (MONUSCO) Joint Intelligence Center (JIC) for the purpose of assessing Intelligence Reports (INTREPs) about the Likasi chemical plant. The questions that have been posed by MONUSCO are as follows:

- What is the purpose of the Likasi chemical plant? Is it CW agent production, pesticide production, dual use, or other?
- If the plant is judged to have a CW role, what agents are being produced? In what quantities? For what purpose? Are they being weaponized? If so, what is the delivery mechanism?

To complete this assignment, your working group or you will be given exact directions by your instructor, but each of these actions have to be completed in some combination to supply your customer with a valid intelligence assessment:

- Create a process flow model of the Likasi chemical plant for one (or each) of the three possible functions of the plant.
- Use the process flow model(s) to develop a target network model (TNM) that includes key players and organizations involved.
- Prepare an intelligence assessment (five to eight paragraphs) that addresses the questions posed (to the extent that you can). Support your conclusions using

the models you have created. Include a section identifying at least ten intelligence gaps.
- In a group setting or during a peer review, critique the assessments presented by other teams or individuals.

ABBREVIATIONS AND ACRONYMS

Abbreviation or Acronym	Description
BND	Bundesnachrichtendienst (German foreign intelligence service)
COMINT	Communications Intelligence
CW	chemical warfare
CWC	chemical warfare convention
DGSE	General Directorate for External Security (France)
DRC	Democratic Republic of Congo
EFT	electronic funds transfer
HUMINT	Human Intelligence
IMINT	Imagery Intelligence
INTREP	Intelligence Report
JIC	Joint Intelligence Center
MASINT	Measurement and Signature Intelligence
MMKK	Mai Mai Kata Katanga
MONUSCO	United Nations Organization Stabilization Mission in the Democratic Republic of the Congo
MV	motor vessel
OPCW	Organisation for the Prohibition of Chemical Weapons (United Nations)
OSINT	Open Source Intelligence
TNM	target network model
UN	United Nations

SCENARIO

Fragmentary reporting suggests that the MMKK is investigating the possibility of producing CW agents with covert assistance from the Angolan government. Because of the serious threat that such a development would pose, MONUSCO has been asked to provide an assessment of the threat. The primary concern centers on the purpose of a chemical plant reportedly being built near Likasi, DRC (see Figure 9.1).

FIGURE 9.1   Katanga Province, Democratic Republic of Congo

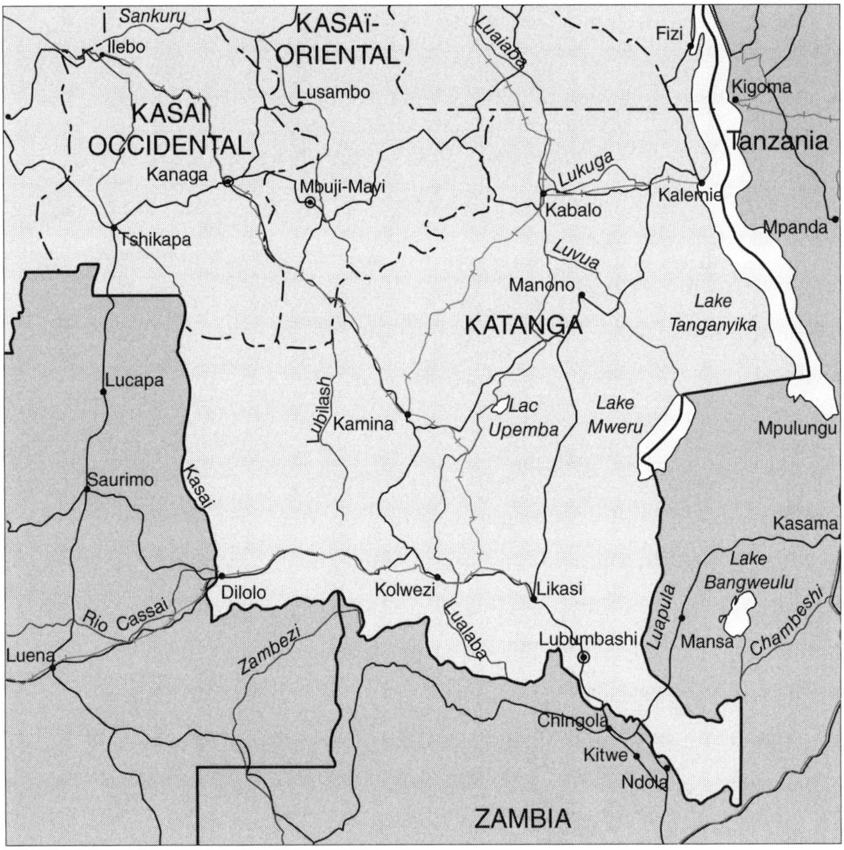

Source: Map courtesy of the University of Texas Libraries, the University of Texas at Austin.

INTELLIGENCE REPORTS

Source/Date-Time Group	Text
Open Source Intelligence (OSINT) June 10, 2015	The United Nations (UN) agricultural commission has released a report on Central African agriculture. It recommended the increased use of pesticides to improve crop yields. In an interview, Paulo Ricardo, a senior official in Angola's Ministry of Agriculture and member of the

Source/Date-Time Group	Text
	commission that produced the report, commented, "Poor crop yields are a long-neglected problem in Angola, and we cannot depend on foreign supplies of pesticide to meet our needs. We must have indigenous production capabilities." (Source: *Manchester Guardian*)
Cyber August 19, 2016	On August 2, 2016, an Angolan government official ordered a Model BKM-334 environmental waste incinerator from the Bù kěkào Machinery Manufacturing Co., Ltd., Henan, China. The price of the incinerator was $123,000 FOB Luanda. The incinerator was to be shipped from Qingdao port on September 3, 2016. (Comment: An earlier model of this incinerator has been associated with scrubbing emissions and hazardous chemicals created by industrial plants.) (Source: French General Directorate for External Security [DGSE] liaison)
Communications Intelligence (COMINT) October 14, 2016	The North Korean motor vessel (MV) *Ku Wol San,* originating from Namp'o, 50 km southwest of Pyongyang, onloaded cargo at Qingdao, China, on September 3 enroute to Luanda, Angola. (Comment: The *Ku Wol San* has a previous history of transporting missile parts between Pakistan and North Korea.) (Source: French DGSE liaison)
Human Intelligence (HUMINT) December 6, 2016	This is a report of an interview with a field engineer employed by Köpenick Hauptmann AG, Mainz, Germany. (Köpenick Hauptmann is a major industrial glass manufacturer, exporting its products worldwide.) The engineer supervised the installation of his company's glass liners on reactor vessels, pipes, and distillation columns at the Likasi chemical plant, Likasi, DRC, October 8–20, 2016. The glass liners specified in the installation were designed to handle extremely corrosive chemicals. (Source: German Bundesnachrichtendienst [BND] liaison)
Cyber December 12, 2016	On December 7, 2016, Paulo Ricardo, a senior official in Angola's Ministry of Agriculture contacted a manager at Mumbai Agricultural Supply, Ltd., in Mumbai, India, about a purchase of phosphorus oxychloride. The Mumbai Agricultural Supply manager declined to bid, explaining that they could not produce the chemical in the quantities Ricardo wanted. (Source: French DGSE liaison)
Cyber December 20, 2016	On December 12, 2016, Paulo Ricardo, a senior official in Angola's Ministry of Agriculture, contacted (FNU) Liu, an official at the Fanzui Chemical Co. Ltd., Guizhou, China, regarding the purchase of 40 metric tons of phosphorus oxychloride, for shipment in January 2017. Mr. Liu

(Continued)

(Continued)

Source/Date-Time Group	Text
	promised to get back to Ricardo with a quote. Ricardo then asked if it would be possible to purchase phosphorus trichloride as well and was told that Fanzui did not manufacture the chemical. (Comment: Phosphorus oxychloride is a common feedstock for pesticides while phosphorus trichloride is not; both, however, are chemical warfare convention (CWC) schedule 3 precursors for the production of nerve agents.) (Source: French DGSE liaison)
Cyber December 24, 2016	On December 18, 2016, Alfonso Kassoma, an official in Angola's Ministry of Agriculture, contacted a manager at Fēifǎ Products Co. Limited, Shanghai, China, regarding the availability of pinacolyl alcohol. The Fēifǎ manager promised to get back to Kassoma with a quote. (Analyst Comment: Pinacolyl alcohol appears on the list of Schedule 2 substances (CWC) as a precursor for the nerve agent Soman.) (Source: French DGSE liaison)
OSINT January 10, 2017	Luanda, Angola: Angolan government officials reported that the Katangans have completed a modern production plant for pesticides and fertilizers in southern Katanga near the city of Likasi. The Angolan Minister of Agriculture, Joao Primo, announced that Angola would be purchasing most of the plant's production. (Source: Luanda ANGOP WWW—Text in Portuguese—government-controlled news agency; http://angolapress-angop.ao)
Cyber February 25, 2017	Monitoring of electronic transfers of funds between banks in Luxembourg, Zambia, and Tanzania suggest that large transfers of funds are occurring. The increased electronic funds transfers (EFTs) also include several offshore banking institutions known to be havens for money laundering. In addition, a number of accounts have been tied to Eduardo Mutumbe, a member of the board of the People's National Bank of Angola. (Source: French DGSE liaison)
HUMINT March 1, 2017	During November and December 2016, Paulo Ricardo, a senior official in Angola's Ministry of Agriculture, contacted several European chemical firms asking for quotes on the purchase of 80 metric tons of phosphorus pentasulfide. When queried about the purpose of the purchase, Ricardo said that it was "for pesticide production in a plant that is under construction." (Source: German BND liaison)
Analysis March 3, 2017	Relations between Angola and the DRC, already poor, have deteriorated sharply during this year. The DRC government is suspected of supporting the independence movement for

Source/Date-Time Group	Text
	Cabinda, an Angolan enclave separated from the rest of the country by DRC territory. The DRC is probably motivated by the potential for acquiring access to Cabinda's extensive offshore petroleum reserves. (Source: MONUSCO JIC assessment, March 3, 2017)
OSINT March 20, 2017	Angola: An article in the *Angolan Peace Monitor,* an online journal cataloguing human rights abuses in Southern Africa, claims that the new chemical plant in Likasi, Katanga province is producing CW agents for use against Angolan rebels. The article claims that the CW agents have not been used yet, because the Angolan military is waiting for an opportune time and target.
OSINT March 21, 2017	Angola: In a press interview, the Angolan minister of information denied reports of an Angolan-supported CW agent production plant in Likasi, DRC, claiming that they were "a pack of lies, spread by the terrorists who are trying to overthrow the legitimate government of Angola." He added, "We have repeatedly said that the Likasi plant will produce pesticides, and we expect to purchase the entire supply to meet our agricultural needs."
OSINT March 25, 2017	Angola: President Eduardo Vicente held a news conference at the conclusion of his four-day unofficial visit to Lubumbashi, DRC. In response to one question about the aspirations of the MMKK, President Vicente responded with this: "All Africans who love freedom and independence support General Mala and the Mai Mai Kata Katanga. They are fighting oppression from the forces of colonial subjugation, which today comes with a black face. Kabila is a corrupt thief, stealing from his own people, and supported by the former colonial powers, which use the United Nations as their surrogate. I support the liberation of the Congo and will work for it diligently." In response to another question, President Vicente stated, "We fought a long struggle against the forces that tried to subjugate Africa. We were victorious, and those who support the oppressors should note that we will continue this struggle throughout the continent until the final vestiges of colonial oppression are destroyed." (Source: Angola in English over Angolan government radio)
HUMINT April 28, 2017	At the invitation of MMKK authorities, an inspector from the Organisation for the Prohibition of Chemical Weapons (OPCW) visited the Likasi chemical plant on April 21, 2017. The inspector's report stated that the plant was

(Continued)

(Continued)

Source/Date-Time Group	Text
	producing an organophosphorus-based pesticide. The inspector observed markings on barrels marked "Malathion Pesticide" along with instructions indicating that the barrels were to be shipped to Angola. The inspector was unable to inspect two buildings in the plant because the plant manager, Damien Mwez, explained that a hazardous chemical spill had occurred there last week. (Source: UN OPCW inspection report)
OSINT Accessed May 3, 2017	Malathion is an organophosphorus insecticide produced commercially by the reaction of phosphorus pentasulfide with methanol in toluene solvent to produce an intermediate, dimethylphosphorodithioic acid, and a byproduct, hydrogen sulfide. The crude material is then stripped of solvent, washed, and filtered to produce technical-grade malathion. (Source: U.S. Agency for Toxic Substances and Disease Registry website)
OSINT May 11, 2017	Numerous online blogs are reporting an outbreak of illness in Likasi, DRC. Over 100 residents have been hospitalized with symptoms that include difficulty breathing, gastrointestinal pain, vomiting, and blisters. The blogs claim that the Likasi chemical plant is the source of the outbreak. (Source: Social media)
Measurement and Signature Intelligence (MASINT) May 28, 2017	On May 19, a RHINO BLUE mission obtained hyperspectral imagery of a chemical plant located near Likasi, DRC (coordinates: S10° 58′30″ E26° 36′ 35″). Analysis of the imagery revealed the presence of chlorobenzene, hydrogen sulfide, and hydrogen cyanide in the area surrounding the plant. Vegetation in an area extending 300 m southwest of the plant was dead or dying. (Analyst comment: Chlorobenzene is used in production of pesticides.) (Source: RHINO BLUE Mission 7327)
Imagery Intelligence (IMINT) June 1, 2017	On May 30, a RHINO RED mission imaged a chemical plant located near Likasi, DRC (coordinates: S10° 58′30″ E26° 36′ 35″). Imagery quality was poor due to mission altitude. The facility consists of six metal-roofed 22x × 116 m buildings and three 20 m × 57 m metal-roofed buildings and an administration building. The entire complex is surrounded by a 3 m high chain link security fence. (Source: RHINO RED to 7347)
HUMINT June 8, 2017	The Netherlands Agricultural Counselor for South Africa, Mozambique, and Angola reported on the result of a visit to observe farming practices in Angola's Bengo and Malange provinces. The counselor noted the extensive use of Malathion pesticide on crops in both provinces. The

Source/Date-Time Group	Text
	pesticide use surprised the counselor, since he had not observed any pesticide use at all in previous visits to the region. Local farmers informed the counselor that the pesticides had begun arriving in late May from a supplier in the DRC. (Source: Netherlands liaison)
HUMINT June 12, 2017	During the early part of 2017, a North Korean ship (name unknown) docked at Luanda port and unloaded 15,000 protective coats designed for protecting the wearer from hazardous chemicals. The shipment also included 28,000 pocket devices that are intended to detect chemical substances. (Source: Netherlands liaison, from a Luanda port official who has a history of reliable reporting)

BACKGROUND READING

From U.S. Congress, Office of Technology Assessment, "Technologies Underlying Weapons of Mass Destruction," OTA-BfP-ISC-115 (Washington, DC: Government Printing Office, December 1993).

Chemical Warfare

Nerve Agent Production   Nerve agents belong to the class of organophosphorus chemicals that includes pesticides. Although many organophosphorus compounds are highly toxic, only a few have physical properties that give them military utility as nerve agents. In general, nerve agents are 100 to 1,000 times more poisonous than organophosphorus pesticides.

From the standpoint of production processes, the nerve agents can be clustered into three groups: tabun, sarin/soman, and VX. Production of the nerve agents requires significantly more sophisticated chemical processing than does pesticide production. Most use corrosive chemicals in the process that require specialized corrosion-resistant construction materials. With the exception of GA (tabun), agent production requires special and expensive construction materials. Reactors, degassers, distillation columns, and ancillary equipment made of high nickel alloys or precious metals are needed to contain the corrosive products and byproducts. Only the last step of the process involves highly toxic material, so that special air handling equipment is needed for only a small portion of the facility.

Tabun. The first militarized nerve agent and the simplest to produce, tabun (GA) is made from four precursor chemicals: phosphorus oxychloride, sodium cyanide, dimethylamine, and ethyl alcohol. Most of these ingredients are widely available. Ethanol and sodium cyanide are commodity chemicals that are manufactured and sold in vast quantities; dimethylamine and phosphorus oxychloride are produced by companies in several countries for commercial applications in the production of pharmaceuticals, pesticides, missile fuels, and gasoline additives.

Tabun synthesis does not require the use of corrosive starting materials and does not produce highly reactive intermediates. The two-step process involves mixing the ingredients with a carrier solvent in a reaction vessel equipped with a sodium-hydroxide scrubbing system to neutralize the gaseous hydrochloric acid byproduct. A relatively simple air-tight enclosure is also needed to prevent the escape of toxic vapors. The ingredients must be added in the correct order, without heating, and the vessel cooled to keep the reaction from building up too much heat. Little or no distillation equipment is required. In sum, tabun production is relatively easy because it does not include the difficult alkylation reaction needed to make the other nerve agents. The major technical hurdle in tabun synthesis is the cyanation reaction (in which a cyanide group is added to the central phosphorus), because of the difficulty of containing the toxic hydrogen cyanide gas used as the reagent.

The Iraqis had difficulties with the manufacture of tabun, although they managed to produce a material with about 40 percent purity that was used in the Iran-Iraq War.

Sarin/Soman. Sarin (GB) and soman (GD) are both made in a batch process with the same basic reaction steps, but they contain different alcohol ingredients: iso-propyl alcohol for sarin and pinacolyl alcohol for soman. (The choice of alcohol changes the toxicity and volatility of the product but does not affect the difficulty of production.) Phosphorus trichloride is the basic starting material for the synthesis of both agents and, depending on which of several alternative synthetic pathways is chosen, two to five steps are required to make the final product. The alternative syntheses all involve the same four reaction steps, which can be carried out in several different sequences.

The synthesis of these two G agents entails three major technical hurdles.

First, the production process involves the use of hot hydrochloric acid (HCL) and hydrogen fluoride (HF), both of which are extremely corrosive. The use of these compounds in reactors and pipes made of conventional steel results in corrosion measured in inches per year. Today, corrosion-resistant reaction vessels and pipes are made of alloys containing 40 percent nickel. Although it is possible to manufacture sarin and soman without corrosion-resistant reactors and pipes, the chance of major leaks is significantly increased compared with using corrosion-resistant equipment.

The second hurdle in the production of G agents is the alkylation reaction, in which a methyl group or an ethyl group is added to the central phosphorus. This step is rarely used in the production of commercial pesticides and is technically difficult.

The third hurdle is that if a high-purity agent with a long shelf-life is required, the supertoxic final product must be distilled—an extremely hazardous operation. Distillation is not necessary if a country plans to produce nerve agents for immediate use rather than stockpiling them.

VX. The persistent nerve agent VX has a phosphorusmethyl bond and a phosphorus-sulfur bond but contains no fluorine. There are at least three practical routes to V-agents that might be used by proliferant countries. As with G agents, production of VX involves a difficult alkylation step. Because the VX manufacturing process avoids the use of hydrogen fluoride gas, however, it is less corrosive than the production of sarin and soman. Indeed, after the alkylation step has been completed, the rest of the synthesis is straightforward.

Production Hurdles. In summary, the technologies required for the production of nerve agents have been known for more than 40 years and are within the capabilities of any moderately advanced chemical or pharmaceutical industry. The technical hurdles associated with nerve-agent production are not fundamentally different from those associated with commercial products such as organophosphorus pesticides. The most technically challenging aspects include the following:

- the cyanation reaction for tabun, which involves the containment of a highly toxic gas
- the alkylation step for sarin, soman, and VX, which requires the use of high temperatures and results in corrosive and dangerous byproducts such as hot hydrochloric acid
- careful temperature control, including cooling of the reactor vessel during heat-producing reactions, and heating to complete reactions or to remove unwanted byproducts
- intermediates that react explosively with water, requiring the use of heat-exchangers based on fluids or oils rather than water
- a distillation step if high-purity agent is required

Pesticide Production Pesticide plants do not normally use hydrogen fluoride—a key ingredient of sarin and soman—and generally use phosphorus oxychloride or phosphorus pentasulfide as a starting material rather than phosphorus trichloride. Phosphorus pentasulfide cannot be utilized as a starting material for nerve-agent production. Converting a pesticide plant to nerve-gas production would mean modifying the production process and stretching the operating conditions to obtain reasonable yields while still maintaining secrecy. For example, the conversion of a parathion plant to the production of G-agents would be extremely difficult, requiring substantial material changes and plant retooling. The modifications would involve rerouting pipes, valves, and mechanical seals to meet minimal operating requirements. For example, a proliferant might design a plant to produce an organophosphorus pesticide that lacks a phosphorus-carbon bond and then change the feed materials and process equipment to add a final alkylation step—either in a clandestine section of the main plant or at a separate location. It would also be possible to design a plant that could make nerve agents and then add on bypass piping to permit the commercial production of pesticides and pharmaceuticals. Thus, in time of need, it would be easy to convert the plant back to nerve-agent production.

In the case of nerve agents, false-positives can arise if the plant is manufacturing or using a legitimate compound that contains a phosphorus-methyl bond and thus breaks down into the same degradation product as a nerve agent. Fortunately, only a handful of commercial products contain a phosphorus-methyl bond, including the pesticide Mecarphon.

Dual Use   If a multipurpose plant were designed for rapid conversion from one chemical process to another, it might be possible to switch over in a few days with little chance of being detected. Even so, a plant specifically designed for rapid conversion from commercial to CW agent production would be costly to build (on the order of $150 million), and would require a high level of technological know-how in plant design, engineering, and operation, and a skilled construction workforce. Design and construction would take about 4 years in most parts of the developing world.

A dual-use plant designed for rapid conversion would also require stringent cleaning measures for the final steps in the production process to prevent the contamination of commercial products, particularly pharmaceuticals, with deadly CW agents. Since seals on pumps and other material handling equipment absorb chemicals from the production process, switching from production of one chemical to another requires removing the pumps and cleaning them off-line, a time consuming process. In a rapidly convertible plant, however, the production line might be configured with modular pumps that could be removed quickly for cleaning and then replaced. Alternatively, two sets of pumps might be installed in parallel so that different chemicals could be produced on the same line without contaminating each other. Nevertheless, a plant that has been specifically designed to facilitate rapid decontamination would probably be uneconomical for commercial production, and would therefore arouse suspicions on those grounds.

10

International Maritime Defense Exhibition and Conference Collection Plan

This case study is set in the year 2015. It deals with real organizations, and the International Maritime Defense Exhibition and Conference (IMDEX) is a real event. The scenario and Intelligence Reports (INTREPs) are notional. The intelligence support is also notional, though based on real organizations and—except for the notional ships *Taina* and *Lorikeet*—real equipment.

The Australian government is concerned about the potential threat posed by a new type of patrol boat being offered for sale by a Russian company. The boat reportedly has a revolutionary propulsion system, is equipped with an antiship missile (ASM), and employs stealth technology. The Russian company plans to demonstrate the boat at IMDEX Asia in Singapore.

Following are the top-level customer needs:

- *The Australian Defence Force (ADF)* has requested any details about planned sales of the craft to countries in the region or to nonstate entities. The ADF wants to know the number of craft sold, the identity of purchasers and their intended uses of the craft, the terms of sale, and planned delivery dates.
- *The Australian navy* wants details on the craft's performance and stealth capabilities, including details about the armament—specifically the ASM performance.

EDUCATIONAL OBJECTIVES

This case study is designed for maximum assignment flexibility. It is also an optimal opportunity for collaboration, either working as a team or through verbal and written peer reviews. The case study consists of three assignments, designed to be completed in sequence. Each assignment has three tasks. Instructors have considerable flexibility in handling the assignments.

1. Each student can independently complete all of the assignments and tasks. Written peer reviews (where students exchange the results of each assignment) work well in this option.

2. Each student can independently complete one task for each assignment. This requires collaboration with students who are assigned the other two tasks. Again, this option can make good use of peer reviews.

3. Form three teams (up to eight to ten members each). Assign each team one task for each assignment. This option requires collaboration with the teams assigned to the other two tasks. Teams then should present their results to the class verbally at the completion of each assignment.

This case study stresses creating a preliminary network model, gap analysis, and collection targeting during a weapons exhibition tradeshow and weapons performance demonstration. It features multiple targets and two customers with different interests. It requires both a target network analysis and an assessment of your collection network, using it effectively to collect against customer needs.

This exercise provides practical experience in the following:

- conducting gap analysis
- collection planning
- dealing with denial and deception
- collaborating with other analysts and collectors in developing and sharing target network models (TNMs)
- conducting system performance analyses

ASSIGNMENT

You are a senior analyst with Australia's Defence Intelligence Organisation (DIO). DIO is the Australian government's source of expertise for matters relating to trends in global security, weapons of mass destruction, foreign military capabilities, defense economics, and transnational terrorism.

Assignment 1: Preliminary Assessment and Gap Analysis

You are to prepare a preliminary assessment and identify gaps in knowledge. This involves answering two broad questions including but not limited to the following:

- What do we know: Who are the potential boat customers? Why are they interested in purchasing the craft? What is your estimate of the boat's design, performance, and stealth capability? What is the nature of the boat demonstration? Where and when will the demonstration be conducted?
- What are the critical gaps in our knowledge?

This assignment has three tasks, all of which require identifying gaps in knowledge:

1. Identify the key participants (including potential purchasers), and create a TNM of the relationships among them.

2. Prepare a preliminary estimate of the boat's design, performance, and stealth capability.

3. Develop a process model of the demonstration scenario (include timing, location, and features to be demonstrated); this task is essential in order to complete assignment 3.

Assignment 2: General Collection Strategy

Next, you are to develop a collection strategy to fill the gaps identified in assignment 1. The strategy must address your customer needs defined in the introduction and should make use of Open Source Intelligence (OSINT), Human Intelligence (HUMINT), and Communications Intelligence (COMINT) assets. This assignment has three tasks, each requiring the preparation of a collection plan.

1. **OSINT:** Identify the open sources that could potentially contribute to the customer needs for your designated customers. Specifically consider the potential for "tip-off" to the other collection efforts. Include possible social media sources.

2. **HUMINT:** Define a collection plan to include tasking as many different HUMINT sources as feasible against your customer needs. Identify the specific assets you propose to use (e.g., attachés, specific recruited sources, or specific liaison sources), and explain what you would task them to collect. Balance what you expect to learn from each source against the risks involved in using that source.

3. **COMINT:** Identify the sources and types of communications that might be collected and likely value of information collected. Possible communications include but are not limited to the following: cell phones, microwave point to point, push-to-talk radios, fiber optic cable, wireless computer networks, and Internet communications. Identify potential COMINT liaison organizations (i.e., COMINT services of friendly countries) that might be in a position to assist, considering geography and mutual interest in the target, and indicate how you would use them.

Assignment 3: Boat Demonstration Targeting

This makes use of the demonstration scenario model that was created in assignment 1. You are to prepare a collection strategy and plan against the weapons system performance needs. The detailed requirements you have received on this subject are next.

Provide details on the performance of the patrol craft (i.e., top speed, range, maneuverability, logistics support).

- If the ship has an ASM, determine the sensor type and performance, missile speed and flight profile, operational profile, and intended targets.

- Provide details on the reported stealth design, its effectiveness, and the hull materials used.
- Determine the type of propulsion used by the vessel.

The purpose of collection, therefore, is to support a weapons systems performance analysis based on reporting from technical collection prior to, during, and after the at-sea demonstration. The plans that come from the collection strategy should follow this process:

- Develop a collection scenario (specific targets, timing, method of collecting—that is, specific sources or assets) based on your demonstration scenario model.
- Develop collection strategies for the different types of collection against the target.
- Prepare a collection plan for the available collection assets, assessing the risk or cost versus probable payoff.

This assignment has the following tasks, each requiring a collection plan:

1. **Imagery Intelligence (IMINT):** Consider the intelligence that you might obtain from the *Taina* in Singapore harbor and when underway using each of the following types of imagery: visible (including video), synthetic-aperture radar (SAR), nighttime infrared, and multispectral imaging.

2. **Signals Intelligence (SIGINT):** This includes COMINT, Electronic Intelligence (ELINT), and Foreign Instrumentation Signals Intelligence (FISINT) targeting during the demonstration. Identify the types of SIGINT collection systems and platforms you plan to use, the targets that you plan to use them against, and the expected intelligence to be gathered.

3. **Measurement and Signature Intelligence (MASINT):** Identify the non-imaging (airborne, land-based, or shipborne) radar types that you plan to use to collect against the vessel during the demonstration and against any weapons exercise. Identify specific targets for materials or materiel collection and the intelligence that you expect to obtain from that target. Describe how you propose to collect the materials or materiel.

ABBREVIATIONS AND ACRONYMS

Abbreviation or Acronym	Description
ADF	Australian Defence Force
ASIS	Australian Secret Intelligence Service
ASM	Antiship Missile
COMINT	Communications Intelligence (a subset of SIGINT)

Abbreviation or Acronym	Description
DIGO	Defence Imagery and Geospatial Organisation (Australia)
DIO	Defence Intelligence Organisation (Australia)
DSD	Defence Signals Directorate (Australia)
ELINT	Electronic Intelligence (a subset of SIGINT)
FISINT	Foreign Instrumentation Signals Intelligence
GEOINT	Geospatial Intelligence
HUMINT	Human Intelligence
IMDEX	International Maritime Defense Exhibition and Conference
IMINT	Imagery Intelligence
INTREP	Intelligence Report
LPI	Low Probability of Intercept
MASINT	Measurement and Signature Intelligence
ONA	Office of National Assessments (Australia)
OSINT	Open Source Intelligence
RCS	Radar Cross Section
SAR	Synthetic-Aperture Radar
SIGINT	Signals Intelligence (includes COMINT and ELINT)
SSM	Surface-to-Surface Missile
SVR RF	Foreign Intelligence Service of the Russian Federation
SWATH	Small Waterplane Area Twin Hull
TNM	Target Network Model
UAV	Unmanned Aerial Vehicle
UWSA	United Wa State Army

SCENARIO

IMDEX Asia is held every two years at the Singapore Expo, 1 Expo Drive, Singapore (close to Singapore Changi Airport—see Figure 10.1). It is hosted by the Republic of Singapore navy. It provides an opportunity for key decision makers from naval organizations and international maritime defense industry to keep abreast of the latest in maritime defense technologies.

During the upcoming exhibition (May 19–21, 2015), a Russian delegation proposes to showcase a new patrol boat at IMDEX Asia. A Russian website describes the *Taina*-class boat as an advanced type of very fast patrol boat, highly maneuverable, and optionally equipped with a new ASM. According to the website, the craft has a new hull design that employs stealth technology and a revolutionary propulsion system. The website provides no performance details about the boat. The craft was designed by the Almaz Central Marine Design Bureau of St. Petersburg, Russia. The

FIGURE 10.1   Map of Singapore with International Maritime Defense
                   Exhibition and Conference Location

Source: Map courtesy of the University of Texas Libraries, the University of Texas at Austin. Map of
Singapore from http://www.lib.utexas.edu/maps/middle_east_and_asia/singapore_physio-2005.jpg with
author annotations.

Russians reportedly plan to set up a booth at the exposition and provide information
about the capabilities of the boat and the missile.

Several of the parties reported to be interested in the boat are a matter of concern
to the ADF customer because they may be associated with gray arms traffickers and
human traffickers. Stealth is a concern because the boat could be used for illicit traffic in arms, drugs, or people. The armament and performance are a concern because
of the potential threat to the customer's naval forces.

INTELLIGENCE SUPPORT

Collection Platforms

Australia operates a fleet of AP-3C maritime patrol aircraft (an upgraded
version of the U.S. P-3C Orion). The upgrades improved the aircraft's radar,
intelligence-gathering, and computing systems. The upgrade included fitting each
aircraft with a new Elta EL/M-2022(V)3 radar, a nose-mounted Star Safire III
electro-optical and infrared system, and a suite of SIGINT and ELINT equipment.

Operation in the Singapore area is possible but expensive because of the long flight time from Australia. And because it is near the limit of operating range from the AP-3C staging area, loiter time in the Singapore area would be limited to a maximum of two hours.

The hydrographic survey ship *Leeuwin* currently is conducting a survey in the South China Sea. It is capable of charting waters up to 6,000 m (20,000 ft) deep. It carries the following sonars:

- C-Tech CMAS 36/39 hull-mounted high frequency (HF) active sonar
- Atlas Fansweep-20 multibeam echo sounder
- Atlas Hydrographic Deso single-beam echo sounder
- Klein 2000 towed sidescan sonar array

The *Leeuwin*'s sonars allow it to produce images of the ocean bottom and to detect underwater explosions. The ship also carries an X-band surface search radar.

The *Leeuwin* can be made available for collection in the Singapore region, but its relatively slow (18 knot maximum) speed means that it would require at least one days' advance notification of the test location in order to observe the test itself.

Signals Intelligence

The Defence Signals Directorate (DSD) is an intelligence agency in the Australian Department of Defence, with its HQ in Canberra. DSD provides SIGINT to the ADF and Australian government to support military and strategic decision making.

The DSD primary collection asset in the Singapore region is the yacht *Lorikeet,* a SIGINT collector operated clandestinely out of Nongsa Point Marina on the island of Batam, Indonesia, across the channel from Singapore. From the marina, the ship can intercept cell phone traffic in Singapore. It also monitors ship traffic and ship communications in the Singapore Channel. It carries an X-band marine radar for sea surveillance.

From the ship's position in the marina, an observer has a clear view of Singapore. The location therefore provides access to most of the cell phone traffic in Singapore. The *Lorikeet* also deploys for at-sea surveillance of targets of intelligence interest.

The *Lorikeet* carries these COMINT and ELINT systems:

- Thales VIGILE 400 ELINT collector, providing instantaneous direction finding and signal measurement on radars in the 500 MHz-18 GHz band, with the ability to detect low probability of intercept (LPI) radar
- Thales ALTESSE COMINT collector, providing maritime communications intercepts and cell phone collection across the HF, very high frequency (VHF), and ultra high frequency (UHF) bands with a direction finding capability

Reporting from the *Lorikeet* intercepts is classified in special COMINT channels carrying the code name KITEFIN.

Open Source Intelligence

OSINT about developments in Singapore is derived from local newspapers and from the Internet. Reporting is the responsibility of Australia's Open Source Centre, which is a part of the Office of National Assessments (ONA). The role of the Open Source Centre is to collect and validate information from open sources and produce reports based on this information for ONA and other Australian and allied government agencies. The centre team is experienced in exploiting social media.

Imagery Intelligence

The Defence Imagery and Geospatial Organisation (DIGO) has the responsibility to provide Geospatial Intelligence (GEOINT), from imagery and other sources, in support of the ADF and national security interests. Its primary imagery source is commercial satellite imagery. Two sources are capable of providing imagery in the Singapore region:

- *Satellite imagery* is provided by the French Pleiades satellite, which produces both visible and multispectral imagery. Visible imagery is very good quality (40 cm resolution), and multispectral imaging is at 1 m resolution. The satellite can acquire imagery anywhere within an 800-km-wide ground strip. It does strip mapping with a 20-km-wide swath and can produce stereo imagery. Imaging requests for a specific target must be submitted at least twenty-four hours in advance.
- *Unmanned aerial vehicle (UAV) imagery* is available from a special source. Pursuant to an agreement between the governments of Australia and Malaysia, two imagery-equipped UAVs operate from a clandestine airstrip near Pengerang, at the tip of the Malay Peninsula on the Singapore Strait. The two Israeli-produced Hermes 900 all-weather UAVs have a payload capacity of 300 kg and can operate for up to thirty hours at 18,000 feet altitude with an airspeed of 105 knots. Both are equipped with a high-resolution video camera capable of imaging at 20 cm resolution. The two-band video (visible and near infrared) is downlinked to the Pengerang site. The primary purpose of the operation is to monitor ship traffic in the Singapore Strait. The terms of the agreement require that all image products be shared with both countries.

Human Intelligence

Unilateral Operations   The Australian Secret Intelligence Service (ASIS) conducts HUMINT operations outside Australia and maintains a base in Singapore. Because of the value of IMDEX as a source of intelligence, ASIS has set up a HUMINT team at a safe house in Singapore for the purpose of doing real-time source tasking and for collecting intelligence during IMDEX. The team includes the Australian Naval Attaché in Singapore and two ASIS case officers with experience at collection during previous IMDEX conventions. In addition, the following collection assets may be available for priority collection requirements:

- An agent, code-named GRAYMANE, is a service technician with Singapore Telecommunications (SingTel). His job allows him to access commercial business telephone and Internet communications. He has a past record of success at emplacing telephone taps and cyber collection equipment in commercial facilities.
- A surreptitious entry team can acquire material from locked rooms and safes or clandestinely emplace audio and video surveillance devices. Team operations in Singapore are considered to be high-risk collection efforts, since the discovery of the team during an operation would be politically embarrassing for the Australian government. Therefore, all team operations must be approved in advance by a senior ASIS official, based on an evaluation of risk versus payoff.

Liaison Operations   The IMDEX HUMINT team maintains close ties to two ongoing multilateral liaison operations:

- A counternarcotics team comprised of intelligence officers from Indonesia, Singapore, Malaysia, and Australia meets weekly in the offices of the Internal Security Department (Singapore's domestic intelligence agency) to share intelligence about drug trafficking in the region. Reporting from these meetings carries the code name PARADIGM.
- A counterterrorism team comprised of intelligence officers from Singapore, Thailand, Malaysia, and Australia meets weekly in the offices of the Internal Security Department to share intelligence about terrorist group activity in the region. Reporting carries the code name PARADOX.

The ASIS station also maintains a liaison relationship with the Singapore Police Force.

INTELLIGENCE REPORTS

Source/Date-Time Group	Text
HUMINT April 2007	In January 2007, a San Diego company, SeaPath Salvage, attempted to purchase the prototype stealth vessel *Sea Shadow*, which was being offered to the highest bidder by the U.S. navy. Investigation determined that SeaPath Salvage was a shell company controlled by the Almaz Central Marine Design Bureau, headquartered in St. Petersburg, Russia. The navy declined the offer. (Source: NATO Counterintelligence Summary, April 2007)

(Continued)

(Continued)

Source/Date-Time Group	Text
HUMINT May 2012	During July 2011, a cyber collection effort bypassed the firewall of the Umoe Mandal shipbuilding company, located in Mandal, Norway. Umoe Mandal specializes in producing high-speed naval vessels such as the Skjold-class coastal corvettes. During a period extending from July through August 2011, the hackers downloaded approximately 2,400 files on ship designs and construction technology. The collection effort has the earmarks of past cyber collection efforts by Russia's intelligence service, the Foreign Intelligence Service of the Russian Federation (SVR RF). (Source: NATO Counterintelligence Summary, May 2012)
HUMINT November 12, 2014	The United Wa State Army (UWSA), headquartered in Myanmar and one of Southeast Asia's largest drug-producing and drug distribution entities, is attempting to expand its narcotics operations into Indonesia, the Philippines, and Australia. UWSA founder Bao Yuxiang does not have the means to deliver the drugs, however. He has rejected the idea of air shipments because the risk of seizure is too great and has opted to make the deliveries by small boat to clandestine locations in the region. He reportedly is considering cigarette boats (aka "go fast" boats) because of their high speed. (Source: PARADIGM reporting)
HUMINT May 10, 2015	The Indonesian terrorist group Jemaah Islamiyah recently established a small cell in a residence on Bedok Ria Drive in Singapore, near the rail yard and expo center. The Singapore police are monitoring the cell's activities. (Source: PARADOX reporting)
HUMINT May 16, 2015	The Russian boat (named *Taina*) arrived sometime during the night of May 15. The boat currently is anchored in Singapore harbor, approximately 200 m from Pulau Bukum (see Figure 10.2). Most of the deck is covered with canvas that extends down to the waterline. Overall size is approximately 40 m in length and 15 m in width. A single armed guard is visible on the deck. (Source: Case officer serving as harbor observer)
HUMINT May 16, 2015	Suspected Burmese drug trafficker Aik Hauk arrived in Singapore with an entourage on May 15. He currently is staying at the Pan Pacific Singapore hotel. (Source: PARADIGM reporting)
HUMINT May 17, 2015	The Australian naval attaché inquired of an IMDEX director as to the possibility of seeing the *Taina*. The Russian advance

Source/Date-Time Group	Text
	coordinator had previously told the director that they do not plan to showcase their patrol boat at the warships display along with the other exhibitors. Instead, they plan to invite a select set of guests onboard sometime during the conference and to take the *Taina* out into the Straits of Malacca for a performance demonstration. The Russian refused to say when the demonstration was to take place or who would be invited, explaining that those decisions had not yet been made.
HUMINT May 17, 2015	Three IMDEX exhibitors are registered from the Almaz Central Marine Design Bureau: the *Taina*'s designer, Sergei Yezhov, Valery Golovin (no title), and sales representative Viktor Vetrov. All Russian attendees are staying at the Pan Pacific Singapore Hotel. (Source: IMDEX exhibitor list)
IMINT May 18, 2015	On its May 17 morning pass over Singapore, the Pleiades satellite obtained an image of the Russian patrol craft. The deck appeared to slant downward away from the centerline toward the water on either side and was covered with a highly reflective material. Visible on the deck, uncovered, was a single cabin, 4 × 5 m in size. See the sketch in Figure 10.3. (Source: French Pleiades satellite imagery)
HUMINT May 18, 2015	Surveillance was conducted on the *Taina*'s daytime guard, Igor, beginning at 1800 local time. An unidentified Russian, presumably the nighttime guard, was taken to the boat on a harbor launch and Igor was aboard on the return trip. Igor spent the evening drinking at Harry's Bar on Boat Quay, a sleazy nightspot that features a live jazz band and jam sessions. Igor was observed to drink heavily and to converse with other bar patrons. He claimed to have arrived in a "fancy boat" a few days ago. In response to a patron's question about where the rest of the crew was, Igor replied that they had to stay at the embassy. After a stay in a local hotel, Igor replaced the nighttime guard at 0600 local time on May 18. (Source: Case officer reporting)
COMINT May 18, 2015	The information came from a cell phone conversation between "Vadim" in Singapore and "Arkady" in St. Petersburg. Vadim complained that there wasn't enough time to do the full demonstration if he had to follow the planned course. Arkady replied, "We have to maintain the appearance of our cover. Head west until you are clear of the harbor and then take up a course to the demonstration area. You're in charge of this. Don't mess it up. Leave early if you must." (Source: KITEFIN reporting)

(Continued)

(Continued)

Source/Date-Time Group	Text
HUMINT May 18, 2015	The source conducted surveillance of visitors to the Russian hospitality suite, located in the Pan Pacific Singapore Hotel, on May 18. At 1745, three Russians who had manned the exhibit that day arrived: Sergei, Valery, and Viktor. There were approximately forty-five visitors to the suite during the evening, some arriving singly, some in small groups. At about 1840, the source recognized a visitor to the suite: Aik Hauk, escorted by three bodyguards. Hauk spent approximately two hours in the hospitality suite before departing with his guards. (Source: Case officer reporting)
OSINT Biographic Report May 19, 2015	Aik Hauk is the managing director of Yangon Airways. He also is a member of the UWSA, headquartered in Myanmar, and one of Southeast Asia's largest drug-producing and drug distribution entities. Hauk is the son-in-law of UWSA founder Bao Yuxiang. (Source: OSINT web search)
HUMINT May 19, 2015	The source conducted surveillance of the Russian exposition booth from 0900 to 1200. At approximately 1120, a tall, gray-bearded individual in seaman's clothing approached the booth and was handed an envelope by Valery, one of the booth attendants. The seaman pulled out a nautical chart of the region around Singapore, looked at it for a minute, and began arguing in Russian with Valery. While the argument was going on, the source was able to get a look at the chart. The chart was marked with a circle centered on a point in the South China Sea approximately 60 nm east of the entrance to Singapore Strait and a line drawn from the Strait entrance to the center of the circle. The seaman apparently noticed the source's presence, hastily folded the map, and left. (The source later was able to estimate the circle's center on a duplicate of the map. The location source pointed to fell at N01° 28′ E105° 42.′) (Source: Case officer reporting)
HUMINT May 19, 2015	Surveillance continued on the Russian boat's daytime guard, Igor, beginning at 1800 local time. Igor again spent the evening drinking heavily at Harry's Bar. In response to a patron's question about how he liked guard duty, Igor replied, "It is hell. The captain—Gavrilov—he is a pig. Kicked me overboard this morning. Said I was drunk on duty. I told him, 'Vadim, you will be very, very sorry you did that.' He just laughed at me." (Source: Case officer reporting)

Source/Date-Time Group	Text
COMINT May 19, 2015	The following information came from a text message between "Vadim" and "Sergei" in Singapore: "Departure is scheduled for 0630. Notify all participants." (Source: KITEFIN reporting)
HUMINT May 19, 2015	On May 19, the Australian naval attaché invited his counterparts to a specially arranged blue-ribbon tour of selected ships in the harbor warship display during the last conference day (May 21). The naval attachés from China, Malaysia, India, and Singapore accepted. The naval attachés from Indonesia, Pakistan, and the Philippines declined, all three pleading prior commitments during that day. (Source comment: Most attachés would jump at the opportunity for this special tour because of the opportunity to obtain valuable intelligence; the refusal of the three is most unusual.)
COMINT May 19, 2015	Communication came from the Indonesian naval attaché to unidentified person in Jakarta, Indonesia; the attaché said, "The Riyadi has to be in position by 0930." In response to a question (undecipherable) from the Jakarta speaker, the attaché said, "Use zero one twenty, one zero four thirty. I'll communicate with the ship on channel 7 when we are in range." (Analyst comment: The speaker may be referring to an Indonesian Ahmad Yana class frigate named the *Slamet Riyadi*.) (Source: KITEFIN reporting)
HUMINT May 19, 2015	The source visited the Russian exposition booth and talked to Viktor Vetrov, who introduced himself as a sales representative. Vetrov inquired as to the attaché's affiliation and was given a truthful answer. Vetrov evaded answering the source's questions but gave the source a brochure outlining the *Taina*'s features. The brochure contained the same information as that posted on the Almaz Central Marine Design Bureau website. The source subsequently observed the Indonesian naval attaché in a lengthy discussion with Vetrov at the booth. The Indonesian received an invitation to the Russian hospitality suite. (Source: Naval attaché)
HUMINT May 20, 2015	Three members of the Indonesian terrorist group Jemaah Islamiyah have been observed at the IMDEX exhibition. The three visited a number of the exhibits and booths on May 19. The Singapore police continue to monitor the cell's activities. (Source: PARADOX reporting)

(Continued)

(Continued)

Source/Date-Time Group	Text
COMINT May 20, 2015	From a cell phone conversation between "Sergei" in Singapore and "Arkady" in St. Petersburg, Sergei said, "The sea state tomorrow is supposed to be 4. Will the system work with the target under those conditions? It would be very embarrassing if we missed." Arkady replied, "The target is very bright; it will stand out from the waves. Be sure that it is upright after you drop it off and everything will be fine." (Analyst comment: Sea state 4 corresponds to a wave height of 1.25 to 2.5 m. The St. Petersburg telephone number matches that of Arkady in the May 18 report.) (Source: KITEFIN reporting)
COMINT May 20, 2015	A text message from Manuel Quirino, Philippines naval attaché, to the Philippines Naval Seas Systems Command, Cavite City, said the following: "Demonstration tomorrow. Will report preliminary evaluation enroute." (Source: KITEFIN reporting)

FIGURE 10.2   Reported Anchorage Location of Patrol Boat

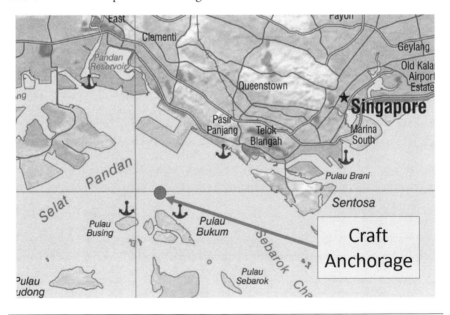

Source: Map courtesy of the University of Texas Libraries, the University of Texas at Austin. Map of Singapore from http://www.lib.utexas.edu/maps/middle_east_and_asia/singapore_physio-2005.jpg with author annotations.

FIGURE 10.3   Sketch of Patrol Boat Taken from Imagery

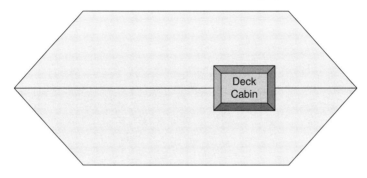

BACKGROUND READING

Stealth Ship Design

A stealth ship uses stealth technology construction techniques to make it harder to detect by radar, sonar, and infrared sensors. It relies on the technologies that came from stealth aircraft design, as well as some specialized technologies that are unique to ships such as wake and acoustic signature reduction.

The highest priority in stealth design is reducing radar cross section (RCS). Two techniques are used to reduce RCS. First, the surface of the ship is made of a material that absorbs radar energy. Second, the ship's hull is constructed to avoid right angles (which strongly reflect energy back to the radar). A commonly used approach is called the *tumblehome* design, where the ship's hull becomes narrower with greater distance above the waterline.

A prototype stealth ship using tumblehome design was the U.S. *Sea Shadow*, built in 1984. Figure 10.4 shows the design. It featured a Small Waterplane Area Twin Hull (SWATH) design. Below the water were submerged twin hulls, each with a propeller, aft stabilizer, and inboard hydrofoil. The portion of the ship above water was connected to the hulls via the two angled struts. The SWATH design helped the ship remain stable even in very rough seas.

To get speed in a stealth design, the preferred approach is a surface effect craft (which has both an air cushion, like a hovercraft, and twin hulls, like a catamaran). The premier example of this design is the Skjold-class coastal corvette, shown in Figure 10.5. These corvettes were first commissioned in 1999 by the Royal Norwegian navy. They are called coastal corvettes because their seaworthiness is comparable to that of corvettes and because they do not carry torpedoes. The Skjold class are the fastest naval vessels in existence, with a top speed of 60 knots.

The Skjold corvettes are constructed using radar absorbing glass fiber/carbon composite materials for stealth. Instead of relying on a tumblehome design, the ships use faceted surfaces that have no right angle structures in the hull.

FIGURE 10.4   Sea Shadow Stealth Ship

Source: Wikipedia, "*Sea Shadow* (IX-529)," http://en.wikipedia.org/wiki/Sea_Shadow_(IX-529).

FIGURE 10.5   Norwegian Skjold-Class Patrol Boat

Source: Wikipedia, "*Skjold*-Class Corvette," http://en.wikipedia.org/wiki/Skjold-class_patrol_boat.

Jemaah Islamiyah

The militant Islamist group Jemaah Islamiyah is active in Southeast Asia, where its goal is to establish a pan-Islamic state. The group conducted attacks against U.S. and Western targets in Singapore, Indonesia, and the Philippines. In 2000, Jemaah Islamiyah teamed with al-Qaida to conduct a series of attacks in Indonesia. The two groups coordinated bombings of churches in nine Indonesian cities on Christmas Eve, killing eighteen people and injuring scores. In 2002, the group detonated three bombs in tourist areas of Bali. In October 2005, Jemaah Islamiyah struck Bali again in a series of suicide bombings that killed 20 people and wounded 129. The group also reportedly was behind the 2009 Ritz-Carlton and JW Marriott hotel bombings in Jakarta.

Jemaah Islamiyah also has conducted or attempted attacks on Australian targets. A plot to blow up the Israeli embassy in Canberra, Australia, on May 28, 2004, was foiled. The group reportedly is responsible for a bombing outside the Australian embassy in Jakarta on September 9, 2004, which killed 11 Indonesians and wounded more than 160.

As a result of these attacks, in 2004 the federal government, in its White Paper on Terrorism, identified Jemaah Islamiyah as the principal terrorist threat to Australia. The Australian government subsequently has concluded that the group may pose a biological or chemical weapons threat.[1]

While Jemaah Islamiyah has kept a low profile in recent years, the federal government continues to regard the group as a threat to Australian interests and to the Australian homeland.

United Wa State Army

The Wa ethnic minority live mainly in Myanmar. The military junta that formerly ruled the country granted the Wa autonomy in the Shan State, near the border with China. Within that region, the Wa have created an armed force, the UWSA. The UWSA is an experienced military force comprising 30,000 full-time soldiers and 10,000 part-time militia fighters. The UWSA is equipped with modern weapons that include armored vehicles and surface-to-surface missiles (SSMs). The UWSA controls towns along the Chinese and Thai borders in northeastern Burma's Shan state.

The UWSA is known internationally for its drug trade in opium, heroin, and amphetamines. It is the main supplier of drugs to northeast India, China, and Thailand. It also is a conduit for supply of arms from the gray market in China to the insurgent groups of northeast India. The U.S. government has named the UWSA as a narcotics trafficking organization.

---

[1]"Australia Fears Jemaah Islamiyah WMD Attack, Cables Reveal," *Global Security Newswire*, February 2, 2011, http://www.nti.org/gsn/article/australia-fears-jemaah-islamiyah-wmd-attack-cables-reveal.

The UWSA also has a commercial arm, the Hong Pang Group. Hong Pang is a true conglomerate, dealing in banks, construction, hotels, logging, telecommunications, gems and minerals, and petroleum. It owns several factories and operates its own private airline.

The USWA has been increasingly pushing in recent years to upgrade its territory to the status of an officially recognized autonomous state. But the Burmese government has been increasing military pressure on the USWA using a divide-and-encircle strategy that has left the Wa in a difficult strategic position. The USWA will need substantial additional funding, probably from its narcotics trade, in order to support military operations if the Burmese government pressure continues.

11

Mara Salvatrucha

This case study is set in the year 2014. It deals with real organizations, and the scenario later in the chapter is real. The Human Intelligence (HUMINT) and Communications Intelligence (COMINT) reporting in the Intelligence Reports section is notional. The analysis and Open Source Intelligence (OSINT) reporting after September 2013 also is notional.

The Federal Bureau of Investigation (FBI) and the Washington, DC, police department have observed an increase in activity by the gang called Mara Salvatrucha (MS-13) during the past five years. Both organizations believe that the gang's numbers and propensity to commit violent crimes are increasing. They have requested a threat assessment that should include the composition of the gang locally, its connection with drug trafficking organizations (DTOs), and its possible expansion geographically.

The Washington-Baltimore High Intensity Drug Trafficking Area (HIDTA) has assembled a team of analysts who have been tasked with producing a special study of the threat posed by MS-13 that would answer the questions posed. The product will also be included in the annual Washington-Baltimore threat assessment.

Customers include local law enforcement leadership, the Washington-Baltimore HIDTA, and the FBI Safe Streets and Gang Unit.

EDUCATIONAL OBJECTIVES

This case provides an opportunity to use intelligence from source types that are not encountered in the other exercises; it includes criminal network analysis and addresses the topics of narcotics and human trafficking.

The exercise provides practical experience in the following:

- preparing a detailed problem model
- developing multiple target network models (TNMs)
- practicing Geospatial Intelligence (GEOINT) analysis
- dealing with contradictory reporting from a variety of sources in preparing an intelligence assessment

ASSIGNMENT

You are a senior intelligence analyst with the Washington-Baltimore HIDTA and have been asked to assess whether or not MS-13 in the Washington region is moving to become a third-generation gang (see the background reading for details on what qualifies as a third-generation gang). Ancillary questions that need to be addressed are as follows:

- What is the organizational structure and geographical distribution of MS-13 activity in the metropolitan region?
- What are MS-13 recruitment patterns?
- What are MS-13 communication methods?
- What are the sources of funds and methods used to conceal funding?
- What are MS-13 strategies and tactics for avoiding or countering law enforcement?

The following tasks are required for you to be able to address your customers' needs.

1. Prepare a detailed problem breakdown model. (Hint: The Background Reading subsection titled "Gang Characterization" will be helpful.)

2. Create multiple TNMs showing:
   o gang composition and external relationships
   o funds flow
   o gang activity (this will be a GEOINT model)

3. Create a predictive model about recruiting patterns and geographical spread of gang activities.

4. Prepare an assessment that answers the primary question posed (Is the Washington-Baltimore MS-13 becoming a third-generation gang?). Answer the ancillary questions listed previously, to the extent that you can.

ABBREVIATIONS AND ACRONYMS

Abbreviation or Acronym	Description
DEA	Drug Enforcement Administration (United States)
DTO	drug trafficking organization
COMINT	Communications Intelligence
FBI	Federal Bureau of Investigation (United States)
GEOINT	Geospatial Intelligence
HIDTA	High Intensity Drug Trafficking Area (United States)

Abbreviation or Acronym	Description
HUMINT	Human Intelligence
IASC	International Assessment and Strategy Center
MS-13	Mara Salvatrucha
NLS	Normandie Loco Salvatrucha (MS-13 clique)
OSINT	Open Source Intelligence
SLS	Sailors Locos Salvatruchos (MS-13 clique)
TNM	target network model
WLS	Western Locos Salvatrucha (MS-13 clique)

SCENARIO

MS-13 is a transnational criminal gang. MS-13 was formed in Los Angeles by Salvadoran immigrants during the 1980s. Since then, the gang has spread to other parts of the United States, Canada, Mexico, and Central America. Originally comprised only of Salvadorans, MS-13 now has members from all of Mexico and Central America. The FBI estimates that more than 70,000 MS-13 gang members now operate in Central America and the United States. Most gang members in the United States are concentrated in California, New York, Virginia, and the District of Columbia.

The Washington-Baltimore HIDTA has provided the following assessment of MS-13:

MS-13 members are known to be involved in all aspects of criminal activity. Because of their ties to their former homeland, MS-13 members have access to sophisticated weapons, thus making firearms trafficking one of their many criminal enterprises. Despite their access to weaponry, there have been many high-profile murders and assaults in which members have used machetes to attack their victims.

The gang is heavily involved in burglaries, auto thefts, narcotics sales, home-invasion robberies, weapons smuggling, illegal firearm sales, carjackings, extortion, murder, rape, prostitution, assault, and witness intimidation. While MS-13 victims are usually rival gang members, incidents have included innocent civilians. The gang constantly creates and runs into turf wars with other gangs because of its aggressive recruitment of new members and expansion into new areas. Currently, the gang's biggest rivalry is with other Hispanic gangs: 18th Street, South Side Locos (SSL) and Street Thug Criminals.

MS-13 members identify themselves through various gang indicators such as tattoos, clothing, graffiti, and hand signals. MS-13 members are known to use various tattoos, some of which are large enough to cover the entire back; others are small enough to fit in the web of a hand. The size of the tattoo is sometimes an indication of the degree of gang involvement with older or more active members wearing the larger, more prominent tattoos. Gang members directly from El Salvador generally have more prominent tattoos than those who become members in the United States.

MS-13 members may represent the number 13 using Arabic numerals, Roman numerals, or a combination of the two. "MSXIII" is also often used. Members may attempt to disguise the MS-13 tattoo within another one.

Gang members may carry or wear a blue or black bandana around the wrist, neck, or forehead. They often wear sports clothing that displays strategic numbers like 13, 23, or 3. They also wear jerseys that show the gang colors of blue or black. Some of their favorite jerseys are those of Allen Iverson (blue 3) and Kurt Warner (blue 13). Members also wear Nike Air Jordan hats with the Air Jordan logo resembling their hand signal. New York Yankees apparel is also a favorite of members. (It is important to understand that many young people wear these colors and sport clothing, and these indicators alone should not be viewed as evidence of gang membership.)

Graffiti is used by MS-13 to mark territory or to promote its image, particularly in a new area. This graffiti can be elaborate or just a scrawl to publicize their presence. Members may scrawl "MS," "Mara Salvatrucha," "MS-13," or "MSXIII," or they may tag their clique's initials.

MS-13 members use several different hand signals, including devil's horns or gang's initials. Other hand signals are used to communicate silently with one another. MS gang members often use the Spanish word *sureno,* meaning "southerner" to identify themselves.

The gang is known to heavily recruit school-aged members between ten years of age and up. Gang members are known to hang around middle and high schools to lure prospective members with "skip parties" that offer sex, alcohol, and drugs.

Membership must continually be earned. In severe cases, failure to carry out an order or mission has resulted in death.

Once a member, it is very difficult to leave the gang without severe consequences. One of the only exceptions to participation is if a member has a child and wants to start a family.[1]

MS-13 operations in the Washington-Baltimore area date to the 1990s. From its beginning among the Salvadoran population in Northern Virginia, the gang expanded into Maryland and the District of Columbia. Figure 11.1 shows the estimated areas of gang activity as of 2012.

---

[1]Washington-Baltimore High Intensity Drug Trafficking Area, "Mara Salvatrucha (MS-13)," http://www.hidtagangs.org/Gangs/MS13.aspx.

FIGURE 11.1   Mara Salvatrucha Past Activity in the Washington Metropolitan
Area

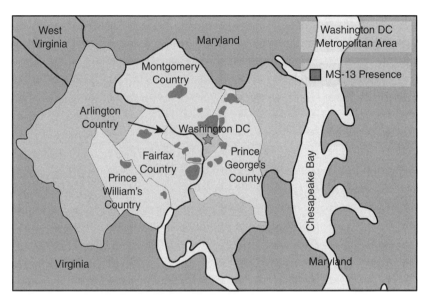

MS-13 has a hierarchical organizational structure. The fundamental MS-13 unit
is the *clica* (clique), which typically has between 10 and 30 members but can range
as high as 100 members. Within its neighborhood, the clica is basically autonomous.

The *clicas* are grouped into larger blocs called *programas,* [programs] with mid-
level leaders known as *palabreros,* who have authority over several dozen *clicas.*
Above them is a *ranflero,* who is generally in prison but whose orders are passed
on and obeyed. Above the *ranfleros* are the *jefes nacionales,* a small group of
national leaders who have the ultimate authority on issues that affect the entire
structure. Within this structure, local gang leaders have considerable autonomy
in deciding which criminal activities to engage in as a clique or group of cliques,
how to distribute criminal proceeds, and which non-gang [transnational criminal
organizations] to work with. Each *clica* is responsible for its own financial well-
being, and thus can decide how to raise that money: through extortions; "taxing"
of local businesses and those who transit the neighborhoods they control for
commerce (vendors, gas suppliers, beer trucks etc.); *narco menudeo* or the small
scale retail of cocaine and crack; and, contract assassinations and other activities.[2]

---

[2]Douglas Farah and Pamela Phillips Lum, "Central American Gangs and Transnational Criminal
Organizations," February 2013, pp. 6–7, http://www.strategycenter.net/docLib/20130224_
CenAmGangsandTCOs.pdf.

There are a number of reports suggesting that MS-13 has the characteristics of a third-generation gang. MS-13 does not have any known connections to terrorist groups, but it has a number of the same traits. It is willing, for example, to use indiscriminate violence, intimidation, and coercion internationally. In the United States, the gang's presence in multiple states and its pattern of criminal activities are indicators that the gang may be moving toward third-generation status.

INTELLIGENCE REPORTS

Source/Date-Time-Group	Text
Analysis November 2007	A Congressional Research Service report concludes that MS-13 appears to be involved in sophisticated transnational activity that characterizes third generation gangs. The report argues that the Maras have "transcended operating on localized turf with a simple market focus to operate across borders and challenge political structures."[3] The report concludes that MS-13 now is strong enough to compete with Mexican DTOs.
OSINT August 2010	MS-13 is well established in the District of Columbia and the surrounding states. The gang is firmly established in Virginia's Fairfax and Arlington counties and has a presence in Prince George's County and Montgomery County, Maryland. Officials believe there are between 1,500 to 3,000 MS-13 members in the metropolitan region. (Source: Geoffrey Ramsey, "Tracking El Salvador's Mara Salvatrucha in Washington, DC," October 12, 2012, http://www.insightcrime.org/investigations/tracking-el-salvadors-mara-salvatrucha-in-washington-dc)
Analysis June 6, 2011	The National Drug Intelligence Center analysts have concluded that MS-13 seems to be increasing its coordination with MS-13 chapters in Los Angeles, Washington, DC/Northern Virginia, and New York City, possibly signalling an attempt to build a national command structure. (Source: U.S. Department of Justice, "National Drug Threat Assessment 2011")
OSINT October 3, 2011	MS-13 has two major cliques that work together in the Washington, DC, region. The Western Locos Salvatrucha, or WLS, operates in northern Fairfax County and Loudoun County. The Normandie Loco Salvatrucha, or NLS, operates in Prince George's County, Maryland, and parts of Fairfax County. (Source: HIDTA reporting)
Analysis December 2, 2011	There are currently six major MS-13 cliques in the Washington area that maintain close ties to the gang's

[3]Congressional Research Service, "The MS-13 and 18th Street Gangs: Emerging Transnational Gang Threats?" November 2, 2007, http://fpc.state.gov/documents/organization/94863.pdf.

Source/Date-Time-Group	Text
	founders in El Salvador. One of them, the "Sailors Locos Salvatruchos (SLS)," was established in 2005 as a subunit of an MS-13 unit based in San Miguel, El Salvador. "Some SLS operations are done for their clique, and some are for their partners in El Salvador," the report concludes. (Source: Assessment by police gang unit in Prince George's County)
OSINT June 2, 2012	Marijuana and cocaine dealers in Baltimore paid $1.2 million to MS-13 members for drugs, according to prosecutors. Wade Coats and James Bostic of Baltimore paid the money to MS-13 member Jose Cavazos of Prince George's County, Maryland. Investigators seized two suitcases containing $610,000 cash and recorded a meeting in which Bostic paid Cavazos more than $590,000 for marijuana and cocaine. (Source: *Washington Post,* June 2, 2012)
HUMINT June 5, 2012	Source reports that Marvin Geovanny Monterrosa Larios (alias "Enano") and Moises Humberto Rivera Luna (alias "Santos") coordinate the MS-13 strategy in the Washington, DC, area. The two are planning a regional coalition of cliques. MS-13 leadership in El Salvador is pushing the formation of regional grouping of cliques (known as "programs"). The Washington, DC, area program is to be called "La Hermandad," or "the Brotherhood." (Source: Informant, code-named Perco, MS-13 member)
HUMINT June 6, 2012	Many MS-13 members in southern Maryland work for local landscape management companies. In that role, they are able to target homes for subsequent burglary by other gang members. (Source: Informant, code-named El Ratón, MS-13 member)
HUMINT July 8, 2012	MS-13 runners make use of several drug concealment techniques in vehicles. The preferred method in the past had been to use natural voids and after-market compartments created in vehicles. Because these compartments were increasingly being targeted by police, runners are using spare tires and gas tanks to transport marijuana. Gas tanks are the preferred method for transporting liquid methamphetamine. (Source: Informant, code-named Perco, MS-13 member)
HUMINT October 11, 2012	Local "cliques" in the Washington, DC, area maintain close contact with MS-13 in El Salvador. The local cliques send a share of their profits from criminal operations to the El Salvador leadership. They also coordinate with El Salvador on planned hits of suspected police informants and rival gang members. Each clique has about 60 to 100 members; WLS has roughly 93 members. (Source: Informant El Pavo)

(Continued)

(Continued)

Source/Date-Time-Group	Text
Analysis October 12, 2012	An independent assessment concludes that "the maras are too spread out and their leadership structures are too weak to amount to a true transnational criminal organization. Instead of conceptualizing MS-13 as a hierarchical group based in Central America, they should be seen instead as 'franchises,' with local interests taking precedence over international coordination."[4]
HUMINT December 6, 2012	The Washington, DC, MS-13 is collaborating with the Mexican drug cartel Los Zetas to gain tactical training and weapons. In return, the Brotherhood provides intelligence and functions as a network for drug distribution. Reportedly, the Brotherhood is trying to establish a similar relationship with a Nigerian drug cartel. (Source: Informant, code-named Perco, MS-13 member)
HUMINT December 14, 2012	MS-13 is making increasing use of the Internet for a number of purposes: for communicating with each another; intimidating police and rival gang members; and handling prostitution, extortion, drug trafficking, money laundering, and identity theft. (Source: Informant, code-named El Ratón, an MS-13 member)
Analysis January 2, 2013	"Drug rips" are occurring more frequently within the metro Washington area. These violent encounters typically involve one drug dealer or DTO stealing a drug load from another individual or group. In November 2012, there was at least one attempted "drug rip" that occurred in Virginia. An area enforcement group was conducting a controlled delivery, following an eighteen-wheeler loaded with 300 pounds of marijuana. Gunmen in three sport utility vehicles cut off and ambushed the tractor trailer. They opened fire on the driver, killing him. A Loudoun County sheriff's deputy was also wounded as law enforcement and the gunmen exchanged fire. At least three of the gunmen were MS-13 members. (Source: U.S. Drug Enforcement Administration [DEA] reporting)
HUMINT February 2, 2013	The MS-13 WLS clique derives its funding primarily from smuggling drugs and illegal aliens. It also collects funds from extortion, kidnapping, and murder for hire. (Source: Informant, code-named El Pavo)
HUMINT February 6, 2013	MS-13 collects protection money from three prostitution organizations operating in Arlington, Virginia. In exchange

[4]Geoffrey Ramsey, "Tracking El Salvador's Mara Salvatrucha in Washington, DC," October 12, 2012, http://www.insightcrime.org/investigations/tracking-el-salvadors-mara-salvatrucha-in-washington-dc.

Source/Date-Time-Group	Text
	for payments, gang members allow the prostitution services to operate in the area. The owner of one prostitution service told police that he was convinced the gang would kill him if he did not pay. (Source: Fairfax County Police)
OSINT February 13, 2013	The Salvadoran national police link at the Salvadoran embassy in Washington, DC, receives an average of 6.3 reports of transnational extortions of U.S.-based Salvadorans by gangs in their homeland each month, based on 2012 data, with payment demands usually ranging from $200 to $3,000.[5] (Source: *La Prensa Grafica*)
HUMINT February 25, 2013	Leaders of the Brotherhood communicate regularly with MS-13 leaders incarcerated in El Salvador and frequently send them funds via international money wire transfers. (Source: Informant, code-named El Pavo, an MS-13 member)
HUMINT March 2, 2013	MS-13 members are making use of free smartphone applications that allow members to talk back and forth using a walkie-talkie type feature. They allow members to send instant audio, text, photo, and location messages to each other. Members prefer to use the applications that have an integrated geolocation feature because of its value in executing operations. (Source: Informant, code-named El Ratón, an MS-13 member)
OSINT March 5, 2013	MS-13 leaders in DC "have expressed interest in setting up cliques in Chile, Peru, Spain, and Argentina, among other countries. According to the report, gang members facing deportation from the United States are being instructed to falsely declare that one of these countries is their country of origin, thus gaining a 'free ride' to the country, and helping the MS-13 to increase its presence there." (Source: International Assessment and Strategy Center [IASC] report, http://www.strategycenter.net/docLib/20130224_CenAmGangsandTCOs.pdf)
HUMINT March 12, 2013	An unidentified MS-13 member in Virginia is providing misleading information to local law enforcement officials. The decision to have the member act as a "double agent" was ordered by a gang leader named "Cobra" located in El Salvador. (Source: Informant, code-named Perco, MS-13 member)

(Continued)

[5]InSight Crime, "Phone Tap Shows U.S.-El Salvador MS13 Connections," October 29, 2013, http://www.insightcrime.org/news-briefs/phone-call-highlights-el-salvador-gang-connection-with-us.

(Continued)

Source/Date-Time-Group	Text
COMINT April 2, 2013	During a phone call originating from alias "Duck" in Fairfax, Virginia, alias "Enano," an MS-13 leader operating out of El Salvador, discovered that some members of a DC clique wanted to remove him from his position. "Enano" told "Duck" that the plot leader, alias "Kamikaze," must be "taken down" and that all participants in the plot should "be taught a lesson." (Analyst comment: The communication indicates an increasingly sophisticated command structure and has highlighted the operational links between MS-13 branches in the two countries.) (Source: FBI COMINT report)
OSINT June 6, 2013	In 2012, the U.S. Treasury labelled MS-13 a transnational criminal organization. The action froze U.S. assets of the gang and prohibited U.S. citizens and businesses from doing business with the gang. The report identified six top figures in MS-13: Jose Misael Cisneros Rodriguez, alias "Medio Millon"; Moris Alexander Bercian Manchon, alias "El Barney"; Moises Humberto Rivera Luna, alias "Santos"; Marvin Geovanny Monterrosa Larios, alias "Enano"; Enrique Borromeo Henriquez Solorzano, alias "El Diablo de Hollywood"; and Saul Antonio Turcios Angel, alias "El Trece."[6]
HUMINT June 7, 2013	Some northern Virginia MS-13 members have been designated as "runners." These "runners" frequently travel between Washington and El Salvador or Los Angeles. Some "runners" recently have been travelling to Spain and Nigeria. The source did not know what the mission of the "runners" was. (Source: Informant, code-named Perco, MS-13 member)
HUMINT August 11, 2013	An NLS-designated runner, Omar "Duck" Pato, travels to El Salvador every month to keep MS-13 leadership informed on developments in Maryland. He brings back instructions from the leadership. (Source: Informant, code-named Perco, MS-13 member)
HUMINT August 22, 2013	The source was told that members of NLS have been sent into northern Virginia because WLS members there were not "representing" or handling gang business properly. (Source: Informant, code-named El Pavo, an MS-13 member)
OSINT October 11, 2013	Police in Milan, Italy, have arrested twenty-five members of the El Salvador-based street gang known as MS-13 following

---

[6]Ibid.

Source/Date-Time-Group	Text
	an investigation into two attempted murders in 2011. Among those arrested was gang leader Josue Gerardo Isaac Flores Soto, alias "Kamikaze." The members were charged with conspiracy, assault, robbery, and illegal weapons possession. Police also seized a manual containing the gang's guidelines and financial accounts.
	Italian law enforcement officials have expressed concern that MS-13 may be expanding its presence in Europe. The arrestees reportedly had extensive contacts with MS-13 units in El Salvador and in the Washington, DC, area. (Sources: *La Prensa Grafica, La Repubblica,* and *Corriere Della Sera*)
OSINT October 12, 2013	Loudoun County police during a routine traffic stop heard a thumping noise coming from the trunk of the stopped vehicle. Law enforcement found a bound and gagged man in the trunk. He was an Arlington County resident who had been kidnapped and held captive for two to three days. This incident stemmed from a load of marijuana that the captive had failed to deliver. Two men confirmed to be MS-13 members were linked to the kidnapping and were arrested. (Source: *Washington Times*)
Analysis October 22, 2013	Crack cookies sold by MS-13 members in DC continue to look thinner and thinner and are typically 15 to 18 g, in comparison to 28 g as in the past. Investigators there say that they used to look similar to an old-fashioned sugar cookie but now tend to look more like a waffle. The Arlington (Virginia) Police Department also reported that crack cookies are now becoming "wafer thin." (Source: Law enforcement reporting)
HUMINT November 15, 2013	Melvin "Joker" Cruz, deported in 2012 after serving his jail sentence, returned to Arlington, Virginia, three months later, bringing with him six Salvadoran MS-13 members and a quantity of cocaine. He was caught late in 2012 and again deported but returned again in mid-2013. (Source: Informant, code-named Perco, MS-13 member)
HUMINT December 2, 2013	SLS leader Noe "Shorty" Cruz had one of his members volunteer for U.S. Army service in 2011. The recruit volunteered to be assigned to an army finance battalion at Cruz' direction (the source does not know the reason.). The recruit engaged in drug distribution while on duty and was caught and discharged from the army for misconduct. (Source: Informant, code-named Perco, MS-13 member)
HUMINT December 2, 2013	MS-13 members are purchasing expensive electronics, primarily smartphones, and shipping them to Los Zetas

(Continued)

(Continued)

Source/Date-Time-Group	Text
	contacts in Mexico where the goods are sold in exchange for pesos by Los Zetas. (Handler comment: This process is known as trade-based money laundering. It is typically used to launder drug funds, which are given the appearance of legitimate proceeds from a trade transaction. DTOs thereby avoid placing U.S. dollars in Mexican banks.) (Source: Informant, code-named El Ratón, an MS-13 member)
HUMINT December 3, 2013	The 2013 murder of Lisa Flores, an informant who had entered the witness protection program, was ordered by SLS leader Noe "Shorty" Cruz. (Background: Flores joined MS-13 in El Salvador at age sixteen. She travelled as a "runner" between Los Angeles, Seattle, San Diego, and Tijuana to transfer money from drug sales. After providing information to law enforcement officers in San Diego, she entered the witness protection program and moved to Virginia in an attempt to escape the gang.) The source reports that Flores was located with the help of an MS-13 member who had infiltrated the witness protection program. (Source: Informant El Pavo)
HUMINT December 8, 2013	MS-13 members hired as baggage handlers and airport employees have recently begun using commercial airlines for drug smuggling. Baggage handlers for airlines leaving Houston and Los Angeles put luggage filled with marijuana on planes bound for Washington Dulles International Airport. In Washington, the bags are unloaded and taken out of the airport using an employee exit. The informant did not know which airlines were used for the shipments. (Source: Informant, code name El Ratón, an MS-13 member)
OSINT December 19, 2013	Two Fairfax County police officers were arrested yesterday for gang-related crimes. Both were reportedly members of MS-13. One officer was involved in the cover-up of a $772,000 bank robbery; the officer shot and framed another person for the robbery. The second officer stole and resold cocaine having at least $800,000 street value from evidence lockers. (Source: *Washington Post*)
HUMINT January 3, 2014	The source reports that "Enano" and "Santos" are insisting that the Brotherhood stop the intergang violence and lower their profile so that law enforcement will back off. The 2013 government-facilitated truce between MS-13 leaders and their rivals in Barrio 18 in El Salvador has benefited MS-13 in El Salvador, and the two leaders believe that it will work in Washington as well.

Source/Date-Time-Group	Text
	The gangs' enforcement of the cease-fire in El Salvador, and the heightened status and positive press that they received from the agreement, resulted in dramatically reduced law enforcement against gang activity. (Source: Informant, code-named Perco, MS-13 member)
HUMINT January 4, 2014	The Brotherhood has created a website and invited visitors to the site to send tweets and use their Facebook site to follow or "like" them. The website depicts pictures of gang members with large amounts of cash and expensive cars. The site highlights the advantages of gang membership and is intended to attract prospective new members. (Source: Informant, code-named El Ratón, an MS-13 member)
Cyber January 5, 2014	An MS-13 website has links to YouTube where several hundred videos show gang members flashing hand signals and displaying signature graffiti and tattoos. The videos include rap songs and photos of celebrities who have been associated with the gangs. Other videos include commercially produced television clips that depict crimes committed by MS-13, prison connections, tattoos, signs, and other related activities. (Source comment: The videos seem to have a recruitment purpose, in that they glamorize gang life.) (Source: FBI cyber operation)
Analysis January 5, 2014	Drug investigators throughout the Washington, DC, area reported that, with increasing frequency, they are seeing "lead" and "follow" vehicles, traveling with a "load" vehicle. These additional escort vehicles are being used as "distracters" to keep law enforcement from focusing on the vehicle carrying narcotics. Drug investigators reported that the additional vehicles are also being used for countersurveillance of law enforcement.
HUMINT January 6, 2014	On January 2, SLS leader "Shorty" Cruz met with Nuhu Buhari, a lieutenant of Nigerian drug lord Joseph Nwafor. Buhari offered a deal to sell supplies of very pure heroin to the SLS for resale. The price quoted was too high, and Shorty rejected the deal. (Source: Informant, code-named El Pavo, an MS-13 member)
HUMINT January 7, 2014	Report of surveillance on informant El Pavo: After meeting with the handler to provide information on a Nigerian drug lord transaction, El Pavo travelled directly to a meeting with WLS leader "Shorty" Cruz at the Restaurant El Salvador in Arlington, Virginia. The two men talked for about fifty-five minutes and then left separately. Cruz seemed pleased with the result of the meeting and hugged El Pavo before leaving.

(Continued)

(Continued)

Source/Date-Time-Group	Text
Cyber January 8, 2014	MS-13 in the Washington, DC, area is apparently using bitcoins in international drug traffic transactions. In the past four months, we have observed a major increase in bitcoin traffic between an MS-13-controlled computer in Arlington, Virginia, and the Bishop Company, a UK subsidiary of Trojan Enterprises, owned by Joseph Nwafor, a Nigerian. Intelligence has linked Nwafor to drug running in the past. Bitcoin transfers between MS-13 and the Bishop Company currently are averaging approximately $1.5 million each month. (Source: DEA cyber operations center)
COMINT January 15, 2014	Salvadoran nationals Marvin Geovanny Monterrosa Larios and Moises Humberto Rivera Luna (both currently imprisoned in El Salvador) authorized several killings in the Washington area during 2013. The two men communicated by cell phone with their MS-13 associates in the Washington, DC, region. The only confirmed target was Ramon Membreno Zelaya, killed on August 16, 2013; he had been trying to leave the gang, going so far as to have his gang tattoos removed. (Source: FBI)
HUMINT February 3, 2014	Currently, both WLS and NLS use Facebook, YouTube, and Twitter for communicating with each other and with other DC-area cliques. They rely mostly on blogging and video sharing. YouTube and MySpace are also used to intimidate other gangs or to form gang alliances. (Source: Informant, code-named El Ratón)

BACKGROUND READING

Gang Characterization

From a U.S. Congressional Research Service Report, "The MS-13 and 18th Street Gangs: Emerging Transnational Gang Threats?" by Celinda Franco, January 30, 2008.

Gangs can be characterized as either first generation, second generation, or third generation.

- First-generation gangs are traditional street gangs. They are turf-oriented and localized, lack sophistication, engage in unsophisticated criminal activities, and tend to have a loose leadership structure. First-generation gangs participate in opportunistic criminal activity and intergang rivalry.
- Second-generation gangs have an organized structure similar to a business. They tend to assume a market rather than a turf orientation. Gang activities

tend to be drug-centered. Such gangs tend to operate in broader areas and have a centralized leadership.

- Third-generation gangs are highly sophisticated, mercenary-type groups with goals of power or financial acquisition and a set of fully evolved political aims. They tend to operate in a global environment and may embrace terrorism to advance their goals.

Most urban gangs fit into the first- and second-generation characterizations.

Connections with Drug Trafficking Organizations

The majority of the illegal drugs sold by gangs within the Washington, DC, area, such as marijuana, methamphetamine, cocaine, and heroin, are produced in foreign countries and trafficked into and through the area from Mexico. Ecstasy is primarily imported from Canada but does enter the region from Mexico to a lesser extent. Some hydroponic marijuana ("BC Bud") is also brought into the region from Canada.

DTOs have a profitable partnership with transnational gangs such as MS-13. The arrangement provides substantial benefits to both the gangs and the drug cartels. The arrangement gives the gangs increased power and access to large quantities of inexpensive drugs. The DTOs use the gangs to expand their sales network. The MS-13 relationship with Mexican cartels varies with time and region. The closest relationship occurs when the gang serves as a U.S.-based extension of the cartel. In that arrangement, gang members take orders from the DTO leadership; acquire weapons, vehicles, and other material for the cartel; and move people and weapons into and out of the United States.

12

Defeating the Balamiran Transporter Erector Launcher and Radar

This case study takes place in a fictional setting and involves a conflict between two countries—Dalistria and Balamira. It presents a typical example of providing intelligence support to counter a system (as described in Chapter 1) that poses a military threat—in this case, the threat posed by an antiship missile (ASM) launched from a transporter erector launcher and radar (TELAR) such as that shown in Figure 12.1. This case study is about exactly that: the intelligence role in making an opponent's system of systems ineffective.

FIGURE 12.1   Transporter Erector Launcher and Radar

EDUCATIONAL OBJECTIVES

Upon completion of this case study, students will have gained experience in:

- creating a target network model (TNM) of a weapons platform system
- identifying exploitable weaknesses from a systems understanding of a major weapons platform
- applying geospatial analysis to an intelligence problem
- developing operational recommendations

ASSIGNMENT

As the lead intelligence analyst in the Dalistrian Joint Operational Command (DJOC) you have been tasked to support mission analysis for Operation Free Sailing (described in the scenario). This means you must advise the commander of the Dalistrian Task Force (DTF) about the risks associated with sailing a convoy north through the disputed Mira Straits. For this preliminary assessment of risk and viability, there is no complete operational timeline; a full concept of operations (CONOPs) will only be developed once the DJOC commander gets governmental approval to do so. The mission analysis must be presented to the government in the near future for approval before operational planning can begin.

The DJOC commander is very much aware that a confrontation with the Balamiran navy on the water is not a serious challenge, as the Balamiran navy is outmatched (see respective orders of battle). It is rather the Balamiran coastal defense cruise missile (BCDCM) network run by their navy that presents the biggest challenge to sailing a convoy through the straits. Therefore the DTF commander has requested the following, based on the intelligence provided:

1. Build a TNM that represents the BCDCM system. The model must be presentable on one slide.

2. Develop a collection plan and sensor exploitation plan that will support a continuing operational status assessment of the BCDCM network and will provide an imminent threat warning. As part of this effort, do the following:

   o Identify the observables (activities and communications) associated with the BCDCM state of readiness that can be exploited by the DTF to provide warning of an intent to attack the convoy.
   o Create a timeline that shows the process from normal BCDCM status to missile launch.
   o Describe the BCDCM collection that is needed to provide warning of an imminent attack. Include details that specify sensor types and target

locations. (Hint: Imagery Intelligence [IMINT] and Electronic Intelligence [ELINT] are especially useful against CDCM targets.)

3. Develop options for the commander's consideration on how to defeat the BCDCM, based on the results of 2. As part of the options, identify a general (not specific) timeline window for the operation to be launched in order to have the best chance of success.

4. Suggest, in very general detail, a route for the convoy to follow westward through the Mira Straits.

ABBREVIATIONS AND ACRONYMS

Abbreviation or Acronym	Description
ASM	antiship missile
BPS	Balamiran People's Ship
CDCM	coastal defense cruise missile
CONOP	concept of operations
BCDCM	Balamiran coastal defense cruise missile
DJOC	Dalistrian Joint Operational Command
DRS	Dalistrian Republic Ship
DTF	Dalistrian Task Force
ELINT	Electronic Intelligence
HMG	heavy machine gun
IMINT	Imagery Intelligence
JOC	Joint Operations Command
RCDCMSB	regional coastal defense cruise missile support bases
RCV	remote-controlled vehicle
ROV	remote-operated vehicle
SAM	surface-to-air missile
SSM	surface-to-surface missile
TEL	transporter erector launcher
TELAR	transporter erector launcher and radar
TLAM	Tomahawk Land Attack Missile
TNM	target network model
VLS	vertical launching system

SCENARIO

Background: The Straits of Mira Conflict

Outside of the East-West Cold War conflict, decolonization was the single most defining dynamic of post–World War II international relations. Worldwide, the dismantling of colonial empires created a patchwork of nation-states that varied in governmental competence and national identity.

Political change in the Mira Straits was swift and uncharacteristically violence-free. Normarkistan, the colonial power in the region, recognized by 1990 that its historic domination of the Mira Straits was ultimately unsustainable. It sought an agreed-upon accommodation with the regional elites campaigning for autonomy or independence. In so doing, Normarkistan was able to disengage at a limited fiscal cost and without having to use its military and police forces to suppress public dissent.

The latter point was central in Normarkistan attempting to maintain close—and profitable—relations with its new neighbors. In this, Normarkistan was largely successful, but after attempting to mediate the regional disputes through the 1990s, it retreated to neutrality by the late 1990s—a position it maintains in the current disputes between Balamira and Dalistria concerning ownership of the Mira Straits.

Balamiran campaigns for autonomy led to the independence of the two countries, though with varying degrees of enthusiasm. Balamira was the most vocally nationalist, with a large Muslim majority historically supporting greater independence. Dalistria did not seek independence but opted for it when it was clear that self-determination was preferable to remaining the sole Normarkistan colony.

Partition itself was quick and notably unjust, with the biggest loser being Dalistria, which lost both its northern industrial heartland and several western counties that had a Dalistrian majority population at the time of partition. Figure 12.2 shows the current national boundaries between the two countries. Balamira was the largest winner at Dalistria's expense, and relations between the Dalistrian administration and the

FIGURE 12.2 Disputed Straits of Mira

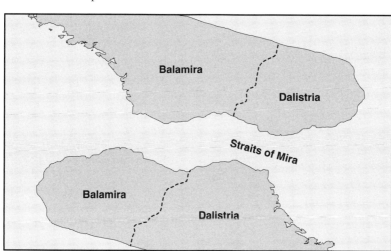

Balamiran government have long been strained over this issue. Balamira has accused Dalistria of sponsoring separatism along its southeastern border and in retaliation has denied Dalistrian shipping access to the Straits of Mira.

The Dalistrian government knows that the situation is not tenable, as the unilateral closing of the straits by Balamira will completely undermine the Dalistrian economy. And though the international courts would probably judge in their favor, the likely ten-year wait for a court ruling would result in irreparable damage to the Dalistrian economy. Therefore, the Dalistrian government has asked its military to prepare a military operation to force the issue. It calls for the Dalistrian navy to sail a small fleet of Dalistrian cargo vessels in a convoy north through the Mira Straits. If the Balamiran navy tries to block the straits, the Dalistrian navy is directed to do whatever is necessary to push through. However, the rules of engagement will likely be only to open fire to defend the cargo vessels and/or in self-defense. The Dalistrian government has asked the Joint Operations Command (JOC) to put together an initial mission analysis for assessment of an eventual operation under the designation "Operation Free Sailing." The mission analysis must be presented to the government in the near future for approval before operational planning actually begins.

Dalistrian Republic Navy Order of Battle

Ship	Speed and Size	Armament
Dalistrian Republic Ship (DRS) NESTRIAL	30/18 kn,[1] L: 209 m, B: 36 m, D: 7.6 m	3xAH-64D, 3xSK MK4, 2xCH-47, 3xLX MK7; place for 22 helicopters in all; diverse self-defense systems
DRS PINEG	28 kn, L: 133 m, B: 16 m, D: 7.3 m	113 mm cannon (22 km); 32x Sea Wolf (13 km); 8x Harpoon (124 km); torpedoes
DRS FERALAS	28 kn, L: 133 m, B: 16 m, D: 7.3 m	1xLX MK8 helicopter; 113 mm cannon (22 km); 32x Sea Wolf (13 km); 8x Harpoon (124 km); torpedoes
DRS RONIN	29 kn, L: 152 m, B: 21 m, D: 7.4 m	1xLX MK8 helicopter; 113 mm cannon (22 km); Aster 15 surface-to-air missiles (SAMs) (30 km); Aster 30 SAMs (120 km)
DRS PLAT	30 kn, L: 154 m, B: 20 m, D: 9.4 m	127 mm cannon (24 km); 1 × 29 cell, 1 × 61 cell Mk 41 vertical launching system (VLS) med 90x Tomahawk Land Attack Missile (TLAM), BGM 109 Tomahawk (1.700 km); torpedoes
DRS MILTIRA	30 kn, L: 154 m, B: 20 m, D: 9.4 m	127 mm cannon (24 km); 1 × 29 cell, 1 × 61 cell Mk 41 VLS med 90x TLAM, BGM 109 Tomahawk (1.700 km); torpedoes

[1]Knot (kn) is the speed equal to 1 nautical mile per hour (1.852 km/hr).

Ship	Speed and Size	Armament
DRS TORMENTER	30 kn, L: 154 m, B: 20 m, D: 9.4 m	2xMH-60R helicopter; 127 mm cannon (24 km); 1 × 29 cell, 1 × 61 cell Mk 41 VLS med 90x TLAM, BGM 109 Tomahawk (1.700 km); torpedoes
DRS MITEN	29 kn, L: 130 m, B: 15 m, D: 4.7 m	1xCH-124 helicopter; 76 mm cannon (16 km); 1 × 29 cell Mk 41 VLS med 29x RIM-66 Standard SAM (170 km); torpedoes
DRS VETEREN	30 kn, L: 134 m, B: 16.5 m, D: 7.1 m	1xCH-124 helicopter; 57 mm cannon (8,5 km); 24x Mk 46 torpedoes; 16x Sea-Sparrow SAM (50 km); 8x Harpoon (124 km)
DRS CONTINUE	20 kn, L: 172 m, B: 23 m, D: 10 m	Helicopter deck with place for 3x helicopters; diverse self-defense systems
DRS RITRIA	20 kn, L: 206 m, B: 27 m, D: 11 m	Helicopter deck; diverse self-defense systems
DRS PROVISION	K15 kn, L: 91 m, B: 17 m, D: 5.5 m	2x 20 mm cannon
DRS TOBRIA	17 kn, L: 60 m, B: 9,8 m, D: 2.2 m	30 mm cannon; SeaFox mine disposal system; diver-placed explosive charges
DRS FOBRIA	17 kn, L: 60 m, B: 9.8 m, D: 2.2 m	30 mm cannon; SeaFox mine disposal system; diver-placed explosive charges
DRS CONRIA	17 kn, L: 60 m, B: 9.8 m, D: 2.2 m	30 mm cannon; SeaFox mine disposal system; diver-placed explosive charges
DRS DALA	13 kn, L: 52.5 m, B: 11 m, D: 2.3 m	30 mm cannon; remote-controlled vehicles (RCVs)
DRS GALA	13 kn, L: 52.5 m, B: 11 m, D: 2.3 m	30 mm cannon; RCVs

Balamira People's Navy Order of Battle

Ship	Speed and Size	Armament
Balamiran People's Ship (BPS) KINGMIRA	28 kn, L: 133 m, B: 16 m, D: 5.50 m	114 mm cannon; 8x Harpoon; 32x Seawolf; torpedoes
BPS DOMINANCE	30 kn, L: 130 m, B: 15 m, D: 6.3 m	76 mm cannon; 16x Sea Sparrow; 8x Harpoon; torpedoes
BPS COUNTERAL	30 kn, L: 139 m, B: 14 m, D: 5.7 m	100 mm cannon; 4x Exocet MM.40; 26x Crotale SAM; torpedoes

(Continued)

(Continued)

Ship	Speed and Size	Armament
BPS TIGERAL	30 kn, L: 55 m, B: 14 m, D: 2.5 m	2x 20 mm cannon; 2x 12,7 mm heavy machine gun (HMG); Mistral SAM; 2x Pluto Plus remote-operated vehicles (ROVs)
BPS STORMBALL	18 kn, L: 55 m, B: 9,2 m, D: 2.9 m	2x 40 mm L70; 2x Stinger SAM; ASQS-11 sonar
BPS FENDER	19 kn, L: 157 m, B: 21 m, D: 10.8 m	1x 40 mm cannon; 6x 12,7 mm HMG; Simbad SAM
BPS TIDALER	20 kn, L: 174 m, B: 24 m, D: 7.6 m	4x 27 mm cannon; 3x Stinger
BPS GAGE	15 kn, L: 100 m, B: 16 m, D: 4 m	2xSAM

Supplemental Intelligence Report 01: Balamiran Navy Coastal Defense Cruise Missiles

The western coastlines of the Straits of Mira are dominated by bays, promontories, lochs, and inlets, making the region ideal for the rapid deployment and redeployment of coastal defense cruise missiles (CDCMs). The Balamiran naval defensive doctrine has long recognized this and has established pre-surveyed TELAR sites along both sides of the strait. Frequently little more than a reinforced concrete hardstand with a free arc of fire, these pre-surveyed launch pads are by road and rail connected to a series of regional coastal defense cruise missile support bases (RCDCMSB). The support bases are physically no more than secured frame buildings. Seven RCDCMSB sites (assessed as probably operational) have been identified and tagged sequentially on both the east and west sides of the Mira Straits (see Figure 12.3).

The RCDCMSBs maintain an infrastructure for the support of deployed CDCMs but are themselves in need of support; the support infrastructure required for a deployment is supplied by HQ CDCM force at Holk. It is assessed that there is insufficient support equipment for all RCDCMSBs to be concurrently operational, meaning that the movement of support equipment has historically provided robust indicators and warnings of force generation.

CDCM convoy training is undertaken as a key part of the annual training cycle. Convoy protection is assigned to the Balamiran navy, but the Balamiran Special Police reportedly has taken over some high-profile convoys on the north side of the straits. The Balamiran Home Guard are responsible for the convoys on the south side of the straits, once the equipment is off-loaded from cargo ships making the run from Port Gonghi on the north side to Port Bawa on the south side.

The training support for the CDCM network is conducted at the only known test range for the surface-to-surface missiles (SSMs) located approximately 40 km north of Holk. It is known as the "Barrens."

FIGURE 12.3   Assessed Balamira Navy Regional Coastal Defense Cruise Missile Support Bases Laydown, August 2009

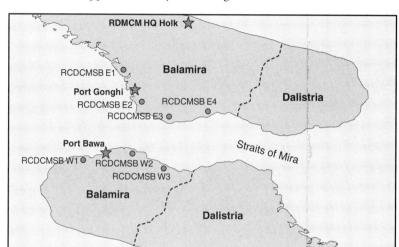

Since October 2007, six highly publicized C-802 firings and one C-704 CDCM firing have taken place on the "Barrens" ranges. These firings have been sporadic and irregular and are assessed to be more closely tied to political maneuverings than to the operational requirements.

The most noteworthy test occurred on August 4, 2009, against a target ship approximately 34 nm east of the "Barrens." At least three missiles were fired, and the target ship (Rusty) was sunk. It is unknown what, if any, signature augmentation was carried by Rusty at the time of the test.

It is assessed that Balamira has approximately 200 cruise missiles, although the exact division between C-802s and C-704s is unknown. The missiles were purchased from the People's Republic of China, and no more than twenty have been fired. It is assessed that up to thirty transporter erector launchers (TELs) were purchased in 1998 and 1999, and there have been unconfirmed open-source reports that the domestic TEL production was due to begin in 2002 and 2003. Despite the parading of an "indigenous" TEL based on a Scania R420SHK 6 × 6 chassis in 2008, it is assessed that this is a prototype only and that series production is yet to begin in Balamira.

In line with their national policy of operational independence, the Balamiran navy purchased a large number of SS-N-2 STYX ASMs. These were initially the baseline P-15 (SS-N-2A STYX-A) supplied in small numbers in the 1980s, followed by the more advanced P-15M (SS-N-2C STYX-C, shown in Figure 12.4), of which more than 300 were procured. Finally, in preparation for a midlife upgrade in the 1990s, between fifty and seventy-five of the definitive P-20M were delivered from 1992 to 2007, prior to the upgrade being cancelled. In addition, a small number of inert training simulators were provided, notably for missile loading drills.

FIGURE 12.4   Balamira Navy P.15M/SS.N.2C STYX Prior to Display in Holk,
March 2006

The operational status of the missiles is uncertain. It is assessed that the SS-N-2A STYX-A stocks were expended in trials and training no later than the early 1990s. There is no evidence that the annual training allowances could have expended upwards of 350 missiles between 1993 and 2006. Therefore, the central assessment remains that at least 200 SS-N-2C STYX-C and probably 30 to 50 P-20M remain extant.

SS-N-2 STYX ASMs are stored and maintained at Balamiran navy facilities at Holk. Reporting suggests that a basic level of maintenance continues on the missiles themselves. Importantly, operational experience has shown that the STYX is a robust design that, while not impervious to poor storage and handling, is more rugged than its western contemporaries. Consequently, it is assessed that the STYX missiles themselves could be made operational in a matter of weeks if required.

With the Chinese HY-2 SILKWORM series as lineal descendants, the STYX series has an inherent land-based CDCM launch capability. Historically, the Balamiran navy has not exploited this capability, preferring instead to rely on systems specifically procured for this role. Should the need arise—either through failure of the CDCM force or from the need to expand the number of deployed missiles—the use of STYX in the shore-based CDCM role cannot be excluded.

All Balamiran missile types, during the final 5 nm of flight, are self-guiding using their own homing radar and have difficulty distinguishing between ship types. Missiles of the same type used by Balamira that have been fired in other conflicts have hit civilian commercial shipping vessels by mistake. See Table 12.1.

Table 12.1   Balamiran Surface-to-Surface Missile Range Parameters

Surface-to-Surface Missile	Minimum	Maximum
C 802	4,5 nm	65 nm
C 704	?	20,5 nm
SSN-2C	4,5 nm	43 nm

Supplemental Intelligence Report 02: Maritime Commercial Activity

There are two major Balamiran civilian fishing areas in the straits (see Figure 12.5) that remain continuously busy with small- to medium-sized trawlers, including some very large freezer ships collecting the catch from the fishing vessels and packaging the catch so that the fishing boats can immediately refill their holds without having to return to port. Fishing season runs from April to September for the eastern fishing ground and from April to October for the western fishing ground.

A civilian ferry crossing between the Port Gonghi and the Port Bawa has a fleet of six large car ferries of which four are relatively modern and are sailing most of the time. Depending on the weather, the crossing can take up to ten or more hours. There is a reserve ferry at each port. Ferries cross each other in the middle of the straits usually between 1000 and 1400 hours and 2200 and 0200 hours. Each ferry has a capacity to carry over 800 passengers and 200 vehicles. The busiest times are usually from July to August with nice sailing weather and vacationers visiting family on either side of the strait.

FIGURE 12.5   Maritime Commercial Activity in the Straits

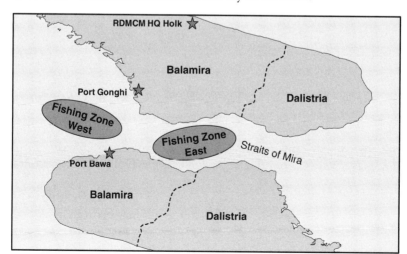

Supplemental Intelligence Report 03:
RCDCMSB Deployment and Threat Coverage

Figure 12.6 shows the threat coverage of RCDCMSB sites. Each RCDCMSB is capable of servicing up to five TELs and their predetermined launch sites that usually are within 5 km of the RCDCMSB. Though not all is known as to the role of the RCDCMSBs with regard to keeping the TELs and the launch sites operational, it is known that they require support material from the HQ in Holk before they can make ready the TELs allocated to them. It is suspected that this is also a command-and-control security measure implemented by the Balamiran government. Furthermore, it is assessed that the TELs are incapable of accurately firing the missiles without functional RCDCMSBs.

FIGURE 12.6   Estimated Ranges of the Individual Regional Coastal Defense
Cruise Missile Sites

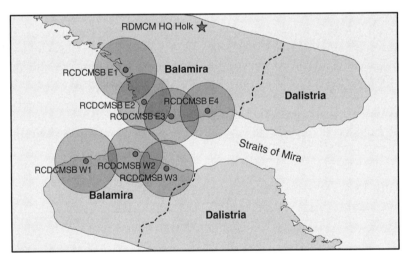

Supplemental Intelligence Report 04: Mines in the Straits of Mira

Figure 12.7 shows the known or suspected mines in the Straits. The estimate of Balamiran waterway mining includes both the older legacy mining around the old colonial power Normarkistan's naval installations as well as recent suspected mining in the Mira Straits along the disputed border between Balamira and Dalistria.

FIGURE 12.7   Suspected Mined Areas

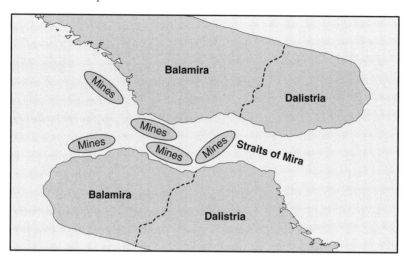

13

Horn of Africa

This case study is set in the year 2015. It uses a fictitious scenario, albeit a projection of the situation based on developments in the Horn of Africa region over the past five to ten years. It is a *netwars* scenario where an interstate conflict is made more complex by transnational militant and criminal networks.

FIGURE 13.1 The Horn of Africa

The first and last sections—Country Background and Situation and Background Reading—are factual. Although the names of actual regions, organizations, and some events are included, the remainder is notional. Any similarities with real force constructions past, present, or future, are purely coincidental. In short, adhere strictly to the knowledge provided in the following text. *Don't fight the setting!*

EDUCATIONAL OBJECTIVES

This case study presents the most complex scenario in the workbook. Its purpose is to provide advanced practice in network modeling as a structured technique for visualization and decomposition, providing practical experience in the following:

- defining threat networks
- representing threat networks in a complex operational environment to facilitate shared situational awareness (SA) and situational understanding (SU)
- managing target network models (TNMs) in order to facilitate shared SA/SU
- generating priority information requests and intelligence collection plans (ICPs)
- identifying and prioritizing targets
- practicing verbal briefings
- practicing the generation of geospatial products

ASSIGNMENT

This assignment works well using teams or individuals. You or your team represent an all-source intelligence analyst in the joint command intelligence organization (J2) at a regional alliance HQ responsible for Africa's Horn and are preparing for campaign planning support. The commander's intent is to take actions to reopen the Strait of Bab el-Mandeb and establish a safe and secure environment for humanitarian organisations. You or your team have been asked to prepare an intelligence assessment of the threat posed to this mission and a prioritized list of targets for the commander to approve.

Task 1: Intelligence Preparation of the Battlespace

1. Read the scenario and produce a TNM to represent your overall understanding of the Horn of Africa situation/battlespace based on *just the scenario reading.* Sub-TNMs may be created here to represent specific threat networks identified from the scenario. Present the TNMs in no more than five to ten minutes.

2. Read the intelligence reporting and adjust your original TNMs, and then brief once again, this time highlighting the changes made in the TNMs.

Task 2: Intelligence Collection Planning

1. Generate a list of ten key questions for your collection assets, based on your TNMs created in task 1. For example, if a smuggling network was identified in the TNM, create questions that will be put out to your collection assets to provide details of that particular threat network.

2. Read the intelligence reporting, and answer those questions that can be answered. Discuss the accuracy of the original ten ICP questions.

3. Develop a new list of ten prioritized questions. Discuss the reasoning behind prioritization of the new questions.

Task 3: Operations Planning: Effects and Target Generation

1. Assuming the commander wishes to *disrupt* the different threat networks, identify a set of targets for each threat network model.

2. Read the intelligence reporting and adjust your TNMs, populate them where possible, and adjust your list of target sets. Do a short brief, highlighting any changes, and develop a prioritized high-value target list (HVTL). An effect for each HVTL must be chosen from destroy, disrupt, or influence.

3. Discuss the HVTLs, and identify any differences between them.

Task 4: Georectification (Optional)

1. Geotag as much relevant information from your baseline TNM as possible. Present and discuss products.

2. Geotag as much relevant information from the intelligence reporting as possible. Present and discuss products.

ABBREVIATIONS AND ACRONYMS

Abbreviation or Acronym	Description
ADF	air defense fighter
AH	attack helicopter
AOTL	replenishment tanker
APC	armored personnel carrier
AQAP	al-Qaida on the Arabian Peninsula
ASCC	Army Service Component Command
ASM	antiship missile
CINC	commander in chief
COMINT	Communications Intelligence
DOCEX	Document Exploitation
FBA	fighter bomber attack

Abbreviation or Acronym	Description
FIAC	fast inshore attack craft
FOC	full operational capability
GEOINT	Geospatial Intelligence
HUMINT	Human Intelligence
HVTL	high-value target list
ICP	Intelligence Collection Plan
IRC	Internet relay chat
IVO	in vicinity of
IMINT	Imagery Intelligence
INTREP	Intelligence Report
IOC	initial operational capability
J2	Joint Command Intelligence Organization
J3	joint command operations organization
LST	landing ship tank
MANPADS	man-portable air defense systems
MASINT	Measurement and Signature Intelligence
MCC	Maritime Component Command
MHI	inshore minehunter
MR	multirole
MRL	multiple rocket launcher
MRX	multirole all-weather
MSF	steel hull fleet minesweeper
NATO	North Atlantic Treaty Organization
NGO	nongovernmental organization
OPEC	Organization of the Petroleum Exporting Countries
OSINT	Open Source Intelligence
PBF	patrol boat fast
PFDJ	People's Front for Democracy and Justice (Eritrea)
PoL	pattern of life
RPG	rocket-propelled grenade
SA	situational awareness
SAM	surface-to-air missile
SAR	synthetic-aperture radar
SAS	British Special Operations Forces
shura	Arabic word for "consultation"; the Quran encourages Muslims to decide their affairs in consultation with those who will be affected by that decision.
SIGINT	Signals Intelligence
SIM	subscriber identity module

(Continued)

Abbreviation or Acronym	Description
SSM	surface-to-surface missile
SU	situational understanding
TNM	target network model
TOW	tube launched, optically tracked, wire guided
UN	United Nations
UNHCR	United Nations High Commissioner for Refugees
UNITAF	Unified Task Force
UNK	unknown
UNOSOM II	United Nations Operation in Somalia II
UNMEE	United Nations Mission in Ethiopia and Eritrea
YRA	Yemeni Regular Army

SCENARIO

Country Background and Situation

1. Somalia   The Horn of Africa has historically been settled by nomadic tribes, organized in four or five clans. The nomadic tribes were African with a strong influence from the Arabian Peninsula due to early adoption of the Muslim faith. The southern part was settled by African animist clans.

The British colonial protectorate of Somaliland was established in the north of Somalia in the middle of 1800. In 1889, Italy bought the southern part of Somalia—henceforth, Italian Somaliland—from the Sultan of Zanzibar. In 1941, Britain invaded and took Italian Somaliland in the south after an Italian incursion into British Somaliland in the north. After the war, the territory was granted back under a United Nations (UN) mandate that the territory would gain its independence within ten years. The republic of Somalia was established in 1960 through an amalgamation of the newly independent British and Italian Somalilands. In 1961, a public vote established parliamentary rule through democratic elections. The foreign policy was neutral and free of alliances. See Figure 13.2 for a map of Somalia.

The years from 1961 to 1969 were marred by internal conflicts between northern and southern clans and border clashes with Kenya and Ethiopia. The economy stagnated, and corruption and nepotism were widespread.

In the wake of the elections in 1969, the reelected president Mohamed Ibrahim Egal was assassinated. General Mohamed Siad Barre led a subsequent military coup, and for almost twenty years, Somalia was without a democratic constitution. Mohamed Siad Barre aligned Somalia with the Soviet Union with a politic called "scientific Socialism" along Soviet lines.

The close ties with the Soviet Union were temporarily severed when Somalia invaded the Ethiopian province of Ogaden in 1977. Somalia's subsequent defeat in the Ogaden war destroyed the Somali economy, and resistance to the autocratic rule of Mohamed Siad Barre grew. The leading clans formed alliances against Barre who had to flee the country in 1991.

FIGURE 13.2   Somalia

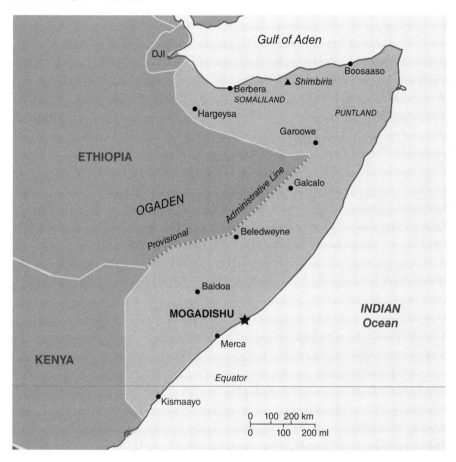

Source: CIA World Factbook.

Several clans and shifting alliances fought each other for dominance of Somali territory during the 1990s. In 1991, the northern clan declared a "Republic of Somaliland" spanning the territory of former British Somaliland. No countries have recognized the Republic of Somaliland.

In 1992, the deteriorating situation led to a UN Security Council ban on all arms exports to Somalia, and a humanitarian operation was decided upon in April after international warnings of an impending hunger disaster.

A U.S.-led intervention force, Unified Task Force (UNITAF), arrived in Somalia in December 1992 to secure the delivery of humanitarian aid. The UNITAF mission encountered heavy resistance from the clans, and regular fighting between the parties ensued. UNITAF was relieved in 1993 by United Nations Operation in Somalia II (UNOSOM II), a mission with a broader mandate. After a spectacular but failed mission in the capital of Mogadishu, the United States decided to pull out of Somalia in 1994. They were followed by the rest of the UN forces in 1995.

Since then the situation in Somalia has been one of lawlessness and anarchy. Repeated attempts to ameliorate the situation have collapsed one after another. In 1998, the autonomous region of Puntland in the northeastern part of Somalia was declared by the politician and warlord Abdullahi Yussuf Ahmed. This declaration is not recognized by the international community.

2. Yemen   Yemen has historically been a diverse country, influenced by many cultures (see Figure 13.3 for a map of Yemen). A number of city-states have thrived in the area and nomadic tribes have lived in the desert expanses. The population adopted Islam early on. The Ottoman Empire obtained a foothold in Yemeni cities for a short decade in 1547. In 1839 the harbor city of Aden was annexed by the British to support their shipping to India. They took over the northern part of the country in 1872 and controlled it until the end of the First World War.

In the wake of the decline brought on by the First World War, the Ottomans left the Arabian Peninsula in 1918, and North Yemen became an independent state under a conservative feudal rule.

South Yemen was at that time a protectorate of Britain. After an increasing insurgency campaign, Great Britain withdrew from South Yemen in 1966, and civil war broke out between the National Liberation Front, who won the conflict, and the Front for the Liberation of South Yemen. Egypt had supported the resistance against the British and subsequently supported the Front for the Liberation of South Yemen.

During the Cold War era, the Soviet Union managed to establish strong connections to South Yemen, which gradually adopted the Soviet way of organizing a society. North Yemen remained a conservative tribal society.

During the 1980s, oil deposits were discovered in North Yemen, resulting in both economic and political progress in that region. In contrast, conditions deteriorated in South Yemen after the Soviet Union withdrew its support. A civil war broke out in 1986. In 1990, there was a peaceful amalgamation of the two Yemens into the modern-day state of Yemen. The peace did not last long, though, as the South Yemeni vice president fell out with the North Yemeni president Saleh. Civil war broke out in 1994. The war ended only when the North Yemeni forces had secured the southern territory.

Yemen has a strained relationship with Saudi Arabia despite many cultural similarities. The tensions spring from territorial and political disagreements. After several years of armed border clashes between Yemen and Oman in the Rub´ al-Khali desert, a peace agreement was settled in 2000.

In 2001, a revision of the constitution of Yemen decreed that the Republic of Yemen, subdivided into nineteen provinces, was to be led by an elected president supported by a two-chamber system consisting of the house of representatives and a Shura Council.

FIGURE 13.3   Yemen

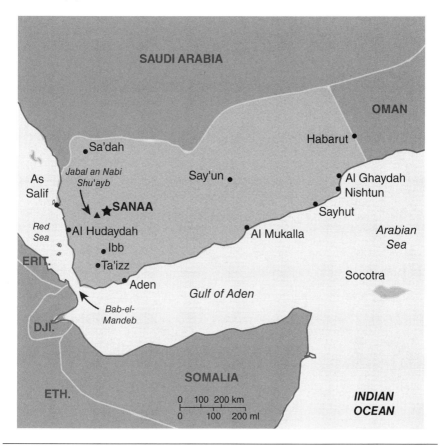

Source: CIA World Factbook.

3. Eritrea   Eritrea was part of an Italian colony from 1890 until 1941. Although Italian colonial rule developed the area's infrastructure and industry, the benefits of these improvements were all channeled to mainland Italy. After invading and expelling the Italians during WWII, Great Britain governed the country until the future of Eritrea could be decided upon. See Figure 13.4 for a map of Eritrea.

The country divided into two political parties, one desiring independence and the other a union with Ethiopia. Violent clashes between these parties ensued, and when Great Britain prepared to leave the country in 1947, the UN decided to have a public vote in Eritrea regarding the future status of the country. The independence bloc won with 55 percent of the votes, but it became clear that the winners would be unable to keep the nation together. UN resolution 390 created the federation of Eritrea and Ethiopia with guaranteed democratic rights and certain autonomy to Eritrea.

This federation proved to be short-lived as Ethiopia annexed Eritrea in 1962 without protest from the UN. The annexation led to armed resistance in Eritrea with

FIGURE 13.4   Eritrea

Source: CIA World Factbook.

several armed wings fighting both against Ethiopian rule and against each other for the next thirty years. The collapse of the Soviet Union, which had been backing Ethiopia, severely weakened Ethiopian military capacity and the armed resistance managed to free all of Eritrea in 1991.

A public vote on formal independence was won by a landslide of 99 percent. The early years of the government for the publicly elected party—PFDJ (People's Front for Democracy and Justice)—seemed bright. A constitution was agreed upon but never implemented, and public dissatisfaction with the government grew as new elections were delayed. This led to a tightening of the government's rule under president Isaias Afewerki; critics were imprisoned and press censorship imposed. The year 1998 saw a renewal of the armed clashes between Ethiopia and Eritrea, and a two-year war ended indecisively. The African Union facilitated a peace agreement in December 2000, and a peacekeeping UN mission was established. The United Nations Mission in Ethiopia and Eritrea (UNMEE) monitors a 25 km zone of separation between the two countries.

Eritrea has the largest army, per capita, in Africa.

4. Djibouti   A former French colony, Djibouti has maintained close relations with France. Strategically located at the mouth of the Red Sea, Djibouti enjoys a fairly stable economy through French support. Wedged between the larger nations of Eritrea, Ethiopia, and Somalia, Djibouti relies primarily on the 3,000-strong French military contingent for security. Several countries, including the United States and Japan, use the port and military base in Djibouti for operations and maintain a permanent presence.

5. Oman   A Portuguese colony until 1560, Oman was colonized by Great Britain in 1871. Gaining independence through a peaceful process, Oman nursed strong connections to Great Britain. A Yemen-backed rebellion in the province of

FIGURE 13.5   Djibouti and Oman

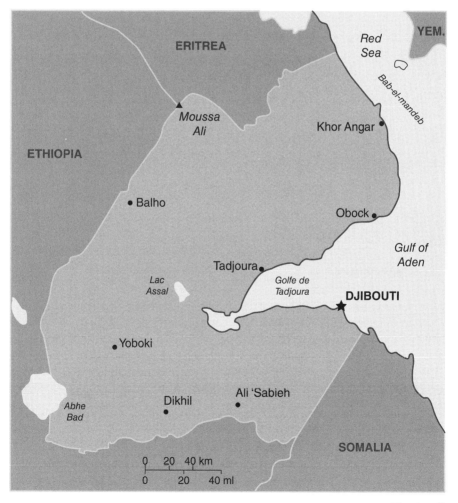

(Continued)

(Continued)

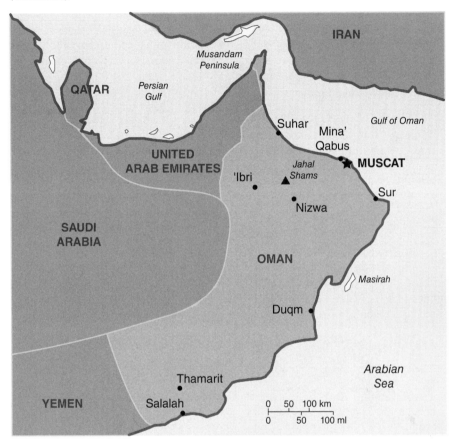

Source: CIA World Factbook.

Dhofar was crushed in 1975 by a combination of Omani army and British Special Operations Forces (SAS). The Omani economy primarily depends on its oil resources and on Saudi Arabian loans. Having to balance between the neighbors of Yemen and Saudi Arabia, Oman has granted the U.S. basing rights to one location where the U.S. military is allowed to station 10,000 troops and operate a minor air base. Please see Figure 13.5 for maps of Djibouti and Oman.

6. Saudi Arabia Abd al-Aziz ibn Abd al-Rahman Al Saud took control of Riyadh in 1902; it was the start of a thirty-year-long conflict that ended with the unification of the Arabian Peninsula. The country has been an absolute monarchy since then, governed by Islamic law and heavily influenced by a fundamentalist branch of Islam called Wahhabism. In 1990, Saddam Hussein's attempted annexation of Kuwait produced 400,000 refugees, including the Kuwaiti royal family, all of whom were given refuge in Saudi Arabia. The king allowed Arab and Western military forces to deploy in his country for the liberation of Kuwait in 1991. After the end of Operation Desert Storm, foreign troops were no longer welcome in Saudi Arabia, and the growing discontent pushed the United States to withdraw its troops to neighboring Qatar in 2003. See Figure 13.6 for a map of Saudi Arabia.

Yemeni Military Capabilities

The Yemeni armed forces are divided into two separate organizations: the regular armed forces and the paramilitary forces belonging to the Ministry of the Interior. The paramilitary forces are tasked with upholding public order and are lightly armed.

The politico-military chain of command is shown in Figure 13.7. The head of the Defence Council is the commander in chief (CINC) of Armed Forces, a post that is rotated between the three services (army, navy, air force) on a two-year basis. The three service CINCs form the Defense Council. This means that the CINC Armed

FIGURE 13.6   Saudi Arabia

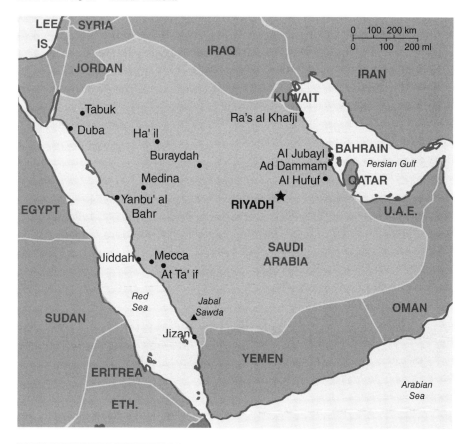

Source: CIA World Factbook.

FIGURE 13.7   Yemeni Military Organization

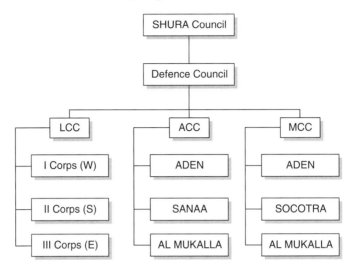

Forces serves in a dual role. The main HQs (including the Defense Council and combat commanders) are all placed in Sanaa's diplomatic quarter.

Yemeni military doctrine is heavily inspired by Soviet doctrine. Yemeni ability to coordinate inter-service activities is moderate to poor.

Army Organization and Materiel   The Yemeni Regular Army (YRA) consists of forty-four brigades. The various brigade types are shown in Table 13.1, and brigade equipment is shown in Table 13.2.

Table 13.1   Yemeni Regular Army Brigades

Brigade Type	Number of Brigades
Armored	8
Mechanized	6
Infantry	16
Special Forces	1
Commando/Airborne	2
Artillery	3
SSM	1
Central Guard	1
Air Defense	6 (each: 1 SAM Bn, 4 ADA Bn)

Note: SSM = surface-to-surface missile; SAM = surface-to-air missile.

Table 13.2 Yemeni Army Brigade Equipment

Unit	Composition	Materiel
8 Armored brigades	3 battalions of 30 tanks each (3 companies per battalion, 10 tanks per company)	T-72, M-60A1, T-62, T-54/55, T-34
	1 battalion of 30 armored personnel carriers (APCs) (3 companies per battalion, 10 APCs per company)	BMP-1/2, M-113, BTR-40, BTR-60
6 Mechanized brigades	1 battalion of 30 tanks (3 companies per battalion, 10 tanks per company)	T-72, M-60A1, T-62, T-54/55, T-34
	3 battalions of 30 APCs each (3 companies per battalion, 10 APCs per company)	BMP-1/2, M-113, BTR-40, BTR-60
16 Infantry brigades	1 battalion of 30 APCs (3 companies per battalion, 10 APCs per company)	BMP-1/2, M-113, BTR-40, BTR-60
3 Artillery brigades	3 battalions of 36 guns each (3 batteries per battalion, 12 guns per battery)	BMP-1/2, M-113, BTR-40, BTR-60

Current deployments appear in Figure 13.8. I Corps is responsible for the capital, Aden, and the immediate access to the strait of Bab el-Mandeb; it maintains a high level of readiness. All units are 50 percent ready at any given time and can achieve 100 percent readiness (to move) within one week. II Corps is at 50 percent readiness and can achieve 100 percent readiness (to move) within three weeks. III Corps is at 50 percent readiness and can achieve 100 percent readiness within two weeks. All surface-to-surface missile (SSM) units are constantly at 100 percent readiness.

The army logistic system is based on a combination of depots and mobile facilities.

Armored, mechanized, and infantry brigades all are allocated a battery of twelve multiple rocket launchers (MRLs) for organic fire support. Artillery brigades are allocated by the Defense Council on a case-by-case basis. See Table 13.3.

Air Force Organization and Materiel Figure 13.9 shows the base deployment of the Yemeni air force. The readiness state of the Yemeni air force is 50 percent initial operational capability (IOC) within twelve hours and full operational capability (FOC) within two days. Each air base is equipped with air defenses (man-portable air defense systems [MANPADS]/guns/missiles) and is assessed to have between two to four quick reaction interceptors on ground alert. See Table 13.4 for inventory and basing for Yemeni aircraft.

Navy Organization and Materiel The Yemeni navy is situated in the Gulf of Aden and the Red Sea at the three bases shown in Figure 13.9. Its main task is to uphold Yemeni sovereignty. It is very much a green and brown water navy specializing

FIGURE 13.8   Yemeni Military Deployment

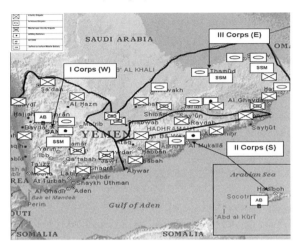

Table 13.3   Yemeni Heavy Weapons Inventory

Category	Type	Total
Main battle tanks	60 T-72, 50 M-60A1, 200 T-62, 450 T-54/55, 30 T-34	790
APC/Armored infantry fighting vehicles	200 BMP-1/2, 60 M-113, 650 BTR-40/50/60	910
Artillery	Towed: 105 mm: 25 M101A1; 122 mm: 200 D-30; 130 mm: 60 M-46; 152 mm: 10 D-20; 155 mm: 15 M-114	310 25 294
	Self-propelled: 122 mm: 25 2S1	
	MRLs: 122 mm: 280 BM-21; 140 mm: 14 BM-14	
Antitank	Sagger, Dragon, TOW	71
Air defense	MANPADS: Gopher, Gaskin, Grail, and Gremlin	800 530
	Guns: M-163 Vulcan: 20; M-167 Vulcan: 50; ZSU-23–4: 50; ZSU-23–2: 100; M-1939: 150; S-60: 120; KS-12: 40	
SSMs	Frog-7	12
	Scarab SS-21	10
	Scud-B	6
	Sardine C-801	UNK

Note: APC = armored personnel carrier; MRLs = multiple rocket launchers; TOW = tube launched, optically tracked, wire guided; MANPADS = man-portable air defense systems; SSMs = surface-to-surface missiles; UNK = unknown.

FIGURE 13.9 Yemeni Air and Naval Bases

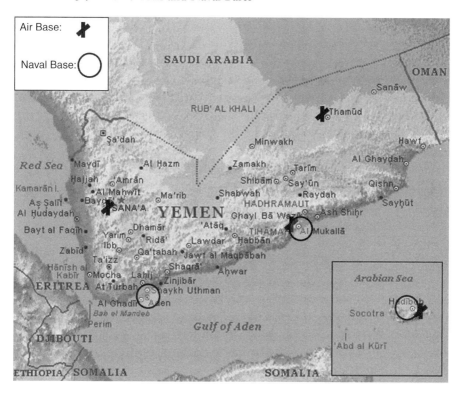

Table 13.4 Yemeni Aircraft Inventory and Basing

Air Base	Squadron/Role	Type	Airplanes in total
Sanaa	FBA	F-5E Tiger II	10
	FBA	Su-20 Fitter C	10
	MRX	MiG-29 Fulcrum	8
	AH	Mi-8 Hip	8
Al Mukalla	FBA	Su-20 Fitter C	10
	MRX	MiG-29 Fulcrum	8
Hadiboh	FBA	Su-20 Fitter C	10
	TP	Il-76 Candid	6
Tamud	MR	MiG-21 Fishbed	15
	TP	C-130 H	12
	AH	Mi-35 Hind	8

Note: FBA = fighter bomber attack; MRX = multirole all-weather; AH = attack helicopter; TP = transport; MR = multirole.

in littoral warfare. The navy's focus point is firmly fixed on maintaining and improving its ability to block the strait of Bab el-Mandeb.

The readiness state of the navy is 75 percent, and it can reach FOC within two days. Each naval base will statistically have one to two patrol boats at sea at any given time. The navy is unable to stay at sea for periods exceeding three to four weeks due to logistical restraints. Its peacetime deployment is at the three naval bases shown, but in crisis and war it will deploy to several smaller locations prepared along the coast. This switch in posture can be achieved in two to three days.

The navy is believed to operate a system of well-concealed caves on the coast along the Bab el-Mandeb. It must be assumed that these hold antiship missiles (ASMs).

All vessels in the navy as well as several civilian ships sailing out of Aden are capable of laying mines. Yemen's sea mine arsenal consists exclusively of MK6-type moored contact mines. See Table 13.5.

Other Forces   The paramilitary forces are approximately 50,000 strong and are under the command of the Ministry of the Interior. They are equipped with small arms and are semi-mobile. They are primarily trained for public safety duties although assistance to military movements in Yemen proper is well rehearsed.

In more isolated parts of Yemen, the tradition of tribal levies remains. If threatened, local tribal leaders can raise the men of the community and direct them against any perceived enemy. Such groups will be poorly equipped with a variety of small arms and edged weapons (no uniforms).

Table 13.5   Yemeni Naval Ship Inventory and Basing

Naval Base	Role	Type/Weapons	Total Number
Aden	PBF (ASuW)	Huangfen Y-1, carries 4 CSS-N-4 Sardine tactical SSM (C-801)	8
	PBF (ASuW)	OSA II, carries 4 STYX tactical SSM	2
	MHI	Yevgenya	5
	MSF	Natya	1
	LST	Ropucha	1
Al Mukalla	PBF (ASuW)	Huangfen Y-1, carries 4 CSS-N-4 SARDINE tactical SSM	6
Hadiboh	PBF (ASuW)	Huangfen Y-1, carries 4 CSS-N-4 Sardine tactical SSM	3
	AOTL	Toplivo	2

Note: PBF = patrol boat fast; SSM = surface-to-surface missile; MHI = inshore minehunter; MSF = steel hull fleet minesweeper; LST = landing ship tank; AOTL = replenishment tanker.

Eritrean Military Capabilities

The poor relationship with Ethiopia remains the sole focus of the Eritrean government. The armed forces of Eritrea are postured along the Ethiopian border in fixed positions, ready to repel any invasion. The military is not likely to engage in any other direction unless the sovereignty of the nation is at stake.

The military, although heavy in manpower (320,000), is poorly equipped and primarily oriented toward static attrition battles in which it excels. It is probably not capable of coordinating mobile battle beyond the battalion level. It is not capable of conducting joint operations. Figure 13.10 shows the deployment of the Eritrean military forces.

Army Organization and Materiel   The Eritrean army consists of four corps with five divisions each. Only one division is mechanized; the rest are infantry divisions (see Table 13.6).

Air Force Organization and Materiel   The Eritrean air force is poorly funded, and due to this, only 50 percent of its aircraft will be operable at any given time (see Table 13.7). Pilots have some experience in fighting air-to-air with the Ethiopian air force and are capable of conducting combat air patrols. The air force is based at Asmara.

FIGURE 13.10   Eritrean Military and Paramilitary Forces Deployment

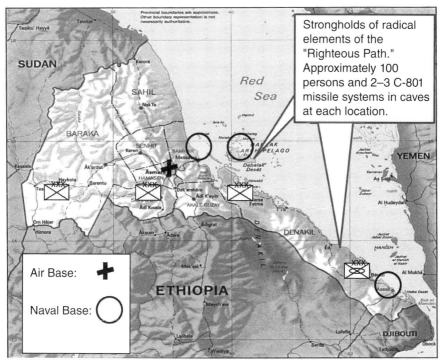

Table 13.6   Eritrean Army Units

Unit	Composition	Materiel
1 Mechanized division	3 battalions of 30 tanks each (3 companies per battalion, 10 tanks per company)	T-55: 150; BRDM: 40; BTR: 40; BMP-1: 40.
19 Infantry divisions	3 brigades, 9 battalions	RPGs, AK-47/74s, Sagger, Spandrel, some lorries

Readiness: It is estimated that the Eritrean army will be capable of reorienting a maximum of three divisions toward the coast within two days (ready to move).

Note: RPG = rocket-propelled grenade.

Table 13.7   Eritrean Air Force Inventory

Air Base	Squadron/Role	Type	Airplanes in Total
Asmara	MRX	MiG-29 Fulcrum	6
	ADF	MiG-23 Flogger	3
	MR	MiG-21 Fishbed	1
	AH	MI-17 HIP	6

Readiness: The air force maintains two quick reaction alert interceptors. Full operational capability (FOC) can be achieved within one week.

Note: MRX = multirole all-weather, ADF = air defense fighter, MR = multirole, AH = attack helicopter.

Navy Organization and Materiel   The Eritrean navy operates three very small naval bases at Massawa, Assab, and Dahlak (see Table 13.8). It suffers from the same weaknesses with regard to funding as the rest of the armed forces, and only 50 percent of its vessels are assumed operational at any given time. The navy is only partly capable of policing its coastline, and there is constant mistrust between the Christians and Muslims in its ranks.

Followers of the "Righteous Path"   French intelligence sources estimate that this movement has approximately 1,500 followers. These are almost exclusively from the Muslim population along the coastline of Eritrea. The movement's strongpoints are considered to be in the Dahlak archipelago and in the Danakil province. The majority of the movement sees no conflict between the movement and the nation of Eritrea. There is an inner hard core of fundamentalists who aspire to spread the Yemeni version of Islam to Eritrea, and this grouping is striving to radicalize the majority of the movement. This core is estimated to consist of two groupings of 100 persons each located in the Dahlak Desert on the Dahlak Archipelago and on the coast of the Danakil province (see Figure 13.10).

Table 13.8 Eritrean Naval Units

Naval Base	Role	Type/weapons	Total number
Massawa	PBF (ASuW)	OSA II, 4 STYX tactical SSM	3
Assab	PBF (ASuW)	OSA II, 4 STYX tactical SSM	2
Dahlak	PBF (ASuW)	OSA II, 4 STYX tactical SSM	2

Readiness: The navy maintains one patrol boat fast (PBF) per naval base as a quick reaction force. Full operational capability (FOC) can be achieved within three weeks.

Note: SSM = surface-to-surface missile.

Intelligence Reports (INTREPs) confirm that the radical wing of the movement has received ASM systems from Yemen during the last half of 2009. These are estimated to be deployed as shown in Figure 13.10 and could be activated on Yemen's request to assist in a confrontation in the Red Sea.

Both the Yemenis and the Eritrean Righteous Path have C-801 ASMs. The specifications for these missiles are shown in Table 13.9.

Figure 13.11 shows the standard deployment pattern for the C-801 truck-mounted version, which is the version used by the Yemeni armed forces and by the Righteous Path in Eritrea. The two missile firing units can operate autonomously but then will depend on external target data or be limited to "lock on before launch" mode.

Table 13.9 C-801 SARDINE Specifications

Contractor	CHETA—China Hai Yang (Sea Eagle) Electro-Mechanical Technology—CASC 3rd Academy
Total length	5.81 m
Diameter	0.36 m
Wingspan	1.18 m
Weight	625 kg (not including booster)
Warhead weight	165 kg high explosives
Propulsion	one solid rocket engine, one solid booster
Max speed	MACH 0.8 at sea level
Effective range	8–42 km
Guidance mode	Initial guidance (coordinates) from organic radar or from external source, terminal guidance from own active radar and final targeting from inverse synthetic-aperture radar (SAR) imaging.
Single-shot hit probability	75 percent

FIGURE 13.11   C-801 Missile Battery Deployment Pattern

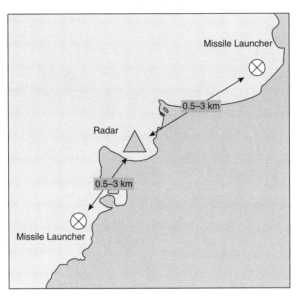

Figure 13.12 shows the area threatened by C-801 units operating from prepared launch sites in Yemen and Eritrea.

Somalian Military Capabilities

Close to being classified as a "failed state," Somalia is fragmented into the three areas shown in Figure 13.13: Somalia, to the south; Puntland; and Somaliland. The government of Somalia exercises no control over Puntland and Somaliland. These areas are ruled by local warlords.

Somalia Proper   Despite the establishment of the transnational government in 2004, national forces have yet to be formed. A militia-like body of 5,000 troops is established but is able to control only Mogadishu and suburbs. The government retains its formal claim to Somaliland and Puntland but is unable to influence these areas in any way.

Puntland   The charismatic clan leader Abdallah Walid controls Puntland with an iron fist through his 20,000-strong militia "Spears of Puntland." After a turbulent period of interclan violence in 2007 and 2008, the Spears of Puntland emerged from the central part of Puntland and its primary stronghold is the city of Quardho. Abdallah Walid rules the region through a feudal-like system in which other clans pay homage and tribute to him. Should tribute fail, his militia will deliver quick punishment often in the form of ritual executions.

FIGURE 13.12   C-801 Threat Area

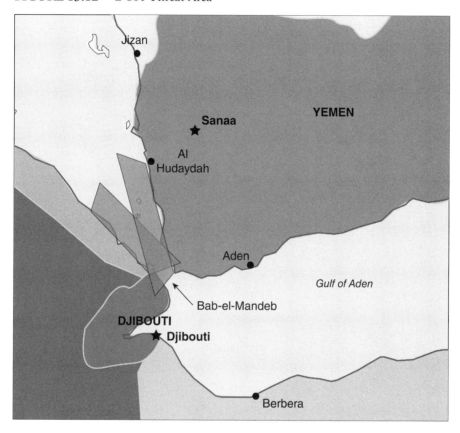

Through this system, Walid is estimated to control approximately 150,000 militiamen across Puntland. The average militiaman is between fourteen and forty, heavily brutalized by years of conflict, and often addicted to drugs and alcohol. The militias are financed by taxing the civil population, guns and drug trafficking, and piracy. The militia operates numerous smaller boats along the coast of Puntland. When a commercial or private ship is sighted, packs of small fast boats will emerge from their hideouts on the coast and the victim will be hijacked. Larger mother ships often support the small attack boats. The pirated vessel and its crew will either be looted or held for ransom. The numbers of pirate attacks has risen alarmingly since 2008.

Somaliland   The situation in Somaliland mirrors the situation in Puntland. The region is ruled by the clan leader Said Al Yusuf and his militia "Buffaloes of Somaliland." Emerging out of the chaos in 2007 and 2008 as the dominant clan, the Buffaloes rule Somaliland through terror and violence. The Buffaloes of

FIGURE 13.13   The Three Parts of Somalia

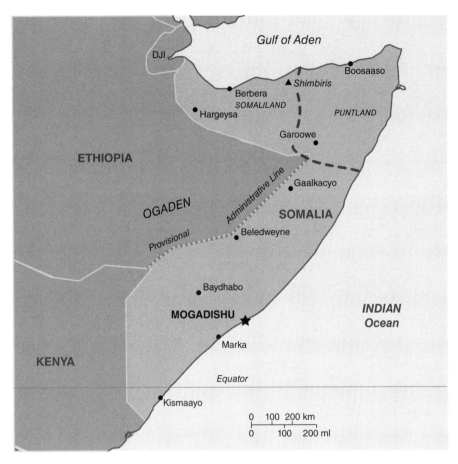

Somaliland is approximately 50,000 strong although many of these numbers in reality come from other subdued clans. The Buffaloes of Somaliland originates from the northern coast area of Somaliland, and its primary stronghold is the coastal town of Berbera.

Like its Puntland counterpart, the Buffaloes of Somaliland relies on extortion from the civil population, guns and drug trafficking, and piracy. After initial clashes with the Spears of Puntland when interests collided, a marriage of convenience was established leading to exchange of information and other forms of cooperation among the clans.

The harsh treatment of the population in combination with scarce resources has prompted large numbers of civilians to flee the province. Approximately a half-million people live in improvised refugee camps near the border with Djibouti.

Increasing Instability 2007–2015

Yemen Autumn 2007 sees a diplomatic crisis between Yemen and Saudi Arabia as both parties claim a newly discovered oil deposit on their common border. After lengthy negotiations, an international court rules in favor of Saudi Arabia. Yemen agrees reluctantly after serious pressure from the Western governments that fear another war on the Arabian Peninsula. The foreign minister of Yemen states in a BBC interview, "The oilfield rightfully belongs to Yemen and Yemen should be compensated for the loss of this crucial asset."

The Yemeni economy deteriorates throughout 2008 as existing oil fields are drained. The population of Yemen experiences a severe decline in living standards, and dissatisfaction with the government grows. The perception of a Yemeni government unable to assert its rightful claims in the diplomatic confrontation with Saudi Arabia becomes widely accepted among the general public. A religious wakening sweeps Yemen, and violence erupts between radical Muslims and government troops. The cities of Aden and Sanaa encounter the worst troubles. The demonstrators demand the government's resignation in favor of a rule based on traditional religious values. The government responds by declaring a state of emergency, and martial law is imposed. A severe riot in Aden claims the lives of 200 demonstrators, including women and children.

The violent response of the government forces a strategy change by the radical fundamentalists. Through a peaceful campaign funded by Iran, a wide range of social programs are launched by the radical movement the Righteous Path. Targeting the poorer part of the Yemeni population, the movement funds schools, education, hospitals, and welfare, earning wide public support throughout Yemen and in particular within the armed forces where the government's use of military force against the population has alienated the common soldier from the government.

After the government issues a ban on the religious schools of the Righteous Path in the summer of 2009, events spin out of control. The population takes to the streets of all major cities, and when police and military are called out, most of the units refuse to fight and side with the demonstrators. The president and his cronies leave the country with the gold reserve.

Autumn 2009 sees the Righteous Path establishing a fundamentalist state, which due to the wide public support and the relatively peaceful revolution gains reluctant international recognition. The state is governed by a Shura Council of nineteen elders.

Although the infrastructure remains intact, the Yemeni economy continues its decline. Dwindling oil revenues and the Organization of the Petroleum Exporting Countries' (OPEC) distrust of the new government lead to further decline in living standards. In an attempt to raise capital, Yemen announces that a tax will be levied on all ships passing through the Bab el-Mandeb straits beginning in the year 2010. The UN promptly protests this unilateral action. However, the idea of rightful taxes continues to be widespread and results in intermittent actions by Yemeni forces to stop shipping and collect taxes off the Aden coastline despite warnings from the UN.

Somalia   The fragmentation of the state of Somalia continues throughout 2007 and 2008. Armed conflicts between rival clans proliferate, and an already long-suffering population is victimized even further. The autonomous provinces of Puntland and Somaliland experience civil war conditions as various clan leaders struggle for dominance. Other countries, the UN, and nongovernmental organizations (NGOs) hesitate to intervene, haunted by the ghosts of the U.S. experience in Somalia from 1992 to 1995.

The Horn of Africa region is marred by piracy, famine, and disorder. However, Combined Task Force 43 (TF 43, a multinational naval task force, set up in 2006 as a response to piracy attacks in the Gulf of Aden and off the eastern coast of Somalia) is disbanded in 2008 due to other commitments elsewhere on the African continent and in the Far East.

At the end of 2008, two clan leaders emerge as dominant in the two provinces. Said Al Yusuf rules Somaliland through his clan, or militia, the Buffaloes of Somaliland while Abdallah Walid and his Spears of Puntland govern neighboring Puntland. A marriage of convenience between the two despots is created through common interests in smuggling and piracy in the waters of the Horn of Africa. The official government of Somalia has neither the will nor the capacity to counter this development and is stretched just to maintain a fragile hold on the southern part of Somalia. In 2009, the level of piracy again reaches a "pre-TF 43" level. From 2010 to 2014, efforts to reduce the piracy risk to shipping through private contractors have had some effect, but piracy remains a serious destabilization factor to the international economy.

As a consequence of the clans' exploitation of the civilian population in the provinces, neighboring Djibouti is seen by many as the "promised land" compared to the harsh realities of Puntland and Somaliland. Many refugees decide to seek a new life there. Djibouti, backed heavily by France, refuses to accept these "displaced persons," resulting in temporary refugee camps along the Djibouti-Somaliland border. The United Nations High Commissioner for Refugees (UNHCR) estimates that by the end of 2009 up to 500,000 displaced persons are living under terrible conditions in these temporary camps.

By the new year of 2010, international media is overflowing with images and reports from these temporary camps that display the signs of an impending hunger disaster as well as an emerging cholera epidemic. The UN and several NGOs launch a major relief operation, relying on the Djiboutian infrastructure for support. By the end of 2012, the relief efforts of the UN and the NGOs have stabilized the hunger situation; however, without a safe and secure environment it cannot be sustained after 2014.

Beginning in 2010, regional and international smuggling networks have exploited the situation to their economic advantage. Human smuggling and slavery have become a lucrative activity, rivaled only by the narcotics smuggling.

Narcotics smuggling from the region has grown since 2010 due to the lack of government control in the region. Along with slavery, it is a major source of income for various insurgent and terrorist groupings throughout the region.

Due to the anarchic character of many parts of the region, both domestic insurgencies and international terrorist organizations have established themselves and enjoy a significant amount of freedom to organize, arm, train, and plan.

Eritrea   The situation in Eritrea is relatively calm in the years 2008 and 2009. UNMEE monitors Eritrea's border with Ethiopia, and as both countries struggle with drought and poverty, neither have the capacity to renew the hostilities. At the end of 2008, a local version of the Yemeni organization, the Righteous Path, establishes itself among the Eritrean Muslims in the coastal areas.

Channeling support from the parent organization in Yemen, the Righteous Path manages to raise living standards among its followers and as a consequence gains local support in the coastal area. This pattern is reinforced in the autumn of 2009 as the Yemeni Righteous Path takes power in Yemen, channeling even more support to the Eritrean Righteous Path chapter.

The presence of the movement in Eritrea is largely ignored by the Eritrean government due to the relatively small number of Muslims in the country combined with the movement's positive economic effect on the coastal region.

At the beginning of the year 2010, French INTREPs of arms shipping from Yemen to the Eritrean coastal areas start circulating in the UN system. As of 2012, the situation between Eritrea and Ethiopia is stable despite a significant buildup of arms and munitions. However, unsettled disputes in neighboring Sudan constitute a continuing source of destabilization and an open sore to be picked at for terrorist or criminal organizations that wish to cause a general destabilization in the region. From 2010 to 2014, increased activity on all criminal and terrorist fronts within the Horn of Africa region has and continues to destabilize the region and is directly threatening the global economy.

Events after January 1, 2014   Yemen imposes the announced tax on ships passing Bab el-Mandeb. Yemeni patrol vessels stop ships in the narrows near Aden to collect the tax. The government of Yemen threatens to mine the strait unless the international society does the following:

- accepts the Yemeni right to tax shipping through the strait of Bab el-Mandeb
- returns the oil fields on the Yemeni-Saudi border to Yemen

The UN refuses this demand and calls for moderation from all parties and for peaceful negotiations of the issue.

The months of February and March are characterized by a fragile and unstable stalemate in the Red Sea and the strait of Bab el-Mandeb. Yemeni vessels continue to tax all unescorted vessels, and semichaotic ship waiting areas develop north of Suez and in the waters off Somalia as commercial ship traffic awaits an escort through Bab el-Mandeb. Stocks related to international shipping plummet because shipping delays continue to occur as a consequence of the crisis. The tension builds as several merchant ships are hijacked, pirated, and plundered by pirates of the Somaliland-Puntland coast.

International agencies report that the relief effort on the Djibouti border is failing due to missing deliveries of aid through Djiboutian ports.

On April 2, as a combined flotilla of British, Spanish, and Italian vessels investigate suspected minefields in the strait, three Sardine SSMs are launched from coastal batteries in Yemen. The British frigate *Daring* is hit by one missile resulting in extensive damage and twelve casualties. Withdrawing toward the Suez, the small flotilla picks up emissions from the Eritrean coast indicating preparations for another missile attack although none is actually launched. The strait of Bab el-Mandeb is effectively closed; only a few civilian companies are willing to take on the combined risk of missiles, mines, and taxation. Most civilian traffic is redirected around the Cape of Good Hope considerably upping the cost and prices of most items on the western market.

As the UN debates a solution to the crisis, a UNHCR report on the humanitarian operation in Somaliland and Djibouti is published on April 10. The report describes how the blockade and the piracy of the Somali coast combines to stop delivery of much needed aid to the approximately 500,000 displaced persons in temporary camps along the border. The militias, exploitation, hunger, disease, and lack of water further combine to enhance the atrocious living conditions in the camps. The report concludes that "unless decisive action is taken immediately, the international society will have a full-blown humanitarian disaster on their hands within two to three months." NGOs entering the camps have been intimidated, assaulted, and in some cases held hostage by armed militiamen.

After a series of extraordinary debates in the UN Security Council, a resolution is agreed upon May 1, 2014. The resolution calls for an immediate reopening of the strait of Bab el-Mandeb and the establishment of a safe and secure working environment for humanitarian organizations in Somaliland. Acting on an offer made by the North Atlantic Treaty Organization (NATO), France, and the United Kingdom, the resolution authorizes NATO to act on behalf of the UN.

Developments from May 1, 2014, to Present

Bab el-Mandeb   Since the UN resolution on May 1, the Yemeni's Righteous Path Shura Council has been trying to reach agreement with the UN Security Council concerning the Bab el-Mandeb straits. As of May 10, there has been a tentative agreement between the Shura Council and the Security Council to reopen the straits as soon as possible, but the Yemenis had to take the agreement back to Yemen for ratification by the Shura Council and the Defense Council.

From May 15 until May 19, the Shura Council debated the issue in heated discussions; representatives from the southeast region of Yemen argued that there would be severe economic consequences if they did not do something with regards to sovereignty in the straits. When the vote followed on May 20, the Shura Council representatives from the southeast, knowing they would lose the vote, walked out of the meeting. It was noted that when the politicians from the southeast walked out, military commanders mainly from the II Corps (S) walked out from the spectator area where the Defense Council was sitting.

On May 21, senior politicians met in Al Mukalla in the southeast region and called for the people to overthrow the Shura Council. Over 50,000 protesters attempted to storm the government buildings at Sanaa; they were stopped by the national forces loyal to the government. The government ordered the II Corps (S) to arrest the Shura Council rebels in Al Mukalla. II Corps (S) refused and said they would stop any attempts by other Yemeni forces to interfere with the establishment of a partially separate state based out of Al Mukalla.

On May 26, the Defense Council chief stated three points to the nation: (1) that he will protect the Shura Council; (2) that the remainder of the Yemeni forces will not interfere with UN forces operating in the region, in accordance with the UN resolution, even if there are clashes between the UN and II Corps (S); (3) but he will not use his forces against II Corps (S) as long as they remain within their II Corps (S) boundaries.

The chief of II Corps (S) responded that he has no intention of leaving those boundaries until the political situation within the Shura Council is settled. However, the II Corps (S) will not support the UN resolution and intends to enforce taxation in the waters surrounding and between Hadiboh and the Yemeni mainland.

II Corps (S) also stated that it will establish a new Joint Operations Command (II Corps JOC) of its own somewhere within its II Corps (S) boundaries. Some of the suggested locations are Habban, Ahwar, Al Mukalla, Sayhut, and on Hadiboh Island. II Corps (S) also called for other units outside of II Corps to join with them.

Al-Qaida on the Arabian Peninsula and Al-Shabab   During the unrest on May 21, al-Qaida on the Arabian Peninsula (AQAP) announced via Sada al-Malahim their support for the forces wishing to overthrow the Shura Council, including carrying out several high-profile raids across the capital region on I Corps (W) installations around At Turbah and Zinjibar. It also successfully penetrated the protected compounds of several of the Shura Council representatives' homes in Eritrea, Saudi Arabia, Somalia, and Djibouti. Furthermore, AQAP said that it will do everything in its power to keep the straits closed to the "infidel hordes sailing under the banner of the UN. We shall send them all to the depths of the ocean." Unlike Al-Shabaab, AQAP has little seagoing experience. AQAP largely conducts operations on the Arab Peninsula in Yemen and Saudi Arabia, but there are indications that they are investing in a capability for activities at sea that could include cruise missile systems, fast attack craft, mini-submarines, drones, and/or slow-flying civilian aircraft.

Al-Shabaab has not officially spoken on the conflict; however, the leadership has expressed concern about the arrival of a UN-sanctioned task force in the area. On May 23, Al-Shabaab said that it would be collecting Somali shipping taxes between

Hadiboh and Somalia but does not want to get involved in the internal politics of Yemen. Al-Shabaab stated that all shipping through the straits south of Hadiboh must pay tax before attempting to go through the straits. On May 27, it sent representatives to Hadiboh to coordinate activities around the straits with Yemeni navy installations on the island. It also offered its support to AQAP and the II Corps (S) if they come into conflict with the UN Task Force.

Organized Crime and Human Trafficking With the separatist declaration on May 21, there was an immediate increase in the number of refugees moving across the straits. The smuggling networks are trying to accommodate the extra demand for passage and are using less seaworthy ships and vessels than before; the number of ships unlikely to make the crossing safely will increase. There is a great deal of money to be made in a short period, and the expectation of war in the straits and internal strife in Yemen has had a direct effect on the supply and demand. More people want out of the region—more weapons want in. However, it is unclear which clans are the most relevant to either organized criminal activity.

Some observers rightly describe the clan system as "me against my brother, me and my brother against my uncle, me and my brother and my uncle against the world." However, some clan levels are more important than others. The large supraclan level consists of the five major clan families of Somalia (some Somalis will maintain that it is just four): the Darod, the Hawiye, the Isaq, the Diir, and the Rahanwhein. These clans today, with some exceptions, are seldom important, and these large clan families are seldom united. At least two of these clans are benefiting greatly from the influx of refugees and the rising demand for weapons.

Before the May 21 rebellion in Yemen, there were three to seven camps along the Somali-Djibouti border that hosted over 50,000 refugees each. As of today, there are five to seven camps with over 500,000 refugees, and boats all along the Somali coast are being commandeered by organized criminal groups. A lot of people want out of the region before the task force arrives and the region likely explodes into open conflict.

INTELLIGENCE REPORTS

Rep #	Date	Text
R1	May 27, 2014	**Human Intelligence (HUMINT)—001-C-3:** Ethiopia is planning a surprise attack on Eritrea in early November 2014.
R2	May 27, 2014	**Signals Intelligence (SIGINT):** Suspect human trafficking investor Bandar Abdul-Rahman Abdullah Al-Dakhil is expecting the completion of all transactions to the casinos in Lebanon once the remaining shipping funds from this month are transferred.

Rep #	Date	Text
R3	May 27, 2014	**SIGINT:** Unhappy Al-Shabaab member Hassan Afrah discusses family issues with UNK person.
R4	May 27, 2014	**HUMINT—005-F-6:** The Walihom (possibly Walidom) subclan intends to assassinate key leaders of the Somalilands' governing body.
R5	May 27, 2014	**Measurement and Signature Intelligence (MASINT):** Pattern of life (PoL): Radar signatures belonging to the Somali coast guard merge routinely with suspected smuggler signatures between 1200 and 1400 on Thursdays and 0200 and 0400 on Tuesday mornings. There are possible boarding activities; however, merging is of a very short duration (in vicinity of [IVO] Bosaso).
R6	May 27, 2014	**HUMINT—005-F-6:** Ali Farah Walid is leader of the Walihom subclan and is giving orders. See R4.
R7	May 27, 2014	**HUMINT—003-B-2:** Because of increasing tensions, Xuseen Khalif Jama (Darood) intends for the majority of "travelers" to be moved to the coastline within the next three weeks, and that fund transfers from Saudi investors will be put in the pipeline to cover shipping (literal meaning—source is referring to boats on the water).
R8	May 27, 2014	**Tearline:** Army Service Component Command (ASCC) and Maritime Component Command (MCC) at Al Mukalla issue official declarations of support for II Corps.
R9	May 28, 2014	**Open Source Intelligence (OSINT):** Somali member of parliament Ahmed Dhimbil Roble from the ISAAQ clan is killed by a drive-by shooting while visiting Djibouti.
R10	May 28, 2014	**MASINT**: PoL: There is a great deal of radar spoofing by Yemeni warships between 0100 and 0500 on Wednesday mornings (Hadiboh).
R11	May 28, 2014	**HUMINT—001-C-3:** Dahir Gamaey "Abdi Al-Haq" in Lebanon is the main international finance advisor for the AQAP.
R12	May 28, 2014	**SIGINT:** Senior Hawiye clan official Caasha Xaaji Cilmi discusses what the role of Islam should be within the clans with UNK person.
R13	May 28, 2014	**OSINT:** Somaliland chat and blog forums indicate a general dislike of the current government in Somaliland and an even greater dislike for the government of Puntland. Several discuss openly their support for Al-Shabaab.
R14	May 28, 2014	**INTREP:** Suspect smuggling ship motor vessel (MV) *Raj Mahali* (Tattoo-2038) (fleet target designation) is

(Continued)

(Continued)

Rep #	Date	Text
		intercepted and boarded by French ships from Djibouti enroute to Hadiboh—over 10,000 rounds small arms munitions, 200x AKs, 20× rocket-propelled grenades (RPGs), 50 × 105mm rnds.
R15	May 28, 2014	**OSINT:** Traditionally the major clans involved in criminal activities along the coast of Somalia have been the Darood and the Hawiye.
R16	May 28, 2014	**Tearline:** UNK member of AQAP is extremely upset with Darood clan leader Abdi Bare Yusuf Jibril—reason is not known.
R17	May 28, 2014	**HUMINT—003-B-2:** Known smuggling investor Bandar Abdul-Rahman Abdullah Al-Dakhil flies to Riyadh from Mogadishu to meet with associates to request a one-year extension on recently invested funds. The meeting was a success, but he flew back with a warning that there would be serious consequences if the money was not repaid within a year. One of Rahman's wives is from the Hawiye clan.
R18	May 28, 2014	**Tearline:** Suspected Yemeni weapons buyer Nasir Al-Rashid has purchased a large load of expensive lightweight high-yield explosives in Riyadh.
R19	May 28, 2014	**INTREP:** About 3,000 to 4,000 Ethiopian refugees unable to pay smugglers for a trip over the gulf are stranded in miserable conditions in Bosaso, Puntland.
R20	May 28, 2014	**SIGINT:** Halawi banker Nuur Iidow Beyle (Hawiye) has banking connections in Beirut.
R21	May 28, 2014	**Document Exploitation (DOCEX):** Receipts for spare motor parts for the detained MV *Raj Mahali* (Tattoo-2038) indicate a bank card issued by an Arab National Bank affiliate in Yambo (U), Saudi Arabia, was used to pay for them.
R22	May 28, 2014	**INTREP:** Two major sources for illicit arms trade for use in Somalia are Yemen and Eritrea. AQAP currently acquires most of their arms from Saudi Arabia and Yemen through a Yemeni arms dealer.
R23	May 28, 2014	**Imagery Intelligence (IMINT):** Thermal imagery of an overcrowded Dhow in stormy waters at 0145hrs at night show crew apparently throwing people—still alive—overboard.
R24	May 28, 2014	**HUMINT—003-B-2:** Sea passage to Yemen currently costs $300 for refugees, but they can pay up to $500 more for the land trip through Yemen over the Saudi border. Prices have almost doubled in a week.

Rep #	Date	Text
R25	May 28, 2014	**MASINT:** A PoL report suggests repeated incidents of relatively small fishing Dhows signatures convoying in groups of four to five from the Somali coast IVO Bosaso to Yemen without stopping to fish.
R26	May 28, 2014	**INTREP:** "Migration Economy" constitutes a lucrative regional network that acts as a powerful disincentive to formally regulate border controls.
R27	May 28, 2014	**SIGINT:** Known Puntland human trafficker Xuseen Khalif Jama attended a friend's wedding in Djibouti recently.
R28	May 28, 2014	**SIGINT:** There is increased "background noise" activity amongst the Halawas throughout the Gulf region as compared to the same time during the past four years.
R29	May 28, 2014	**INTREP:** Transshipment hubs in Aden and Djibouti City handle large volumes of international container traffic, while smaller ports in Al-Hudaydah, Mocha, Al Mukalla, Berbera, and Bosaso cater to local traders shipping fish, livestock, and charcoal. These minor ports are often used by smugglers.
R30	May 28, 2014	**SIGINT:** Hassan Afrah (Al-Shabaab) and Khaleed Bin Ibrahim Mahmoud (AQAP) discussed a common investment project at a shipyard assessed to be in Yemen.
R31	May 28, 2014	**SIGINT:** Suspected Saudi smuggler banker Abdul-Majiid Mohammed al-Mani rings from Beirut to UNK person in Riyadh reporting that over 90 percent of Abdi's casinos are now "stocked with our paper."
R32	May 28, 2014	**OSINT:** Twitter analysis indicates strong support for the Shura Council in Aden and Sanaa.
R33	May 28, 2014	**Communications Intelligence (COMINT):** Suspected MV *Jakel* (Tattoo-2389) was heard last Thursday around 0245 in Bosaso being raised by the Somali coast guard and was told "hold her steady then throw the money over."
R34	May 28, 2014	**SIGINT:** Commander Rakan Mushin from I Corps (W) discusses standing orders with a member of his staff, indicating that there should be no trouble with UN forces coming through the straits of Bab el-Mandeb. And that they should secure the coastline to ensure no trouble occurs.
R35	May 28, 2014	**Geospatial Intelligence (GEOINT):** Major excavation activity is observed on Hadiboh.
R36	May 28, 2014	**HUMINT—001-C-3:** Members of AQAP working out of Sayhut include Abdullah Said Mob 967 777635467; Mustafa Ibrahim Mob 967 779787976.

(Continued)

(Continued)

Rep #	Date	Text
R37	May 28, 2014	**Tearline:** Xussen Khalif Jama has asked Abdullah Jama Hussein to send all the travelers he has to Bosaso ASAP.
R38	May 28, 2014	**MASINT:** Spectral analysis of imagery indicates the airbase on Hadiboh now has sixteen FBA Su-20 Fitter C, multirole all-weather (MRX) 4 MIG-29 Fulcums, and 6 II-76 Candids.
R39	May 28, 2014	**OSINT:** Media reports inside Yemen are promoting the legitimacy of the Shura Council's decision to deal with the UN.
R40	May 28, 2014	**INTREP:** The influx of refugees and migrating persons has almost doubled in the past week in the region between Djibouti and Somaliland out of fears of war in the straits blocking all passage over to Yemen. Conditions in the camps are brutal but ripe for AQAP and Al-Shabaab recruitment of fighting age males.
R41	May 28, 2014	**HUMINT—001-C-3:** The Darood clan has good connections within the Somali coast guard, and payoffs are the only way for the slow moving fishing vessels to get by them.
R42	May 28, 2014	**SIGINT:** Known AQAP weapons specialist Mehmas Bin Mohammed Mehmas Al-Hawashleh Al-Dosari instructs Jubran Ali to tell the Saudis to fly the three doves to Hadiboh tonight. Arrangements have been made with Al Mahdi Maxamed from the Yemen navy to allow them in. When asked if Al Mahdi could be trusted, Mehmas states he is the uncle of my wife. (Al Mahdi is from the Hawiye clan.)
R43	May 28, 2014	**OSINT:** Background noise on all open sites affiliated with promoting AQAP has increased over the past week.
R44	May 28, 2014	**SIGINT:** "Al-Afghani" is a smuggling expert who often works for Sheik Aden Hashi Farah (Hawiye), a leader in Al-Shabaab.
R45	May 28, 2014	**HUMINT—005-F-6:** PUNTLAND coast guard captains Axmed and Roble are all Darood and are corrupt. They let human traffickers through their patrols on Wednesdays and Thursdays for a price.
R46	May 28, 2014	**DOCEX:** Subscriber identity module (SIM) cards from MV *Raj Mahali* indicate there has been recent communication with official members of the Yemen Defense forces on Hadiboh.
R47	May 28, 2014	**HUMINT—001-C-3:** AQAP is planning a suicide attack on naval installations in Djibouti.

Rep #	Date	Text
R48	May 28, 2014	**COMINT:** MV *Tonkjin* requests assistance in heavy seas; however, it refuses help from French naval vessels in the area.
R49	May 28, 2014	**OSINT:** Some media in Yemen are reporting that there is a tight family connection between some of the II Corps leadership and the leading rebel Shura Council members.
R50	May 28, 2014	**HUMINT—012-A2:** Several military aircraft left the Al Mukalla air base on May 27 and did not return.
R51	May 28, 2014	**OSINT:** Al-Shabaab threatens to close the waters between Somalia and Hadiboh to all shipping.
R52	May 28, 2014	**OSINT:** Media in Djibouti report another large influx of refugees from Ethiopia and Eritrea.
R53	May 28, 2014	**IMINT:** Thermal imagery reveals a convoy of nine fishing boats full of people off-loading near Al-Ghadir harbor in Yemen.
R54	May 28, 2014	**SIGINT:** Junior officers in III Corps (E) report an increase in nighttime border crossings over their border with Saudi Arabia—going in both directions.
R55	May 28, 2014	**DOCEX:** Members of II Corps and AQAP have been communicating via Internet relay chat (IRC).
R56	May 28, 2014	**HUMINT—012-A2:** Large MV *Jotika* has left Al Mukalla for Hadiboh. Embarked are four air defense brigades and several large containers with markings Gopher and Gremlin.
R57	May 28, 2014	**COMINT:** MV *Tonkjin* is heard hailing MV *Kemal*, asking for assistance. MV *Kemal* replied they could not as they also had a full load. MV *Kemal* is a human trafficking vessel (Tattoo-2089).
R58	May 28, 2014	**HUMINT—012-A2:** Follow-up subsource reporting states there were 10 x 105 mm towed cannon off-loaded from MV *Jotika* at Hadiboh.
R59	May 28, 2014	**IMINT:** Imagery of known FROG-7 and SCUD-B sites in Yemen indicate no unusual activity. All known sites are outside of II Corps boundaries.
R60	May 28, 2014	**HUMINT—005-F-6:** Eritrea plans to fire a STYX missile at UN forces passing through the straits and blame it on Ethiopia.
R61	May 28, 2014	**Cyber:** AQAP have attempted to hack into French Military servers in Djibouti.
R62	May 29, 2014	**HUMINT—012-A2:** There are now at least two batteries of SSM C-801 operational on Hadiboh.

(Continued)

(Continued)

Rep #	Date	Text
R63	May 29, 2014	**COMINT:** Doves are cleared for landing at Hadiboh military airfield.
R64	May 29, 2014	**HUMINT—001-C-3:** There is frustration among the Al-Shabaab with regards to available funds for weaponry. The group intends to collect a large sum from a coming smuggling operation.
R65	May 29, 2014	**DOCEX:** E-mails recovered from a laptop found on MV *Raj Mahali* show communication with Ali Mahdi Maxamed.
R66	May 29, 2014	**SIGINT:** II Corps commanders order all essential C2 equipment moved to the military port area of Al Mukalla, packed, and ready to be shipped.
R67	May 29, 2014	**IMINT:** Hadiboh Harbor imagery indicates at least sixteen fast inshore attack craft (FIAC) type boats docked in groups of four.
R68	May 29, 2014	**INTREP:** The arms market for RPGs in Yemen has run dry. Remaining RPGs are being sold for seven times the normal price.
R69	May 29, 2014	**INTREP:** Senior leadership of the Hawiye under Samira Xasan Cabdulle has called for a large clan meeting ASAP. There is no obvious event that would trigger this meeting.
R70	May 30, 2014	**OSINT:** AQAP launches a website blitz calling for jihadists to assemble on Hadiboh ready to fight.
R71	May 30, 2014	**Cyber:** Nasir Al-Rashid has been talking to a Hassan Afrah in an online chat room about "the packaging for a very delicate gift from a family in Riyadh that weighs 200 kg."
R72	May 30, 2014	**MASINT:** Multiple sensor reporting is indicating that Hadiboh has become a major C2 node for various electromagnetic emissions, including a notable augmentation of activity at the airport.
R73	May 30, 2014	**IMINT:** Another convoy of fishing boats is caught on thermal imaging disembarking people just outside Zinjibar.
R74	May 30, 2014	**MASINT:** C-801 batteries on Hadiboh are confirmed operational.
R75	May 30, 2014	**DOCEX:** Further exploitation of laptops from MV *Taj Mahali* provided the bank account number 5786 9585736 for Nuur Iidow Beyle (Hawiye), a known Halawi banker for the Hawiye clan.
R76	May 30, 2014	**MASINT:** GMTI indicates some major troop movements within II Corps boundaries with convoys heading toward Al Mukalla.

Rep #	Date	Text
R77	May 31, 2014	**HUMINT—003-B-2:** Abdullah Jama Hussein is in charge of smuggling and is from the Hawiye clan. He answers only to Samira Zasan Cabdulla, a senior leader of the Hawiye clan.
R78	May 31, 2014	**IMINT:** Imagery of naval installations in Aden indicates there is no unusual activity among forces stationed there.
R79	May 31, 2014	**Cyber:** Records "liberated" from servers associated with "Abdi" in Lebanon indicate money laundering for bankers in Riyadh that are connected to both AQAP and Al-Shabaab clan smugglers.
R80	May 31, 2014	**OSINT:** Media inside Somaliland are criticizing the smugglers for going too far in the current situation. This is a rare criticism.
R81	May 31, 2014	**HUMINT—012-A2:** Four HUANGFEN Y-1s have sailed from Al Mukalla to Hadiboh.
R82	June 1, 2014	**GEOINT:** The refugee camps are now severely overcrowded along the Djibouti border, and they are encroaching on Darood clan living space.
R83	June 1, 2014	**HUMINT—001-C-3:** Al-Shabaab is to coordinate a large smuggling operation from Somalia to Hadiboh to Yemen in order to make some money for weapons.
R84	June 1, 2014	**SIGINT:** Khaleed Bin Ibrahim Mahmoud reports to Mohammed Othman Abdullah Al-Walidi Al-Shehri that the doves are ready to splash.
R85	June 2, 2014	**SIGINT:** Notable increase in denial and deception SIGINT activity amongst targeted Al-Shabaab members.
R86	June 2, 2014	**COMINT:** Tower to flight intercepts indicate that two of the doves at Hadiboh military airport have call signs YT548 and V109R.
R87	June 2, 2014	**HUMINT—012-A2:** Discussions between members of the Defense Council indicate that they are quietly hoping for the destruction of the troublesome II Corps (S) capability to threaten the Shura Council.
R88	June 3, 2014	**OSINT:** AQAP has released martyr videos on their sites for the suicide attackers of I Corps (W) installations earlier in the week.
R89	June 3, 2014	**SIGINT:** Negotiations between the Shura Council and breakaway Shura members have failed.
R90	June 3, 2014	**MASINT:** PoL radar indicates that Huangfen Y-1s out of Hadiboh are training attack formations.
R91	June 4, 2014	**HUMINT—005-F-6:** The Eritrean secret service is supplying Al-Shabaab with weapons.

(Continued)

(Continued)

Rep #	Date	Text
R92	June 4, 2014	**Cyber:** AQAP has hacked into the major C2 nodes of I Corps, crashing their servers in the west of Yemen.
R93	June 4, 2014	**OSINT:** Journalists in Al Mukalla are reporting a curfew is now in effect from 2000 hours.
R94	June 4, 2014	**SIGINT:** Commander of II Corps tells the Shura rebel leaders that the time for talk is over and that he is now in control.
R95	June 4, 2014	**HUMINT—003-B-2:** Darood clan leaders are not happy with the refugee influx and want to stop it.
R96	June 5, 2014	**DOCEX:** A USB stick from MV *Raj Mahali* indicates that there were a significant number of high-speed motors delivered from Yambo to Hadiboh earlier in the week.
R97	June 5, 2014	**DOCEX:** A SIM card reveals that Bosaso Port official Aadan Dhaayow (Darrood) is corrupt with regard to human traffickers.
R98	June 5, 2014	**Cyber:** Known AQAP profiles found bragging about mini-submarines in a not so well-protected known AQAP chat room.
R99	June 5, 2014	**IMINT:** Imagery indicates that excavation on Hadiboh resembles that necessary for a fixed scud missile site.
R100	June 5, 2014	**HUMINT—012-A2:** II Corps on Hadiboh have received up to thirty MANPADS courtesy of financial backers within the Hawiye clan.

BACKGROUND READING

Supplemental Intelligence Report 01: Hawala

The following is reprinted from *Convergence: Illicit Networks and National Security in the Age of Globalization* by Michael Miklaucic and Jacqueline Brewer, Washington, DC: National Defense University Press, 2013.

Illicit networks including terrorist groups use an informal banking system known as hawala to move their assets in some regions, taking advantage of the system's non-transparent and liquid nature. A remittance is a transfer of money by a foreign worker to his or her home country. An informal banking system is one in which money is received for the purpose of making it, or an equivalent value, payable to a third party in another geographic location whether or not in the same form. Such transfers generally take place outside the conventional banking system through nonbank money services businesses or other, often unregulated and undocumented, business entities whose primary activity may not be the transmission of money. Traditionally, expatriates—traders and immigrant labourers—used informal banking systems to send money home from or to countries lacking formal and secure banking systems. Informal systems are still used by immigrant ethnic populations in the United States and elsewhere today. Such systems are based on trust and the extensive use of connections such as family relationships or regional affiliations.

These systems also often involve transactions to remote areas with no formal banking system or to countries with weak financial regulations, such as in Somalia, where the AL BARAKAAT informal banking system moved funds for al-Qaida. It is believed that the perpetrators of the Mumbai attacks of November 2008 relied on hawala transactions to fund their operations.

Supplemental Intelligence 02: al-Qaida on the Arabian Peninsula

The following is reprinted from *Yemen and Somalia: Terrorism, Shadow Networks and the Limitations of State-building,* by Sally Healy and Ginny Hill, London: Chatham House, 2010.

[AQAP] is a transnational al-Qaeda affiliate with dual nationality leadership, formed in 2009 after a merger between groups in Yemen and Saudi Arabia. Its leader, Nasser al-Wuhayshi, is a Yemeni. His deputy, Said al-Shihri, is a Saudi national, former Guantánamo detainee and graduate of Saudi Arabia's flagship rehabilitation programme for former jihadists. Al-Wuhayshi served bin Laden in Afghanistan and in 2001 al-Shihri was captured on the Pakistan border with Afghanistan.

In 2010, the U.S. government designated AQAP a foreign terrorist organization and imposed sanctions against both men. AQAP's online magazine, Sada al-Malahim (the Echo of Battles), communicates the organization's aims and grievances. In line with al-Qaeda's standard international narrative, AQAP aims for the creation of an Islamic caliphate and encourages attacks on Western interests, including the oil industry. Although AQAP is based in Yemen, the group has a transnational agenda that reflects the composition of its leadership. In 2009, it tried to assassinate a senior Saudi prince in Riyadh, and al-Shihri has urged Saudi cells to kidnap members of the Saudi royal family as well as Christians living in the kingdom.

AQAP also targets Yemen's security services as a result of the alleged torture of AQAP members in detention. AQAP tries to link widespread anti-American sentiment in Yemen with opposition to the domestic regime by tapping into public perceptions of elite corruption, militarism and the concentration of power. At times, President Saleh has alleged that AQAP supports Yemen's Houthi insurgents, who belong to a unique local branch of Shi'a Islam, as well as the southern separatists, who consider the president's northern clan to be running the country in its own interests. However, all three rebellions against President Saleh's authority are rooted in different histories; they are framed by distinct identities and reflect contrasting notions of an ideal, reformed state. They present themselves as social justice movements, arguing that President Saleh's regime is simultaneously sustained and discredited by opportunist military alliances with Riyadh and Washington.

14

Cyber Attack in the North Kelon Sea Region

This case study takes place in a fictional setting in the year 2015. It is designed to demonstrate the application of a problem definition model (PDM) and target network model (TNM) to cyber threat analysis. The fictional setting is called the North Kelon Sea Region, a region best characterized as being economically productive but increasingly volatile. The countries of Arknad, Trent Gokland, Haldun, and the Basillic Federation make up this unstable region. The narrative centers on the fact that the country of Arknad has just endured a cyber attack of unknown origin. Arknad has no organized cyber defense command of its own, so it has discreetly asked one of its main trading partners, Trent, that does have a fully developed cyber command, to help identify those responsible for the cyber attack. Failure to resolve the issue properly will give fodder to more nationalistic and radical actors, risking instability and conflict in the region, which would hurt everyone's economy. This is a traditional "who done it and why" challenge packed into a basic cyber context.

EDUCATIONAL OBJECTIVES

This exercise is designed to introduce cyber operations, specifically the following:

- working with basic concepts related to cyber intelligence
- managing digital typologies of tags and identifiers
- creating PDMs and TNMs of cyber attacks

ASSIGNMENT

You work at the Trent Cyber Command as an all-source analyst and have been assigned as the lead all-source analyst to assist the Arknad government with the full spectrum of Trent Cyber Command's resources to support you.

Your task is to identify those responsible for a massive cyber attack on Arknad and present your conclusions to both Trent and Arknad authorities. To complete this assignment, you must do the following:

- Create a PDM and appropriate TNMs that include those entities involved in the attacks and the targets of the attacks.
- Determine how and why the attack was carried out.
- Storyboard your conclusions concerning the attack for both Trent and Arknad authorities.

ABBREVIATIONS AND ACRONYMS

Abbreviation or Acronym	Description
CIC	Cyber Intelligence Command
DoS	denial of service
GSM	Global Systems for Mobile Communications
HUMINT	Human Intelligence
HVTL	high-value target list
ICP	Intelligence Collection Plan
IDS	intrusion detection system
INTREP	Intelligence Report
IP	Internet protocol
IVO	in vicinity of
MASINT	Measurement and Signature Intelligence
OSINT	Open Source Intelligence
PDM	problem definition model
SIGINT	Signals Intelligence
SNA	social network analysis
SUPINTREP	Supplemental Intelligence Report
TNM	target network model
UNK	unknown

SCENARIO

The North Kelon Sea Region (see Figure 14.1) consists of five countries: Haldun, Arknad, Gokland, Trent, and the northern tip of the Bassilic Federation. It has a long history of conflicts over everything from border definition to fishing rights. There are many crosscutting cleavages in the region concerning language, religion,

FIGURE 14.1   North Kelon Sea Region

politics, and history, but, for the last half century, a relative peace has reigned, despite ongoing rivalries.

Arknad was founded in 1865, with the city of Diva as its capital as a result of an east-west civil war in the country of Haldun. After an armistice divided the country, Haldun was left with the western part of the region with Tasuk as its capital, and Arknad controlled the eastern half. Despite the passing of more than a century, a strong rivalry still exists in almost every aspect of political, military, economic, and social development. However, there have rarely been serious threats of open conflict.

On April 1, 2014, the country of Arknad found itself under cyber attack for several hours between 0100 and 1300 hours. When the attack was over, a large amount of data had been stolen from several military and other national servers. Since the attack, the Arknad authorities have been reviewing traffic preceding the attack and have found that a great deal of what they think was cyber reconnaissance occurred in the last half of March, with some noticeable activities on or around March 23. This included denial of service (DoS) attacks and a great deal of pinging. (Within the context of cyber warfare, pinging is essentially a reconnaissance technique to support the planning of DoS attacks. A targeted website or Internet protocol (IP) address is forced to respond to a communication test, allowing an assessment of the connection based on time delay by the sender.)

The Arknad government has immediately ordered a full investigation into the cyber attack and has publicly stated that it will "reserve the right to treat the cyber attack as an act of war, invoking its inherent right to self-defense under international law." Internally, the government has told the investigating bodies to review all aspects surrounding the lead up to the attack, the actual attack, and after the attack, in order to establish who is responsible. Arknad has no real cyber warfare specialists and has turned to its key trading partner Trent for assistance. Trent has an established national cyber command and has agreed to assist.

Groups Referenced in Supplemental Intelligence Reports and Intelligence Reporting

Arknadians in Exile are second-generation Arknadian political refugees who were given asylum status by Trent in accordance with international law despite the protests of its main trading partner Arknad. With Trent's interest in maintaining peace in the region, the political refugees have been tightly controlled by Trent authorities to ensure stability. The group is based in Trent.

Bassilic Electronic Army is a self-proclaimed cyber warfare group officially disowned by the Bassilic Federation but suspected of unofficially conducting activities in support of government policies. Many believe it is simply a front organization that offers *plausible deniability* to the Bassilic Federation. It is well funded and very professional. The group is based in the Bassilic Federation.

Cyber Lion is a very recent addition to the plethora of activist groups in the region, and little is known about it.

The *Gokland Bureau of Informatics* is a Gokland government department. It is responsible for managing the greater part of Gokland's infrastructure, from medical records to traffic lights. It has obtained legendary status in the region because of its purchase of one of the most powerful computers available. Gokland is proud to be one of the leaders in cyber social management but has invested very little in cyber defense.

The *Titan Environmental Group* is an environmental activist group that is based in the Bassilic Federation. It is known for acts of civil disobedience in the Bassilic Federation and has often been blamed for disruptive cyber attacks on industries. It has fought information wars directly on social media with the Bassilic Electronic Army.

The following Supplemental Intelligence Reports (SUPINTREPs) detail the IP addresses assigned to countries in the region and the details on IP addresses and files targeted in the cyber attacks.

Supplemental Intelligence Report 01:
Regional Major Internet Protocol Address Blocks

ARKNAD		
FROM IP	TO IP	OWNER
203.215.32.0	203.215.47.255	Navy Command
202.86.16.0	202.86.31.255	Army Command
182.50.176.0	182.50.191.255	Air Force Command
175.106.32.0	175.106.63.255	National Bank
61.5.192.0	61.5.207.255	National Police HQ
121.127.32.0	121.127.63.255	Ministry of Defense
190.104.96.0	190.104.111.255	Ministry of Transport
27.0.96.0	27.0.127.255	Ministry of Agriculture
58.97.128.0	58.97.255.255	Arknad Defense Intelligence Agency
61.247.176.0	61.247.191.255	Fishermen United (Union)
114.31.0.0	114.31.31.255	Arknad University

HALDUN		
FROM IP	TO IP	OWNER
64.37.32.0	64.37.47.255	Army
66.55.112.0	66.55.127.255	Navy
76.8.32.0	76.8.47.255	Air Force
206.53.176.0	206.53.191.255	Haldun Intelligence Agency
209.240.32.0	209.240.47.255	University of Haldun
216.249.32.0	216.249.47.255	Great Western University
61.6.192.0	61.6.192.0	Haldun Connect
119.160.128.0	119.160.191.255	Teleho

GOKLAND		
FROM IP	TO IP	OWNER
41.67.192.0	41.67.255.255	Gokland University
41.92.128.0	41.92.255.255	Gokland Internal Security Service

GOKLAND		
FROM IP	TO IP	OWNER
41.202.192.0	41.202.223.255	Gokland Ministry of Finance
41.204.64.0	41.204.95.255	Gokland Bureau of Informatics

BASSILIC FEDERATION		
FROM IP	TO IP	OWNER
41.67.0.0	41.67.63.255	Titan Environmental Group
41.95.0.0	41.95.255.255	Bassilic Electronic Army
41.202.160.0	41.202.191.255	3rd Joint Army Brigade
41.209.64.0	41.209.127.255	Federal Ministry of Commerce
105.238.0.0	105.239.255.255	Federal Ministry of Transport
196.29.160.0	196.29.191.255	Federal Ministry of Fishery
197.254.192.0	197.254.223.255	Federal Parliament
197.254.224.0	197.254.255.255	8th Fleet Kelon Sea
212.0.128.0	212.0.159.255	King's Harbour University
223.200.0.0	223.260.15.255	Memorial University of Bassilic
223.136.0.0	223.143.127.255	North Bassilic College
223.27.32.0	223.27.63.255	Stan Petroleum
223.143.64.0	223.143.255.255	Bassilic National Petroleum Consortium
223.144.0.0	223.144.255.255	Tophat Telecoms

TRENT		
FROM IP	TO IP	OWNER
41.224.0.0	41.231.255.255	Defense
193.95.0.0	193.95.127.255	Army
196.203.0.0	196.203.255.255	Navy
197.0.0.0	197.31.255.255	Air Force
213.150.160.0	213.150.191.255	Cyber Intelligence Command (CIC)
41.207.160.0	41.207.191.255	Arknadians in Exile

Supplemental Intelligence Report 02: Targeted Files

Date-Time Group	Targeted Internet Protocol	Owner	File Name	Description	Attacking C2 Internet Protocol
April 1, 2014 0120 hours	202.86.19.122	1st Division	TOR19AB	Current manning status with some specializations named	41.67.201.130
April 1, 2014 0120 hours	202.86.29.88	1st Division	TOR 19AC	Weapons readiness of various platforms including artillery	41.67.201.131
April 1, 2014 0120 hours	202.86.18.210	1st Division	TOR 19AD	Ammo inventory in tonnage not rounds	41.67.201.132
April 1, 2014 0120 hours	202.86.24.34	1st Division	TOR 19AE	Uniform sizes in stock	41.67.201.133
April 1, 2014 0120 hours	202.86.18.186	1st Division	TOR 19AF	Spare parts receipts	41.67.201.134
April 1, 2014 0205 hours	202.86.24.45	4th Division	TOR 49AE	Uniform sizes in stock	41.204.84.56
April 1, 2014 0205 hours	202.86.29.60	4th Division	TOR49AB	Current manning—no specializations named	41.204.84.57
April 1, 2014 0205 hours	202.86.19.159	4th Division	TOR 49AF	Spare parts receipts—maintenance records by proxy	41.204.84.59
April 1, 2014 0303 hours	203.215.35.231	12th Naval Task Group	AS102-hfgui	Destroyer escort—landside air radar data backup	41.204.84.62
April 1, 2014 0303 hours	203.215.35.216	12th Naval Task Group	AS105-rtuie	Destroyer escort—landside backup of recorded surface radar pattern of life for last exercise	41.204.84.66
April 1, 2014 0303 hours	203.215.35.209	12th Naval Task Group	AS106-sdjfk	Destroyer escort ship—landside backup of ammunition specs	41.204.84.67

Date–Time Group	Targeted Internet Protocol	Owner	File Name	Description	Attacking C2 Internet Protocol
April 1, 2014 0303 hours	203.215.35.202	12th Naval Task Group	AS109-vdnoi	Destroyer escort ship—landside backup of crew roster	41.204.84.64
April 1, 2014 0303 hours	203.215.37.149	12th Naval Task Group	AS202-wroif	Minesweeper—landside backup of ship capacity values	41.204.89.7
April 1, 2014 0303 hours	203.215.37.134	12th Naval Task Group	AS205-lskdo	Minesweeper—landside backup of ship capacity values	41.204.89.14
April 1, 2014 0303 hours	203.215.40.45	12th Naval Task Group	AS304-csdjk	Amphibious assault prep-ship oceanographer—landside backup of last month's measurements along the south coast	41.204.90.3
April 1, 2014 0303 hours	203.215.43.178	12th Naval Task Group	AS305-qajdr	Amphibious assault ship—launch capacity stats including timings on flooding and launching	41.204.89.24
April 1, 2014 0303 hours	203.215.45.37	12th Naval Task Group	AS402-lokij	Air assault ship—helicopter fuel stats	41.204.89.45
April 1, 2014 0303 hours	203.215.45.22	12th Naval Task Group	AS403-wrsse	Cruiser—communications specs	41.204.89.77
April 1, 2014 0147 hours	182.50.185.14	3rd Air Wing	KAS83754	Patrol timings for Region South	41.95.93.102
April 1, 2014 0147 hours	182.50.185.23	3rd Air Wing	KAS83952	Maintenance specs for the past six months	41.95.93.104
April 1, 2014 0147 hours	182.50.185.34	3rd Air Wing	KAS83209	Fuel depot locations and capacities	41.95.93.105

(Continued)

(Continued)

Date-Time Group	Targeted Internet Protocol	Owner	File Name	Description	Attacking C2 Internet Protocol
April 1, 2014 0233 hours	121.127.44.12	Ministry of Defense	JAK24	Last year's procurement projections	41.67.32.45
April 1, 2014 0233 hours	121.127.46.18	Ministry of Defense	JAK 25	This year's procurement projections	41.67.32.49
April 1, 2014 0233 hours	190.104.102.59	Ministry of Transport	AGAHxt	Personnel files	212.0.143. 104
April 1, 2014 0233 hours	190.104.99.230	Ministry of Transport	AGAHst	Management files	212.0.143. 105
April 1, 2014 0233 hours	190.104.103.15	Ministry of Transport	AGAHty	Traffic stats	212.0.143. 106
March 23, 2014 0239 hours	61.247.184.77	Fishermen United	CAB4506	IP addresses	41.207.180.37
April 1, 2014 0356 hours	114.31.19.109	Arknad University	HALO Files	Related to university exchange system	41.67.201.9
March 23, 2014 0244 hours	61.5.202.37	National Police HQ	Hfhf000002	IP monitoring data	41.207.180.114
April 1, 2014 0349 hours	175.106.52.31	National Bank	Rutame2007 Files	Old accounting files	41.67.201.133
April 1, 2014 0233 hours	27.0.113.5	Ministry of Agriculture	wheatgen360	Last year's grain auction results	41.67.201.134
April 1, 2014 0325 hours	58.97.191.11	Arknad Defense Intelligence Agency	YTTelecad	Internal telephone	41.67.201.130

INTELLIGENCE REPORTS

Rep #	Date	Text
R1	April 7, 2014	**Open Source Intelligence (OSINT):** Regional media are reporting that tensions are extremely high between Arknad and Gokland as sources inside the Arknad government suggest they have indications that Gokland is behind the massive cyber attack of April 1, 2014.
R2	April 7, 2014	**OSINT:** Some Arknadian media are pointing directly at the Arknadians in Exile group living here in Trent. The media note that the group defaced several Arknadian government websites last year.
R3	April 7, 2014	**Cyber:** The Arknadian anomaly based intrusion detection system (IDS) reports that the following IP ranges were likely scanned or reconned between March 15 and 16, 2014.

121.127.40.0	121.127.45.255
202.86.18.0	202.86.29.255
203.215.35.0	203.215.45.0
182.50.185.0	182.50.185.255
58.97.191.0	58.97.191.255

Rep #	Date	Text
R4	April 7, 2014	**Human Intelligence (HUMINT) 043—C3:** Source reports that the Bassilic Federation is investigating the Titan Environmental Group for possible involvement in the attack on Arknad.
R5	April 8, 2014	**Cyber:** Unauthorized network scans were executed from workstations within the IP range 41.67.201.120 to 41.67.201.140 (Unauthorized network scanning is essentially using unauthorized software to map the architecture of the network with regard to servers and stations.)
R6	April 8, 2014	**HUMINT—020-B2:** There was a great deal of panic at the Gokland Bureau of Informatics in the morning as everyone arrived at work.

(Continued)

(Continued)

Rep #	Date	Text
R7	April 8, 2014	**Signals Intelligence (SIGINT):** On April 1 at 1130 hours, Chris "Slackjaw" Wilson, a known member of the Bassilic Electronic Army, rings an unknown member, asking, "What's going on? Did you okay that?" The contact replied, "No, but it was big, and I think we should lay very low for a while."
R8	April 8, 2014	**Cyber:** An attempt to infect working station IP 61.5.202.20 with malware via e-mail was thwarted by signature-based IDS on March 20, 2014.
R9	April 8, 2014	**Cyber:** An attempt to infect working station IP 175.106.52.14 with malware via e-mail was thwarted by signature-based IDS on March 20, 2014.
R10	April 8, 2014	**ARKNAD Intelligence Report (INTREP):** Domain names for all Arknadian Ministry IPs went offline by 0400hrs April 1 due to malware infections.
R 11	April 9, 2014	**Cyber:** Social media sock puppets report a genuine feeling of surprise amongst online Titan Environmental Group members. (Sock puppets are fake social media personalities that penetrate open sources to collect information. They are essentially a digital disguise for attending digital meetings or forums.)
R 12	April 9, 2014	**Cyber:** DoS attacks disabled IP range 41.92.176.0 to 41.92.177.255 from 0100 to 1300 hours on April 1.
R 13	April 10, 2014	**HUMINT—012-A2:** Arknadians in Exile leadership are very concerned that they will be blamed for the recent mass cyber attack. They do not have the capability for such an attack.
R 14	April 10, 2014	**Cyber:** DoS attacks disabled IP range 206.53.181.10 to 206.53.181.95 from 0100 to 1300 hours on April 1. These IPs are known to be used by Haldun intelligence for cyber security issues.
R15	April 10, 2014	**INTREP:** An unauthorized network scan was conducted using complex signature scanning software from a workstation on the Haldun University Campus IP 209.240.39.145, a library workstation.
R16	April 10, 2014	**ARKNAD INTREP:** The Arknad Ministry of Transport has reported that the only file of a sensitive nature that was copied was the file AGAHxt. The file was not destroyed, and no sleeping malware has been detected. Data in the file is mostly personal information about employees, including some evaluation results.
R17	April 10, 2014	**ARKNAD INTREP:** The Arknad Ministry of Agriculture reports that no sensitive data was stolen and information was already available in the public domain.

Rep #	Date	Text
R18	April 10, 2014	**HUMINT—076-B1:** IP range 41.204.90.0 to 41.204.90.20 are workstations belonging to one of the most powerful servers in the region—the Gokland Bureau of Informatics.
R19	April 10, 2014	**OSINT:** The Bassilic Federation has launched a crackdown on known members of the Bassilic Electronic Army.
R20	April 11, 2014	**SIGINT:** Known hacker "Quiet Charley" took an unknown caller on April 1 and started the conversation with "I knew he had something going. . . ."
R21	April 11, 2014	**Measurement and Signature Intelligence (MASINT):** The overall assessment is that there was very little physical damage to software and systems on the April 1 attack. This has been confirmed by Arknadian specialists.
R22	April 11, 2014	**ARKNAD INTREP:** Most of the stolen military files contained information available in the public domain. The following files were *not* available in the public domain: TOR19AB TOR49AB TOR19AC AS105-rtuie AS304-csdjk AS402-lokij AS403-wrsse KAS83754
R23	April 11, 2014	**HUMINT—043-C3:** The infamous "Ronin" hacker Michael Schenke has been boasting in hackers' circles about making a year's salary in four weeks. His mobile number is 09305077.
R24	April 12, 2014	**ARKNAD INTREP:** Arknadian cyber security reports that though some of the attacks on the military servers were stopped almost immediately, the attackers had a second backup line into the targeted servers and possibly a third where it concerns the navy.

(Continued)

245

Rep #	Date	Text
R25	April 12, 2014	**HUMINT—021-F6:** The source overheard members of radical environmental group Titan planning for something "very big" March 19 while sitting at the student bar of King's Harbour University.
R26	April 12, 2014	**OSINT:** Known radical social media chat rooms are themselves doing a lot of speculation about who executed the attack.
R27	April 13, 2014	**SIGINT:** Global System for Mobile Communications (GSM) data traffic monitoring software indicates abnormal increases in the amount of data transferred between 0030 and 0100 hours, as well as 0400 and 1500 hours, or during the period surrounding the attack.
R28	April 13, 2014	**SIGINT:** "Commander" John R. Rutherford from the Bassilic Electronic Army called his best cyber specialist (known as Darren "Screen Flash" Walsh) and stated, "If this comes back to haunt us, it will be your fault for not thinking about the security of our systems . . . (condescending laugh) the famous hijacker gets hijacked."
R29	April 13, 2014	**HUMINT—020-B2:** The government of Gokland has launched a secret investigation as to who and how someone could take over one of the most powerful computer systems in the region—that of the Gokland Bureau of Informatics.
R30	April 14, 2014	**Cyber:** Arknad National Police HQ found malware on workstation 61.5.202.9 on March 25. It appears it was intended to erase file Hfhf000002 at 0000 hours on April 1. They removed the malware.
R31	April 14, 2014	**HUMINT—043-C3:** Bassilic Federation Authorities believe that the Titan Environmental Group's main server was hijacked by an unknown IP in Haldun, possibly Haldun University. (Officially, they are blaming Titan Environmental Group.)

Rep #	Date	Text
R32	April 15, 2014	**Cyber—RFI01 April 8, 2014, CIC Response:** Major regional IP blocks *not* considered pinged, scanned, or reconned between March 10 and 31 are as follows:

114.31.0.0	114.31.31.255
64.37.32.0	64.37.47.255
66.55.112.0	66.55.127.255
76.8.32.0	76.8.47.255
64.37.32.0	64.37.47.255
209.240.32.0	209.240.47.255
223.27.32.0	223.27.63.255
223.26.64.0	223.143.255.255
223.144.0.0	223.200.255.255
41.224.0.0	41.231.255.255
193.95.0.0	193.95.127.255
196.203.0.0	196.203.255.255
197.0.0.0	197.31.255.255
213.150.160.0	213.150.191.255

Rep #	Date	Text
R33	April 16, 2014	**OSINT:** It is assessed from media communications that all telecom and data providers in the North Kelon Sea Region were surprised by the cyber attack.

(Continued)

247

(Continued)

Rep #	Date	Text
R34	April 16, 2014	**Cyber—RFI02 April 8, 2014, CIC Response:** Regional IP blocks that suffered *no* form of attack on April 1 with a high degree of certainty are as follows: {| 41.224.0.0 | 41.231.255.255 | | 193.95.0.0 | 193.95.127.255 | | 196.203.0.0 | 196.203.255.255 | | 197.0.0.0 | 197.31.255.255 | | 213.150.160.0 | 213.150.191.255 | | 223.27.32.0 | 223.27.63.255 | | 223.144.0.0 | 223.200.255.255 | | 197.254.224.0 | 197.254.255.255 | | 41.209.64.0 | 41.209.127.255 | | 105.238.0.0 | 105.239.255.255 | | 196.29.160.0 | 196.29.191.255 |}
R35	April 16, 2014	**OSINT:** Another group called the Cyber Lion is taking credit for the cyber attack in the media. Little is known about them.
R36	April 17, 2014	**INTREP:** Michael Schenke is a full-time geology PhD student at King's Harbour University. His head supervisor is Professor Derik Hammel. His secondary supervisor at Haldun University, Dr. Sheena Stevens, is a specialist in marine geology.
R37	April 17, 2014	**HUMINT—021-F6:** The hackers behind the attack have mobile numbers 07456738, 05464675, and 08328764. All are members of the Titan Environmental Group.

Rep #	Date	Text
R38	April 17, 2014	**SIGINT—RFI03 APRIL 13, 2014, Mob. 09305077:** Cross-referenced GSM tags with masting nearest provided IP blocks (essentially cross-referencing the approximate whereabouts of Mob. 09305077 with already geo-located IP blocks) are as follows: March 17 IVO (in vicinity of) IP 212.0.128.0—212.0.159.255. 1100–1600 hours March 18 IVO IP 223.27.32.0—223.27.63.255 1900–2100 hours March 19 IVO IP 209.240.32.0—209.240.47.255 1600–2100 hours March 20 IVO IP 209.240.32.0—209.240.47.255 1600–2100 hours March 21 IVO IP 209.240.32.0—209.240.47.255 1000–2200 hours March 22 IVO IP 209.240.32.0—209.240.47.255 1200–2200 hours March 23 IVO IP 209.240.32.0—209.240.47.255 0700–2200 hours March 24 IVO IP 212.0.128.0—212.0.159.255. 1000h–1500 hours March 25 IVO IP 223.27.32.0—223.27.63.255 1900–2100 hours April 1 IVO IP 209.240.32.0—209.240.47.255 0030–0100 and 0400–0500 hours
R39	April 17, 2014	**Cyber:** There were at least five attackers coordinating the complex cyber attack from 0030 to 1300 on April 1, with DoS attacks providing cover for exploit operations.
R40	April 18, 2014	**Cyber—RFI04 APRIL 13, 2014:** The following is a response to your request for a list of active IPs at Haldun University for April 1, 0000–0500: 209.240.32.0—209.240.47.255 209.240.34.2 Library (off at 0044 hours) 209.240.34.3 Library (off at 0120 hours) 209.240.34.4 Library (off at 0130 hours) 209.240.42.14 Sedimentology/Marine Geology Dept. (off at 0500 hours) 209.240.42.15 Sedimentology/Marine Geology Dept. (off at 0500 hours) 209.240.42.16 Sedimentology/Marine Geology Dept. (off at 0500 hours) 209.240.42.17 Sedimentology/Marine Geology Dept. (off at 0500 hours)
R41	April 18, 2014	**INTREP:** Dr. Sheena Stevens is married to Wayne Stevens, son of Donald Stevens, executive head of exploration at Stan Petroleum.

Index

$\circledS$SAGE video

We are delighted to announce the launch of a streaming video program at SAGE!

SAGE Video online collections are developed in partnership with leading academics, societies and practitioners, including many of SAGE's own authors and academic partners, to deliver cutting-edge pedagogical collections mapped to curricular needs.

Available alongside our book and reference collections on the *SAGE Knowledge* platform, content is delivered with critical online functionality designed to support scholarly use.

SAGE Video combines originally commissioned and produced material with licensed videos to provide a complete resource for students, faculty, and researchers.

NEW IN 2015!

• Counseling and Psychotherapy
• Education
• Media and Communication

sagepub.com/video
sagevideo